LC 1011   The Liberal arts and teacher
L45   education

LC 1011   The Libseral arts and
L45   teacher education

DATE	ISSUED TO
JUL 1 6 1987	Lillian Jarvis

DEMCO

+LC1011 .L45

COLL. FOR HUMAN SERVICES LIBR.
201 VARICK ST. N.Y.C. 10014

The Liberal Arts and Teacher Education

COLLEGE FOR HUMAN SERVICES
LIBRARY
345 HUDSON STREET
NEW YORK, N.Y. 10014

The Liberal Arts and Teacher Education

A Confrontation

Edited by

Donald N. Bigelow

University of Nebraska Press · Lincoln

Acknowledgments for the use of copyright material
appear on page xiii.

Copyright © 1971 by the University of Nebraska Press
All rights reserved
International Standard Book Number 0–8032–0209–1
Library of Congress Catalog Card Number 73–136024

Manufactured in the United States of America

*This book is dedicated to
all NDEA Title XI Institute Directors
and those of the Experienced Teacher Fellowship Program
whose tribulations, errors, and experimentation
have helped to make more evident
the necessary confrontation
between the Liberal Arts and Teacher Education*

Contents

Foreword, by Don Davies — ix
Preface and Acknowledgments — xiii
Introduction: Revolution or Reform in Teacher Education? by Donald N. Bigelow — xvii

I. Give: *Datta*

Teaching and the Liberal Arts: Notes toward an Old Frontier, by William Arrowsmith — 3
The Liberal Arts, Open Admissions, and the Training of Teachers, by Timothy Healy — 27
The Future of Teaching, by William Arrowsmith — 37

II. Sympathize: *Dayadhvam*

The Liberal Arts and the War against Stone Men, by Benjamin DeMott — 57
Some Additional Aspects of the War against Stone Men, by Charles Z. Wilson — 69
The Condition of Being at Home in the World, by Paul Olson — 75
Stone Men, Accountability, and the Evolution of Teachers of Teachers, by Richard Foster — 85
Stone Men and the Neo-Dantesque Hell of Environment, by Charles Leyba — 91

III. Control: *Damyata*

The Liberal Arts: Antidote to Simplism, by Charles DeCarlo 99
The Liberal Arts and Teacher Education, by B. Othanel Smith 110
The Simplicity of the Liberal Arts Colleges and Mexican-American Community Needs, by José Maria Burruel 120
Questions without Answers: A Response to Dr. Charles DeCarlo, by Bernard C. Watson 123

IV. Panel Discussion: The Education of Teachers and the University of Public Interest, by David Brumble 127

V. Report from the Black and Brown Communities

Minority Report: Observations of Minorities in Attendance 159
Liberal Arts and Teacher Training: A Pan-African Perspective, by Preston Wilcox 164
Haraka, by Edward C. Powell 183
My People Are Crying, by Rev. Henry J. Casso 189
Rescuing the Perishing, by Les Whipp 192

VI. Reflections and Recommendations: The Jesuit and the Trappist 199

VII. A Bibliography: Rapping about the University, by Peter Brooks 233

List of Contributors 249

Foreword

Before becoming a civil servant and before the passage of the Education Professions Development Act of 1967, I wrote that teacher education was the slum of American education. It appeared to me to be an economically disadvantaged, largely neglected, and dangerously isolated enterprise. Included in my indictment were the liberal arts academic departments (which, after all, do so much of teacher education) and their faculty and administrators, as well as those in schools of education, where, all too often, research is emphasized at the expense of training. The indictment necessarily included all related parts of teacher education—the graduate schools, professional associations, state and local educational agencies, and the Office of Education. Together they testified unmistakably to the unbelievably low priority that society was giving to the education of our teachers.

It seemed important then, and is no less important today, that unless all of these groups do everything in their power to reform the way our educators are trained; and unless they do it *together*, our separate efforts will fail to produce better schools. Since 1954 there has been some progress made possible by the civil rights movement, Sputnik and the interest in school reform which it triggered, large-scale student dissatisfaction with the quality and spirit of education, foundation and federal support for innovation, and growing support for reform inside the education professions themselves.

During the past three years the Office of Education, through its new Bureau of Educational Personnel Development, which is single-mindedly dedicated to training educational personnel for elementary and secondary schools, has helped to continue the national dialogue and to bring about an awareness that the system, as a whole, should and can be reformed. It has focused and will continue to focus on the problem of developing teachers and other educational personnel to work effectively with young people of all backgrounds—those who come to school well equipped to learn, as well as those who come to school ill equipped for the conventional school experience. In pursuit of this goal the bureau has helped to stimulate the necessary confrontation between the producers and employers of educational personnel. In this effort it has built upon the pioneering work that Don Bigelow and his colleagues began in the mid-1960's under earlier federal legislation by attempting to get at the education of the educators themselves as one part of the necessary confrontation. The TTT Program; the Phoenix conference, "The Year of the Liberal Arts," which TTT sponsored; and this publication are all important parts of the confrontation and of the strategy of reform. But they are not enough.

Most university scholars and administrators are strongly (and often accurately) critical of the elementary and secondary schools. They see them failing to provide basic practical and intellectual skills. And recently they have recognized that the schools have also failed to provide basic confidence and competence to a large number of low-income and minority-group children. Generally, the liberal arts faculties have seen in the schools an atmosphere that is, at the same time, profoundly antiintellectual and profoundly dehumanizing. Certainly, it is now clear that we are too often impoverishing children in the process of educating them.

What these same critics fail to see (or don't want to admit) is that they themselves are an important, perhaps the major, cause of the failure of our schools. It is they who, more than any other group, have produced the crisis in the classroom. For what happens —and what doesn't happen—in higher education has a strong and often deadening impact on the schools. The reverse is also true. Both higher and "lower" education continue to poison each other's wells; in fact, it turns out to be a common well. On the one hand, elementary and secondary education cannot be improved without the reform of higher education. On the other hand, neither will succeed without genuine participation by the community, which is, after all, the interested and main consumer of education. Otherwise "reform" becomes nothing less than a whitewash job and a reshuffling of the various parts of the hierarchy which make up the established educational system. Outside ideas, pressures, intervention, and stimulation of the real world are needed if we are to change anything important. We must have them. They are a central part of the whole endeavor, and they are already emerging.

In order for our schools to teach youngsters how to think, to learn, and how to apply knowledge from several disciplines, and in order to solve particular problems, we require schoolteachers who know a discipline as a rigorous and imaginative way of thinking, a discipline of intellectual love, not just a bundle of facts tied up with the blue ribbon labeled "B.A." We require teachers who are emotionally, intellectually, pedagogically, and *humanly* equipped to work with students of all sorts. And we now know that this must and can be done in ways vastly different from the traditional ways of telling and testing. It is this kind of teacher that we are not now getting from our undergraduate colleges.

The situation cannot be corrected by changing certification requirements. It cannot be changed by packaging and labeling educational content in slightly different ways. It cannot be corrected by inviting academics and pedagogues to serve on the same committees, in the hope that dialogue will result in significant improvement of what is called, pejoratively, "teacher education." A much more fundamental change is required—a change in the spirit and in the content of the undergraduate preparation of teachers, perhaps even a change in the very purpose and ethos of our institutions of higher education. Professor Arrowsmith in the pages which follow writes with feeling and clarity about the kind of spirit and content that is needed. Now is the time to make our reexamination of the undergraduate preparation of teachers a major and essential national priority; now is the time to reevaluate the nature of the liberal arts education itself.

There are a few themes which I believe are of fundamental importance in this reorganization of the liberal arts for teachers and, hence, for all undergraduates. Some of them can be found in the pages that follow. Some can be found in the plans and programs of the Bureau of Educational Personnel Development, as we look to the improvement of undergraduate teacher preparation. Some can be found elsewhere, inside and outside of the Office of Education. In the briefest way, they include:

the integration of knowledge so that people can solve problems which do not conform to the conventional disciplinary boundaries;
the integration of the cognitive and affective development of human beings;
bringing important new talent, from neglected or excluded sources, into programs of preparation and into the schools;
individualizing education;
the provision of a richly multicultural experience for all who will teach;
joining the content and style of the liberal arts to the modes of professional education;
creating working coalitions among schools, colleges, communities, professional organizations, and government agencies.

As chief administrator of the major legislation for training educators, I believe that we must learn, to our immense cultural advantage, how to use those voices and resources which until now have been excluded in the making of educational policy. As this book indicates, the well-planned conference on "The Year of the Liberal Arts" failed to utilize all of the available resources and, as a consequence, asked more questions than were answered. But if that experience and this book can help to translate these general themes and promises into some commitment and immediate action on the part of those who are in a position to reform the education of teachers, then it will have been worth the time and effort involved. Do these essays, speeches, reports not indicate that if the time is not *now*, tomorrow has already been lost?

Don Davies
Associate Commissioner for
Educational Personnel Development
U.S. Office of Education

Preface and Acknowledgments

"The Year of the Liberal Arts" was the title given to an invitational conference conducted at Phoenix, Arizona by the West Coast and Southwest clusters of the TTT Program (Training the Trainers of Teachers), which is supported by the U.S. Office of Education. The West Coast and Southwest clusters of the TTT were joined at Phoenix by the Great Lakes, Midwest, Southern, and Northeastern TTT clusters, all of which represent regional groupings of forty-three individual TTT projects.

"The Year of the Liberal Arts" was held April 30–May 2, 1970. The conference cochairmen were Hobert W. Burns, then Acting President, San Jose State College (California) and Eugene E. Slaughter, Head, English Department, Southeastern State College (Oklahoma). The former is chairman of the West Coast cluster and the latter of the Southwest cluster.

Each of the fourteen TTT projects belonging to the two clusters west of the Mississippi sent six people to the conference: the director and one other person, generally a staff member, and representatives from the four major sectors of a TTT project (that is, the schools of education and arts and sciences, the school system, and the community). All of these sectors work together, in one way or another, in a TTT project. All of the TTT projects from east of the Mississippi sent two representatives, the director and someone representing the liberal arts. In addition to these 150 individuals, another 75 invited guests, mostly deans from liberal arts colleges, attended the conference.

Several members of the Leadership Training Institute (LTI) for the TTT Program were also present, including its director, Dean Harry Rivlin of Fordham University at Lincoln Center. The purpose of the LTI, supported by the Office of Education, is to help provide appropriate training for TTT project directors, to determine program problems of national concern, and to disseminate information about the TTT Program. In addition, the executive committee of CONPASS was present at Phoenix. CONPASS is a consortium of professional organizations representing the liberal arts disciplines and other concerned educational groups which figure significantly in the training of teachers.

The Phoenix conference was made possible by grants from the U.S. Office of Education to the TTT projects and by grants originally made to Michigan State University, the University of Georgia, and Hunter College of the City University of New York, all of which established institutes to train individuals who helped to develop the TTT Program. The planning for this program began in 1967.

This book is organized roughly to follow the program of the conference, following the introduction by Donald N. Bigelow, Office of Education, which sponsored the TTT project. On Thursday evening, April 30, William Arrowsmith spoke and Timothy Healy commented on his presentation (major contributors and their roles are listed, pp. 249–50). On Friday morning, Benjamin DeMott spoke, and Charles Wilson, Paul Olson, Richard Foster, and Charles Leyba commented on his speech. The Friday afternoon program included group discussions (reported in the "Reflections and Recommendations" section), and Charles DeCarlo's speech, commented on by B. Othanel Smith, José Burruel, Bernard Watson, and Jack Gordon, whose speech was inadvertently not recorded. Finally, on Saturday morning, the large panel discussion was held (Part IV). Out of this discussion grew most of the materials contained in "Report from the Black and Brown Communities" (Part V). The "Reflections and Recommendations" included in Part VI are reports from the small groups which met on Friday during the conference and letters written after the conference by individual participants. Finally, Peter Brooks's bibliographical article was commissioned to permit readers of the volume to follow up the context of this conference in other books having a similar concern.

Preface and Acknowledgments xv

Grateful acknowledgment is made to the following persons and publishers for permission to reprint the material specified:

The University of Nebraska Press for selections from John G. Neihardt's *Black Elk Speaks*.

Harcourt Brace Jovanovich, Inc., and T. S. Eliot for excerpts from T. S. Eliot's "The Waste Land" and "The Love Song of J. Alfred Prufrock" in *Collected Poems, 1901–1962*.

William Arrowsmith for "The Future of Teaching," originally delivered as a speech to the annual meeting of the American Council on Education, New Orleans, October, 1966, and reprinted in the volume *Improving College Teaching*, edited by Calvin T. Lee and published by the council. Copyright 1967 by William Arrowsmith.

Mr. Richard Snyder, Mr. Sidney Whigham, and Miss Tracie Palmer for their poems quoted in Paul Olson's "The Condition of Being at Home in the World."

THE EDITOR

DONALD N. BIGELOW

Introduction:
Revolution or Reform in
Teacher Education?

Throughout history man has interpreted man. He has done this sometimes rigorously, and in almost every age vigorously and regularly. From those civilizations which have produced written histories comes much of the raw material of self-understanding. Sometimes a knowledge of history gives one a sense not only of self-understanding but of universal understanding. As the poet has said:

> I am owner of the sphere,
> Of the seven stars and the solar year,
> Of Caesar's hand, and Plato's brain,
> Of Lord Christ's heart, and Shakespeare's strain.

However, historians do not generally entertain such grand illusions. Some of man's early annals, such as Herodotus' history of the great invasion of Greece by Persia, and some more recent biographies, such as Carlyle's life of Frederick the Great or Tolstoy's historical sections in War and Peace (concerning Napoleon), do play recurrently with the question of whether the times make the man or vice versa. Within the framework of that question, the biographer may ask himself whether what his subject did was to develop a genius which created events or merely a rhetoric which appeared to fit events and so seemed, but only seemed, to determine the direction of a historical movement. In the continuing dialogue "between the idea / and the reality" man has sometimes interpreted man in simple terms, extolling hard work, a good education, or patriotism. But when the going gets tough, when the events are complex and their causes obscure, historians often resort to determinism or to predestination as explanations of man's behavior. What becomes clear for much of the history written about both men and events is that the personal set of the historian—his mythos, belief system, life-style, experience—may determine which events get rendered and what explanations are assigned to the events rendered. Thus, every partial history needs an "introduction," and this book is no exception.

I have taken an Emersonian view in editing this report of the Phoenix conference on the liberal arts. (Happily, but quite coincidentally, ours appears to be a decade in which Emerson again speaks to people who are listening.) This is a book of documents from, and about, the conference;[1] the order which the reader creates must be primarily his order. The function of my introduction will be to describe some of the events which surrounded the creation of the conference and its records and to offer one participant's subjective ordering of those events.

In the end, each reader will have to make his own interpretation of the Phoenix conference's discussions about man and liberal arts and determine the importance of what happened. As Emerson reminds us, "We are always coming up with the emphatic facts of history in our private experience and verifying them here." In his essay on history—and the emphasis is mine—he states: "All history becomes subjective; in other words there is properly no history, only biography. Every mind must know the whole lesson for itself—must go over the whole ground. What it does not see, what it does not live, it will not know."

THE CONFERENCE MAN

In the day of the quick conference, where amorphous groups of men meet to discuss quickly and quickly to determine courses of action (courses of action as often as not initiated by mere attendance at the conference), the problem of "interpreting man" has come to be compounded by several variables, and one's interpretations are thus rendered the more subjective. Men in groups will give off a variety of wave lengths to a variety of observers. A conference, instead of providing for examination and understanding on a one-to-one basis,

[1] Included is one speech given before and independent of the Phoenix conference, one essay by Peter Brooks requested in advance of the conference, and an essay by Preston Wilcox written especially for this book.

requires many levels of comprehension since it includes several sets of interpersonal activities occurring together. Decision-making groups have always worked in this fashion, but today people seem to engage in more conferences, to organize them more complexly and to seek closer interpersonal relations and instant policy decisions. And often not everything is visible. (It has always been this way, of course, but today's conference-initiated actions occur more frequently and spontaneously; the media people have pictured the notion of the multiple perspectives of men acting in groups by using several screens and many pictures simultaneously.)

A conference usually presents an additional dilemma in that seldom do any intelligent or meaningful documents emerge from it except for the program, which may either be forgotten or carried home like a young lady's invitation to her first dance. Usually the participant at the conference has but spotty notes on which to rely, and the conference which exists for him is mostly a conference which exists in imagination and memory, one which becomes in memory all too often like a hall of mirrors into which one has been placed naked and exposed like a bug in a box. What is left is locked away in the computer of the mind. The thinking which was done is often lost. The purpose of this book is to recall as fully as possible the intellectual content of what may have become only a nuance and an emotion in memory, to digest some of the episodes in retrospect, and to provide a written record of most of what was said at one conference, the Phoenix conference on the liberal arts.

My assumption is that it was a useful conference. It may not have offered final solutions, but it does, in the form rendered in this book, release the imagination to deal with the many grievous problems which afflict American education. No one doubts that the pressing problems of this emerging democracy (some would call it both a participating and an emerging democracy) can be solved only if, here and now, the question of how we educate better this and subsequent generations is given top priority. And a solution to that problem is a solution, or at least a beginning, of the solution to many other problems. The egg we lay today may be tomorrow's swan; or as W. B. Yeats said, looking at an ordinary schoolgirl and thinking how like her Helen of Troy must have looked as a child, "Even daughters of the swan can share something of every paddler's heritage."

xx   Introduction

GEOGRAPHICAL DETERMINISM

The circumstances surrounding the Phoenix conference are such as to demand a good deal of explanation. The conference emphasized rather than deemphasized the pressure of history. In this respect, it was unlike some other earlier national conferences of significance—the Bowling Green conference on the education of teachers (1958), the Woods Hole conference on what is known about learning (1959), and the Dartmouth conference on the teaching of English (1966). Without doubt, the processes of the conference—what happened and what did not happen—are as important as the words which were spoken. Several aspects of the conference itself, some of the goals of "The Year of the Liberal Arts," have never been explained or understood adequately. The *time* at which the conference was held proved to be of great importance; so did the *place*. But neither the former nor the full meaning of the latter was taken into consideration when the conference was being planned. The symbolism of the place could have been known; the symbolism of the time could hardly have been foreseen so as to have made the event deliberately fall in the midst of dramatic national events which drove home the importance of what the conference was all about. There were prosaic, workmanlike reasons for getting the group together at the place where it got together. That *what happened* was something other than a prosaic, workmanlike event was an accident. Yet, the time and place of the conference may well have made the difference.

The original reason for the conference, which was an outgrowth of the national TTT Program, was to talk about what liberal arts colleges can do to serve the education of teachers and to improve teaching. The West of the country was the conference host; that is, the two sponsoring cluster groups represented all of the TTT projects west of the Mississippi River. The point in so organizing the conference may not have been evident to all of the conference participants, that is, that the hosts at the conference should be all the TTT participants west of the Mississippi and that the guests at the conference should be, with but a few exceptions, all of the TTT people who came from east of the Mississippi. This was made obvious by the red and green "Guest" and "Host" badges given to each person who registered; but even so, this symbolism may have been entirely lost, as is so much of the symbolism that one intends when he plans the symbolic. The fact is that the West was made host as part of an effort to avoid the patronizing influence of what has since been called "the northeast philosophy" and as part of a conscious attempt, psychologically, to remove the eastern establishment from its natural habitat in the hope that it might turn expansive under western skies.

The location of the conference was also an intentional gesture to permit the westerners from the land-grant universities and state university systems which have grown out of the state teachers' colleges (once normal schools, in many cases) to be the intellectual hosts. The forms of liberal arts work which are growing up at these western universities are as surely now establishing national trends in our country as did once the forms developed by eastern colleges. California today is, for better or for worse, the state which most probably best predicts what the United States of the future will look like. Not that the movement is one way. It could be argued that the West's and the Midwest's oversized universities, those which are setting trends and suffering such anguish of student and faculty revolt, could profit from looking at the methods of teaching and organizing people into units for learning of one of the East's proudest possessions, the liberal arts colleges: in size, residential pattern, provisions for relating teacher and student outside the classroom, these older schools may be models. In any case, geography *is* important. William Arrowsmith advised the conference participants soon after they arrived in Arizona that "mapmakers should place their Mississippi in the same location, and avoid originality. It may be boring, but one has to know where he is." By the host-guest symbolism, the conference attempted to suggest where American liberal education was and where it ought to direct itself.

But in holding the conference in Phoenix, no extra symbolism was intended. There was no desire to suggest that the conference would resurrect the dead body of the liberal arts as Lactantius' phoenix bird reconstitutes itself from the ashes of its own pyre; nor was it being suggested that the liberal arts, having acquired a concern for black culture in recent years, should now develop a concern for Chicano culture. Indeed, just as surely as the sun sets in the West, the designers of the conference clean forgot about the fact that in selecting Phoenix they were placing the meeting in the homeland of a Mexican-American population that had only recently organized itself, a population which had many members and which, in the manner of today's politics, was becoming increasingly militant.

While the significance of where the meeting was held escaped everyone except the Mexican-Americans, and although location was not understood to be an issue until the day before the conference began, it does not follow that the planners of the Phoenix conference were either unaware of militancy throughout the country or indifferent to the wide demands being represented. Neither does it follow that they were less than slightly stupid. "Stupid" they were accused of being immediately when the conference began, as these documents will indicate. There may have been madness in the method of those who planned the conference, but their madness was not the madness of people who were either deliberately illiberal or deliberately insulting, although both charges may have superficial support. What is clear is that the planners of the conference did not know about all of the resources at their disposal and that they were insensitive to the possible value of many individuals who were not known to be available. Because of this, perhaps, one dean from the West Coast, who thought that "the conference was noteworthy in several ways, all negative," wrote that it mainly revealed "something about the mentality of USOE bureaucrats." Perhaps so. But letters of this sort work both ways; such a comment on the material which follows must surely also reveal something about the mentality of this dean as well.

Phoenix was also chosen because previous experience had shown it to have ideal conference facilities; another dean, this one from the East Coast, wrote that "the physical arrangements were superb (I almost said sublime)." Richard Lid has written:

> Phoenix was a good place to hold a conference—if a sense of place can in any meaningful way be said to contribute to the mood of a conference and to direct its agenda. Phoenix had sun, warmth; it offered hospitality and informality. It had the grandeur of mountains and a sweep of sky and an accompanying feeling of expansiveness; it had its arena of stockyards, prime beef on the hoof and on the table; it had Frank Lloyd Wright's legacy in the nearby desert. All-in-all Phoenix was a good place to hold a conference at which East meets West, and the meeting of the Eastern establishment with its Western counterpart was certainly among the purposes and priorities of the conference planners.

That the Phoenix conference was to seem for so many of us a time of enormous emotional urgency—almost of dying and rebirth or of going numb and coming awake—was an accident. So much for geographical determinism.

The Time and Its Events

April is the cruellest month, breeding
Lilacs out of the dead land, mixing
Memory and desire, stirring
Dull roots with spring rain.

Datta. Dayadhvam. Damyata.
Shantih shantih shantih

The notions of "Giving, sympathizing, controlling" (*Datta, dayadhvam, damyata*) were all basic to the Phoenix conference in a special way. For still another unplanned factor was introduced as we all basked under the warming sun of Arizona on the last day of April, 1970, being treated to the physical and esthetic arrangements basic to the success of any conference; the conference guests, hosts, and planners had been speaking casually, as they arrived, of such subjects as "giving to" and "sympathizing with" other human beings or learning humane sorts of cultural self-control. This other unplanned factor worked, like the unplanned aspect of the selection of the place, to the advantage of the conference. It helped to intensify the talk about what a humane man and what a humane society are. It helped to give one the feeling that the "idea and the reality" of history were coming together in an especially powerful way. On the day that people began to arrive in Phoenix, the president of the United States announced the invasion of Cambodia. The great sweeping forces that seem from time to time to descend on man and to make the sort of "history" which clearly changes the course of the human world's actions, and sometimes its destiny—these great forces seemed to engulf even the Arizona desert. So significant was the event that, instead of being perceived as an event thousands of miles away, it was perceived as a campus event. It was almost as if the invasion had occurred at home, on campus after campus. And so it was also in Phoenix: people felt the fear of physical invasion. Men's minds were tormented. Since many of the invited guests, from East and West, were high-ranking administrators of the country's colleges and universities, the timing probably proved to be just as decisive, in what happened and what people thought happened at Phoenix, as the choice of the place.

As one participant said: "President Nixon's decision to go into Cambodia frankly threw me into a psychological depression." Others were equally troubled. Excitement and adrenalin were there in almost equal parts; the first speaker following the keynoter, the vice chancellor of one of the world's largest systems of higher education, said that when he had left New York that morning, of the twenty campuses in his system, "two were absolutely peaceful— they're brand new and have no students; three were in relative calm —they're graduate and upper division schools; twelve were under siege; two had been taken and we hadn't heard from one." Hobert Burns, cosponsor of the Phoenix conference, left for his campus after the first evening to deal with events which soon led to his own resignation. Given the fact that even when the participants came to the conference, Kingman Brewster was under attack by the vice-president and the spotlight was on New Haven with its Panther trial and student discussions, few who were at Phoenix could be unmindful that the world crisis and the campus crisis had come together in a way that did not permit anyone to believe that the liberal arts and the arts of teaching had worked together everywhere in American education for good and reason, for sweetness and light. One had cause to wonder what fabric of generosity, sympathy, or self-control could hold the colleges or the culture together.

Yet, to question, "Is your campus still intact?" or to say, "My university has been gripped in a crisis," was to ask questions and to make statements which might have emerged in these forms had there been no invasion. For similar questions and statements were normal since the college crisis began some six years before at Berkeley. Granted that Kent State and Jackson State are the most recent and most terrible of a long series of episodes, nevertheless it is clear that things between Berkeley and Cambodia had not changed very much. If anything had happened, the cries had gotten louder and the mystery of *why* had deepened. Involved individuals on and off campus had already seen both how much was at stake and how much was unknown about what was at stake.

Since World War II, the undergraduate years in a student's life had become the vulnerable years. The B.A. had become as essential to him as had TV to Americans generally, and he had become the victim of an affluent society which, increasingly and routinely, demanded both the B.A. and TV as "inalienable rights." Ironically, at the same time, many citizens were rediscovering the more important fact that many an individual's political "inalienable rights," seemingly guaranteed since the time of the Declaration of Independence, were not guaranteed—not those of the Indians, the Mexican-Americans, or the Puerto Ricans; not those of black people or of many poor whites. Since 1954, by virtue of the Supreme Court's school integration decision, pressure for civil rights had become more real; it had become more intimate, in a physical sense, and more specific in an ideological sense, because it had been focused on the schools—and, hence, on the students and on their families. As all of this was occurring, the streets of our cities were also exploding. Jefferson had warned that our great cities would become to the body politic as "sores do the human body." And the streets and schools became the rallying centers of opposition to "establishment control" of America; what was at stake in the struggle was more personal than Vietnam or the cities or the lack of rights. What was at stake was the education of children and its domination by elite groups, groups which up until now had been unmolested in their use of the country's colleges and universities as command stations designed to protect the traditions of the nineteenth century. The groups which controlled the school boards and schools had, in many cities and rural areas, shown only surface regard for the public interest.

What was wrong in the schools began in the colleges. While old undergraduate customs—including undergraduate admissions requirements and academic requirements—were becoming increasingly meaningless, graduate school and professional school requirements were having the effect of further reducing the meaningfulness of the undergraduate degree. It was, more and more, becoming a preprofessional degree, one which crammed into students more and more of the techniques of a discipline and less and less of its wisdom, excitement, and meaning. What was becoming quite apparent, as President Charles DeCarlo of Sarah Lawrence observed, was that "the whole packaging of education with its unitizing of knowledge had all but destroyed any meaningful relationship between the teacher and the student." William Arrowsmith had been talking to campus audiences about this destruction; he had been writing about it, beginning with his article in *Harper's* in March, 1966, entitled "The Shame of the Graduate Schools." A few months later, he delivered an important blast to the stunned and somewhat shocked college administrators who were gathered in New Orleans attending the annual festive rites in tribute to the American university which are sponsored by the American Council on Education. Arrowsmith said that he spoke "for the classroom teacher" who must perform a "kind of teaching which alone can claim to be called educational, an essential element in all noble human culture, and hence a task of infinitely more importance than research scholarship," and, he added, a "kind of teaching . . . with which this meeting is apparently least concerned."

It was appropriate that the first step should be talk. A few institutions began, in the mid-1960's, serious reform measures designed to make learning a more democratic thing, to ensure student rights and to make the work between professor and student more collaborative and more meaningfully related to the securing of the rights of individuals, rights long promised them: a Brown influenced by an Ira Magasiner, a scattering of cluster colleges, some promising and some pretty horrible "free universities" in various places about the country. Anyone can name places which have changed, apparently with profit. Generally, faculty evaluations were made, some students were placed on committees, and more books were written. Books and books and books. In most places, talks, words, and books seemed about the extent of it. Much of what was being said was written by people limited by the perspectives of their own institutions, people who had what Peter Brooks has described as "a mental set derived from the forms, the implicit assumptions and rationale generated within the university establishment over the years." As Mr. Brooks observes, few of the books broke through to "radical reassessment and proposal"; few looked closely at the relation between the knower and the known as suggesting what a teacher ought to be to a student, and a teacher to a student; few considered what the "counter university" which might reform the university ought to be like. Indeed, Brooks asserts that only a few people were

> encouraging the growth of a counter university within the university—counter courses, counter curricula, perhaps counter colleges, which would reexamine the basis on which the more "standard" curriculum was proceeding. [In such counter universities,] the standard work of the university could go

forward while at the same time its necessity was being radically questioned. [They] would allow us to live in our house while we were wrecking and rebuilding it.[2]

Brooks offers the hope that by such a dialectical interplay it would be possible to emphasize that "education is primarily neither old structures nor new ones, but process. It would put at the center of undergraduate education the principle of the *agon*, or dispute, central to Greek philosophy and literature."

The events on college campuses triggered by the Cambodian invasion seemed to represent the death of an old order—an old set of structures. During the period which we spent at Phoenix, what "remained to be seen" was whether or not the university could recover until the country was at ease with the world and out of Vietnam. The so-called Amherst declaration had earlier seemed to suggest that the problems of higher education could be largely solved in foreign fields; the Cambodian invasion tended to make many at Phoenix agree.[3] As to the surfaces of the case, there could be no doubt: for reasons which are not always clear, many colleges and universities administrators had been unable to keep order on campus; by coincidence or conviction, these same administrators had become involved in politics. They were questioning the meaning of a world crisis on campus to a degree unknown in recent times. Some critics have said that the presidents had moved toward the political arena unconsciously as a means of explaining their own failure. Whatever the reasons for their failure to "keep order," whatever the sources of their political involvement, they were dropping like flies. Yet, even before Sputnik it was apparent that the basic problems of American higher education—especially those of undergraduate education—would not go away easily and that they were rooted in what institutions of higher education were doing *as centers of teaching and learning*. The concatenation of Phoenix and Cambodia, what was said at Phoenix, may suggest that college administrators are willing to look directly at American education for answers to their problems and perhaps for answers to the problems which the country will face across a period of time into the future. To do so would be to turn the Amherst declaration around.

[2] See below, p. 246.
[3] The text of the Amherst letter to President Nixon is in the *New York Times* of May 3, 1969.

I was gratified that the Phoenix conference placed responsibility for the problems of education so squarely on American higher education itself. The notion that what is wrong with higher education —with students, strikes, tensions over Vietnam, and so forth— relates to what is wrong with the colleges or universities as centers of teaching has long preoccupied me. On February 6, 1969, I had occasion to speak to some three hundred college administrators and teachers from all over the nation, most of whom were directors of federally supported programs to train other teachers. My speech was entitled "The Fourth Revolution." What I am reproducing here is a shortened version of that speech. It explains some of my reasons for holding high hopes for "The Year of the Liberal Arts" conference.

THE FOURTH REVOLUTION

You have all heard the tale of Thoreau languishing in the Concord jail over a matter of civil rights. It is a famous, oft-told story. One of its more engaging moments occurs when Emerson, visiting him, is asked by the blunt Thoreau: "Why aren't you here, too, Waldo?" My question to those who are on campuses where there has been no student revolt, no sign of teacher militancy, must be much the same. Put in my terms, why business as usual? How come? ". . . when all 'round us bombs are bursting in air" and nothing is quite as usual? Let me quickly add, and quite purposefully—as one must in these early days of what I would like to call the Fourth Revolution— that I, too, am against the wanton destruction of property; I, too, believe in academic freedom and the liberal arts (whatever they are), and also in sweet reason to boot. I, too, fully appreciate that there is often more need than seems apparent from afar for teachers to be discreet, to continue to work hard at giving their students "an education," and, above all, to avoid such disturbing phenomena (called confrontations) as have occurred at Berkeley and Columbia and, with such remarkable vigor, at San Francisco State College.

Alas, even as we continue with business as usual—even if the education being given is not so very well done—there is every indication that we are about to forget another point Thoreau made when he suggested that if you give a soldier an education, you will make of him a deserter. And, thus, the question remains: "Why aren't you here, too, Waldo? Is everything jake on campus? Are things that good?" And, if the answer were, "Yes, things are rosy, I'm still doing my thing at the same old stand to my utter satisfaction," then one must ask *why aren't you listening?*

No doubt it is sometimes difficult to know exactly what the shouting is all about. But, nonetheless, the question remains: What is going on elsewhere that isn't happening at home—*and why not?* Why isn't it happening at home? Are you sure it won't happen? Perhaps far too many of us are ignoring the fire bell that rings in the night, warning us of the Fourth Revolution. It may even be that there is still time, but there is not as much as we would like. The academic community seems ever ready to agree with T. S. Eliot's Prufrock who was able to rationalize himself into a state of inertia with the belief that "there will be time."

> ... time yet for a hundred indecisions,
> And for a hundred visions and revisions....

What's happening, or so it appears to this bureaucratized historian, is that the campus revolts are beginning to add up to the first great protest of modern times against the academic community at large. They are really announcing to one and all, it seems to me, the failure of the university to serve adequately the society which supports it. The student protest movement is a protest against nineteenth-century educational methods being applied to students who will live much of their lives (and whose children will live all of their lives) in the next century. It is a protest against colleges and universities which remain places where the professor's education may continue, while the student's may not start; it is a protest against the Ph.D. credit card which is validated by scholarly ghosts of the nineteenth century and universally accepted as a criterion of excellence in the twentieth; it is a protest against teachers who go to "think-tanks," to foreign countries (yes, even to Washington), in order to serve their country while not always serving their students. Finally, it is a protest against teachers who do not teach, a protest against those who are unable to unite "the young and the old in the imaginative consideration of learning."

The causes which I assert to be basic to the student revolution may momentarily be obscured by other, but nonetheless related, causes. But all of the revolts add up to one charge, they all come down to one central issue: our American democracy is not delivering the "inalienable rights" which were promised. It would appear that American education, the handmaiden to democracy, at least as it presently operates, is unable to play its role in making the delivery of what was promised any easier at this particular time in our history.

Many students, many teachers, and, I suspect, even more parents view the present disturbances on campus as so much hippielike activity, reflecting genuine enough teen-age frustration but still, even when destructive, merely traditional frustration and only a sign of momentary youthful rebellion. Or they view the disorders (read: riots) as manifestations of black power, indiscriminately tied in their minds to crime in the streets, slums, and civil rights. The danger is that these revolts may all too easily be dismissed as merely a passing phase. They may be seen as having little, if any, relationship to the destiny of the American university. All too often we are ready to exile students to Siberia as if they were traitors. Or, merely embarrassed, we pretend they are not here but rather off on some kind of private Teddy Roosevelt-like war in other, not so very important, parts of the country—almost as if in other parts of the world. In short, those students who protest may often appear quite unrelated to us and to our lives; certainly they often seem unrelated to the college of our choice.

My thesis, in case you have missed it, is that these revolts represent a major attack on higher education as we know it—an attack from which higher education, and we along with it, may never recover. And if the university and college world does recover, the way in which it recovers will depend upon the way teachers react here and now.

But of course, there are other problems. Almost no one in the country doubts that the intensity of the present struggle taking place in the forum of the streets and on certain campuses is further heightened by reason of the black man's demanding his inalienable rights; almost no one doubts that the intensity of the struggle is heightened by reason of the city, with its seemingly incurable problems; almost no one doubts that its intensity is heightened by reason of the general public's indifference to or ignorance about large cities and the challenge minority groups present to established America. Finally, whether you come from a school district or a college campus, almost no one can doubt that the intensity of the struggle is doubly heightened because of the transparent and demonstrable ease with which teachers can so comfortably escape "East, North, and West" from

cities, slums, and crime,
civil rights for the Indian,
the Mexican-American,
the Spanish-American,
the Negro and others including
those vagrant white Anglo-Saxon Protestant groups. . . .

With irony the WASPS are deserted—left high and dry in the eastern citadels of learning and elsewhere.

Is it not wrong to be content and complacent? And has the academic community not been complacent on campus after campus and in school after school? Regardless of exceptions, and there are many, is it not all too evident that, Babbitt-like, many teachers still find little, if any, relationship between what they do and what happens elsewhere, whether in Berkeley and Columbia or in Tokyo and Paris? Or, to paraphrase a now justly famous comment, does it not appear as if they, too, believe that after you've seen one student revolt, you've seen them all?

On many campuses, and in many schools, teachers are serene. Last fall I gave a lecture on the place of scholarship and the future of higher education. Only one paragraph in that speech referred to student revolt and teacher militancy, and it, in connection with other "evidence," supported my contention that the "high church" of graduate education is, as presently constituted, a deterrent to decent teaching and to meaningful learning. But as soon as I mentioned student revolts and teacher militancy, I lost my audience of some eight-hundred faculty members. A moment later, but still too late, I remembered that I was in an area of the Midwest where probably there had never been a Negro college student—in fact, there was none to be had, unless bused in by a "Berlin airlift." Afterwards, commenting on my lapse, a member of the faculty told me that "yes, the student body was mostly Scandinavian in origin, and the rest were white." It was also clear that the faculty didn't really have any more reason for letting down its hair than the students at this particular place would have had to let theirs grow. How lucky, we think. After all, you say, one can't blame them. Without doubt things are different "out there."

But my point is that things *can't* really be that different out there. Berkeley and Columbia, to cite extreme cases, can't be that different, either. For a common thread does run throughout the academic community. There is a remarkable sameness in our schools, in spite of our dedication to diversity. The area of agreement is far greater than the degree of difference. Airport-modern and motel-madness prevail among architects who design the schools to which we all send our children so that they might "get an education." Almost no one doubts that everybody is entitled to a college education, even if not to equal education. And everywhere, there is that sense of mass-produced colleges which, like a chain of Howard Johnson restaurants, stretch from coast to coast, providing all 57 varieties to the innocent bystander—your child and mine.

So the student revolts. At least, some students revolt. And in spite of a mixture of motives (all highly classified, some never to be analyzed or fully understood), the students—more than meet the eye, at least—protest against one set of clear and present conditions discernible by us. The common theme of the student protests, whatever the diversity of the "hills" they attack, is a concern with *the quality of instruction* offered in our schools, *the type of instruction* being provided, and *the purposes of the instruction.*

The students are involved with black power, they have had an effect on Vietnam, they have an ability to fight fire with fire and to take on Dow Chemical, they know how to knock down some decrepit university administrations, mostly administrations ready to fall—but these world or national or statewide political issues are not the student's primary concern. Their primary cause relates to their conditions *as students.* As students, they are, however inadvertently, penetrating to the very heart of the matter in order to achieve educational justice and a decent local or world community. The heart of the matter is *the teacher in the classroom* (or the teacher *not* in the classroom, as the case might be) and *the courses offered.* Courses of study, the orthodox corollary of the lecture system, are anomalies—vehicles no longer able to transport students into the ecstasy of learning. We all know this. Created in the previous century to serve other and earlier generations of students, courses remain the seemingly solid basis on which the academic community is operated. And such an assumption of solidity is archaic beyond belief.

The present generation of students is interdisciplinary minded, ahead even of those few teachers willing to pay lip service to interdisciplinary studies. Students know that the solutions to many of today's pressing problems, like air and water pollution, poverty and urban renewal, space exploration and American education itself, cannot be learned from a textbook and are not going to come out of a "course" since they cannot be put in a discipline-oriented box. They also know that solutions to these problems really can't be explained by bright young men waving their arms about.

The student in revolt is conscious of things in today's society that older people cannot always see or feel as easily. It has always been thus. But the students of this particular generation have additional abilities which enable them to see, and therefore to revolt against, the rigidity of Gutenberg, the persistence of Shakespeare, and the horrors of American history, not only because our history distorts even Plymouth Rock, not only because there is nothing inherently relevant about Shakespeare, but also because there is so much more to communication than Gutenberg ever suspected.

One might attribute the student's awareness to television. But there are so many other factors, not the least of which is the absence of a third world war and the insistence of a smaller, but nonetheless killing, war. This generation of students has what the generation of pacifists and isolationists prior to the Second World War didn't have—time and leisure and the money to be a nonviolent and revolution-bent generation. And somehow, they know formal learning is no longer only in books and, furthermore, that education cannot be packaged by, or tied to, or directed by, the teacher—as once it was.

Can any one doubt that the current set of riots and the present sense of revolt herald a deep distrust of the American academic system in its entirety? It is a distrust which begins with its system of recruitment and the insistence upon credentials. It is a distrust gained by looking at its power structure and the domination by school boards and boards of trustees and regents, which are all too often composed of men too rich, too old, too white, and too much out of touch. It is a distrust nourished by its reward system—the rewarding of teachers who neither gladly teach nor seem to learn much at all. The revolt touches on the little things in American higher education—its continuation of the sacred rites of college with five courses each year, four times over, as if they could add up to a liberal arts education waiting at the end of the rainbow. It also touches on the big commitments of higher education, particularly its determination to leave the education of teachers in the hands of those who lack the resources necessary to do the job.

It is all too easy to dismiss the whole movement, whether the movement touches civil rights and black power or student-faculty relationships, partly because established America can see and measure the "student enemy" and they are so very few in number. But it should be recalled that it only took a few men and women to start three of the greatest revolutions of our time—in America, in France, and in Russia. Who among us doubts that we are witnessing the beginning of the Fourth Revolution? And who among us will not play his part?

My motive, as "The Fourth Revolution" makes clear, for encouraging the Phoenix conference was simply this: that I felt that our educational, and even our political, crises to be rooted in *bad* education. I wanted to get *good* people to argue cogently about this notion—to give it visibility. While it is at once apparent that the times have outstripped some of the references in my two-year-old speech, nonetheless it appears to have withstood the test of the intervening time as an analysis of the seriousness of the student protest movement and as an attempt to explain a set of assumptions about the root causes of it all. Had I given the speech at Phoenix, I would have referred to Kent State instead of Berkeley and Columbia. Had I spoken later, I would have spoken of Jackson State. Instead of referring as I did on February 6, 1969, to "bombs bursting in air," I would have referred to bomb bursts in college buildings, bombings which, by 1970, were killing people. Instead of making a somewhat playful reference to "confrontations and similar phenomena," with a wave of the hand, I would have treated confrontations with a seriousness which I could not have imagined two years earlier.

On the other hand, the students' concern with national and political issues has broadened beyond expectation, partly perhaps because the rights of undergraduates have been reconsidered and redefined; undergraduates now have, on many campuses, rights which are different and probably better. The tone of our national life has changed and become more tense, perhaps more tragic, certainly more melodramatic. Yet I believe that the central issues in higher education remain the same: *the inadequacy of higher education to serve its clientele, and hence the country.* We, and others involved in planning the Phoenix conference, know that there are major revolutionary forces at work in American society. All of us have witnessed, even experienced, black power and student power and we are not about to underestimate their importance, but we doubt that they can explain *all* that has happened or that they, any more than the

Vietnam war, can be asked to carry the burden of what so many of us are responsible for.

The Birth of Institutions

> And was Jerusalem builded here
> Among these dark Satanic Mills?
> ....
> I will not cease from Mental Fight
> Nor shall my Sword sleep in my hand
> Till we have built Jerusalem
> In England's green and pleasant Land
>
> William Blake, from "Milton"

> But to form a *free government*, that is, to temper together those opposite elements of liberty and restraint in one consistent work, requires much thought, deep reflection, a sagacious, powerful and combining mind. This I do not find in those who take the lead in the National Assembly.
>
> Edmund Burke, "Reflection on the Revolution in France"

Revolutions are born of the sense that institutions do not serve the desires, needs, wills of those who have been invited or forced to be part of those institutions. The transformation of institutions is a much more subtle process than is a revolution, for basic human behavior patterns, basic human conceptions of values and roles and ways of relating to other human beings must change for an institution to change. Hence it is not surprising that so many of the institutional patterns which have emerged in modern Russia seem an extension of the bureaucratic pattern, the rural land-usage pattern, and the movement toward industrialization which characterized Czarist Russia in the late nineteenth and early twentieth centuries. It is not surprising that many of the ritualistic institutions which undergird Maoism—the curious combination of the secular, the ritualistic, and the religious under an aphoristic political leader and seer—seem to be very like the ritualistic institutions which undergirded the Confucian era.

Revolutions have occurred which did not change institutions. When institutions were changed, it was due to plodding, long-term, careful, detailed work developed in terms of a new style and set of values; the work was work which genuinely fulfilled a need (consider, for instance, the institutional transformations which have occurred in Sweden, England, and rural United States in the last eight years). The USOE Training the Trainers of Teachers Program attempts to fulfill such a need: it attempts the building of new institutions to handle problems not being handled by present institutions. It also tries to make room for the transformation of those leaders of present educational institutions who act as if their institutions ought primarily to serve their private will to exercise power over other people and for the enlightening of those more subtle leaders who sense that an educational institution which *serves* their will to power will probably *also serve* the needs of students. Unless the power center is challenged, unless new options are given to school children, to high school and college students, as well as to graduate teaching assistants and young professors across the country, the question of educational reform will be academic and social revolution will occur.

We may, of course, be in a period when planning for new institutions—which of necessity implies pattern, order, decorum, reasoning, and some willingness to find meaning in a ritualistic reenactment of that which has been done before—is in vain. Benjamin DeMott, writing in an article in the *New York Times* Sunday magazine (which mentions the TTT Program as an effort to build new institutions) speaks of the emptiness or wildness which we may face. Speaking of the planning of the men who saw the need for change in the late sixties, he writes:

> The immediate experience of the multiple-selved cause contains within it an antinominian, anti-intellectual ferocity that has thus far created fears only about the safety of institutions—universities, high schools, legislatures, churches, political conventions. But the serious cause for alarm is the future of mind. The love of the Enveloping Scene as opposed to orderly plodding narratives, fondness for variety of self rather than for stability, puts the very idea of mind under extraordinary strain. [In confronting this scene, the planners of the sixties, according to DeMott, were] aware that "planning" would necessarily henceforth be in bad odor; yet, they were unconvinced that the future could be met with any hope whatever minus the resources of intellect. One question addressed was: "Can society be reorganized in a manner that will accommodate the appetite

for self-variousness and possibility—without insuring the onset of social chaos?"[4]

That question, as formulated by DeMott, is a primary question of the TTT Program.

The main thrust of TTT is to identify and "educate" teachers and administrators in the schools and teachers and administrators in the colleges. These people may teach by what they say or by what they do or by the power they have over a "system" and the way in which they use it. The purpose of the TTT Program is to confront these people with the crisis of the times and with the necessity of building new institutions within the present system.

The assumption is that the schools which are going to pieces and the communities in which the schools are going to pieces have the power to educate those "teachers" who seem to control their lives; such people are identified as the third "T" in TTT. The schools and the communities have the political power, once they are organized and come alive to their situation. School superintendents and school boards can demand and get from higher education better teachers; communities such as those in Rough Rock or I.S. 201 can demand and get new teachers and new patterns of education.[5] But the communities and schools do not have power merely by virtue of their political sense; they have a power which resides in the emblems which are formed by their crisis state—emblems which have been rather dramatically described by the Holts and Kohls and Kozols and Dennisons and Silbermans and Colemans and, long before, by Carter G. Woodson in his book *The Mis-Education of the Negro*.

Sometimes for a man simply to confront the realities which his life creates is enough to change him. The TTT project has tried to develop arrangements which will force those who "govern" American education to confront the reality of the schools and the power of their awakening constituencies. But unfortunately, to confront realities is not necessarily to change; it may only make one more defensive, fixed in position, angry, repressive, and vindictive. To confront an elite without offering it the reserves to change may

[4] Benjamin DeMott, "The Sixties: A Cultural Revolution," *New York Times Magazine*, December 14, 1969, p. 28.

[5] I.S. 201 is a black community-controlled school in Harlem; the Rough Rock Demonstration School is located in Rough Rock, Arizona, and is the first school controlled by a Navajo school board in all of its aspects; hiring, curriculum, the handling of the children's behavior, etc.

simply encourage an inflexibility in the elite which is no better than inflexibility anywhere else. At Phoenix there was an attempt to provide a strategy to keep people from becoming defensive.

However, describing the resources offered people at the Phoenix conference requires a description of what, before the conference, we had thought to be the *power realities* and the *classroom teaching realities* in American education, the realities from which the TTT Program derives its reforming energies:

Item: We believed that the minimum essential freedoms and rights had not yet been secured for many students in America's elementary school classrooms or in their college classrooms: the freedom to pursue the sort of learning and information which interests them; the freedom to learn about one's own people, their history and their past; the freedom to have one's feelings respected; the freedom to learn without physical beating or other forms of institutional intimidation.

Item: We believed that most of present education is folklore rather than thought—shopworn approaches passed down willy-nilly without regard to what we know about how man learns, where he can learn, or what sorts of institutions make learning and rational change possible.

Item: We believed that the subtler abuses of intellectual power in America's classrooms are matters of the relationship between *what we know* and *how we use what we know* in the political, the social, and the educational arena: "The abuse of power in the schools has to do with the importation into them, at their earliest levels, of a silly competitive system inimical in the long run to study; a linguistic decorum indicative only of the power of a class or race, an age group or a professional group, to demand from another group's children (as the price of success) language behaviors stylized as it wants them. The abuse of power is the importation of curricular structures reflective of the power of an administrative hierarchy—or a scholarly interest group—to dictate to the teacher, to prevent any humane granting to him of the freedom to create or reshape his own curricula in the classroom."[6]

---

[6] Paul A. Olson, *The Craft of Teaching and the Schooling of Teachers* (Reports of the First National Conference of the Tri-University Project, September 18–20, 1967), p. xi. This report is one of five conference reports issued by the Tri-University Project which was a predecessor of the TTT.

Item: We believed that the securing of freedom, the development of more intellectual, self-conscious approaches to education and the overcoming of the conventional abuses of power in education, required the creation of a new vehicle for discussion and negotiation, for reasoning together and change. This vehicle would bring together those who control the educational institutions which are training teachers but who are not talking to their constituencies *and* those in school and community who have never learned to adopt an educative, helping role with respect to those who are producing death at an early age in their neighborhoods. The controllers may not have talked to their constituencies because they unconsciously feared that they could not defend what they were doing or because they feared to look at the consequences of their actions in the "killing" of children. Many communities simply have never been asked to adopt a helping role with respect to those who control an aspect of their lives.

The introduction of the community into TTT was urged by the original TTT National Advisory Group in the spring of 1968 at a time when I.S. 201 was having its troubles, when the Oceanhill Brownsville difficulties had just reached a crest, and when the Rough Rock arrangement was not too old. The Office of Education's acceptance of this urging was, perhaps, the most significant step toward decolonializing the university which has been taken by the Office in recent years. It was also an important step in establishing what has since been called, in relation to many federal training programs, the principle of "parity," the principle according to which, as the first annual report of the Commissioner of Education on the Education Professions puts it, "representatives of the communities should take an equal part with representatives of institutions of higher education and the school system in negotiations concerning matters of budget, staff and program planning." The report goes on to observe, that "in the conduct of the [federally sponsored] program, the same equality should prevail."[7] It has been established practice since 1968 that any Office of Education program for trainers of teachers should be developed jointly by local staffs from professional (teacher) education, the liberal arts, and the schools "and [by] the community affected by the work of the teacher trainer."

[7] Don Davies, *The Education Professions—1968* (Washington, D.C., 1969), p. 51.

In the institution-building process, TTT has attempted to set up some forty-three small-scale "systems" within the established systems of education where the production of teachers is based on the notion of parity. In each of these programs, the consumers (i.e., the schools and the communities they serve) have direct political access—in the construction of budgets, the planning of programs and so forth—to the producers (i.e., the liberal arts colleges and the schools or departments of education). Problems of raw power and who gets the money (therefore the day-to-day power) interfere with the ideal of parity at times. However, the step—the thrust—in this direction has, according to most participants in the national TTT Program, been both beneficial and meaningful.

With the 1968 step toward community participation, the management of the TTT projects nationally took on a new dimension, so much so that they took a great deal of Bureau of Education Personnel Development time and energy and made the first year of the TTT Program into what could well have been called "The Year of the Community." Clearly, the TTT enterprise was volatile, given the introduction of parity into a training program. Its success was dubious, given our insistence that, minimally, the professional educator must combine forces with his colleagues in the liberal arts; and its outcome was uncertain, in that the attempt was to bring the schools themselves into the production of teachers.

As TTT leaders concerned themselves with the involvement of one new constituency, another seemed to walk away. This was particularly the case with the liberal arts people. Important figures in the liberal arts had been central to the early planning of the National Advisory Committee for the TTT Program, and some significant work in individual projects on the part of liberal arts people seemed probable when the project began; but as the actual training programs got under way, several things seemed to happen: project directors said they were unable to get good liberal arts people to work with them; important liberal arts people whose names appeared on proposals seem to have walked away from the barricades—back to their footnotes and collating and editing. Others left in a huff because the community was giving them a "hard time" and was wasting their time. The militant positions of low-income people, whether taken as strategy or a final position implied a rhetoric, a logic, and a style of going at things which seemed hard for the mind of the professor in the liberal arts to comprehend (a professor is supposed to be the most cosmopolitan of men).[8] The schools were willing to cooperate; they were eager to find ways to get whatever help they could in bringing to the fore a new kind of teacher and teacher of teachers. They often faced an educative daily scene in which the air was filled with anger and revolt, sit-ins, walk-outs, and burn-ups.

If the community was uneasy with its new power and uneasy that it might not have power, the schools were, in their upper echelons, eager but preoccupied with numerous federal projects. Hence, in most TTT projects, the schools of education were in the saddle. The professor of the liberal arts—with his probity and his faculty clubs (as DeMott said, "those bastions of privilege") and his sherry—had faded like the ghost of Peter Quint seen across the lake in *The Turn of the Screw*. But we had to get at him if we were ever to get at his college and its ally, the graduate school, if we were ever to get at those forces in American education which are pushing it away from teaching: the force pushing it away from the Socratic contact of mind with mind in the presence of a problem. These were also the forces pushing it toward the carrel and communication through publication. Hence "The Year of the Liberal Arts."

How to involve the liberal arts professor without making him defensive was a question of crucial importance. He was needed, and badly needed, we felt. His knowledge of linguistics was needed if we were to destroy the myths about language development which were destroying kids (cf. Burruel, infra); his knowledge of Third World history and culture was needed if we were to build institutions tempered to culture in architecture, spacial arrangement, administrative format, life rhythm, or cultural style. But the men whose "knowledge" was needed were themselves part of the problem. They were part of what Tom Wicker, in commenting on the Kerner report, has described as "white, moderate, responsible America," the America where, in his words, "the trouble lies" as regards the division of the country. If the nation, in the words of the Kerner

---

[8] The schools were deeply involved in the program. This was important since the whole enterprise depended on the school's allowing teacher trainers to be really involved with children from black, Chicano, Indian, and poor white schools. Too much of the education of teachers has involved giving teachers findings based on experiences with laboratory rats and giving them experience with conventional laboratory school children—that is, professors' kids. The schools were, however, much less receptive than were the colleges to community participation from locked-out communities.

report, was moving toward two societies—"one black, one white, separate and unequal"—the responsibility for turning things around must lie with the people more equal than others, the white professional establishment which has had such an important role in providing the myths by which men have lived in polite society, myths which accorded to them a professional style which gave to them, as part of an unkind system, a feeling that they were kind.

Black militants had tried to change that professional style—at Cornell, at San Francisco State, and elsewhere; white radicals had tried to change it at Columbia and elsewhere. While it is clear that such moves changed the people who moved on the university, it is not clear that they changed very many professors in their heart of hearts. Preston Wilcox, whose comments on what we were doing at Phoenix are harsh and are contained below, advised one of the TTT Programs to stop the confrontation between black and white in a black-white psychology course and advised the white participants to work on their own racism in all-white groups. His notion of asking white to talk to white came from his sense that only in such circumstances would people give up their defensiveness.

For various reasons, our strategy could not be quite so simple. It was not to be simply to suggest that white establishment speakers confront a white establishment audience. Rather we thought we would get, as our mainspeakers, men who had conventional academic credentials and reputations, but also men who had come to a new conviction and vocation: a William Arrowsmith, who had, in his own words, become a Johnny One-Note on the subject of the importance of authentic teaching; a Benjamin DeMott who had carried a similar crusade across the country into the Washington ghettos, into the backwaters of Mississippi in an SNCC project, and even into the white suburbs and the Ivy League; a Charles DeCarlo who was a former IBM manager and now the president of a small college which was, as a total institution under his direction, on a quest similar to that of Mr. Arrowsmith and Mr. DeMott. We had chosen as commentators on these speeches men who had had various, and differing, experiences in black and poor white communities: a Charles Wilson, a Richard Foster, a Bernard Watson. We had no one who could speak with authority of Chicano or Indian problems until we added, in response to a Chicano community request, Professor Leyba, Father Casso, and Mr. José Burruel. Each TTT project was asked to bring a strong community representative to comment, in the general discussions and small group meetings, on what was said.

We had hoped that where the vision of the establishment, of those "inside" outsiders who were the main speakers, coincided with the vision of the community persons, where both said the same thing at the conference, there would be some possibility for movement in the commitment of the people in the liberal arts. If one looks upon the community representatives on the one hand and the uncommitted liberal arts people that walked away from the job on the other hand as adversaries, one perhaps can better understand the psychology of what we were doing. Carl Rogers has spoken of what can be done to make large groups come to spend more time "listening with" and less time "evaluating about" one another:

> Even with our present limited knowledge, we could see some steps which might be taken, even in large groups, to increase the amount of listening *with,* and to decrease the amount of evaluation *about.* To be imaginative for a moment let us suppose that a therapeutically oriented international group went to the Russian leaders and said, "We want to achieve a genuine understanding of your views and even more important, of your attitudes and feelings toward the United States. We will summarize and resummarize these views and feelings if necessary, until you agree that our description represents the situation as it seems to you." Then suppose they did the same thing with the leaders in our own country. If they then gave the widest possible distribution to these two views, with the feelings clearly described but not expressed in name-calling, might not the effect be very great? It would not guarantee the type of understanding I have been describing, but it would make it much more possible. We can understand the feelings of a person who hates us much more readily when his attitudes are accurately described to us by a neutral third party, than we can when he is shaking his fist at us.[9]

Such a strategy is what we had in mind in organizing the conference as we did.

Self-knowledge comes through introspection; it comes also from

[9] Carl R. Rogers, "Communication: Its Blocking and Its Facilitation," in *Rhetoric: Discovery and Change,* ed. Kenneth L. Pike, Richard E. Young, and Alton L. Becker (New York, 1970), p. 288.

having other persons such as the persons on the podium or the members of the community present mirror their impressions of us back—the mirror which we initially *perceive* as a faithful mirror will most strike us as providing self-knowledge; self-knowledge comes further when people are taken away from their traditional institutional supports, their traditional hours of conducting business, and their traditional roles. It comes when the familiar and the unfamiliar, the threatening and the nonthreatening are appropriately mixed.

We may have missed entirely with our strategy, as the minority report section suggests. However, that the notion that the white establishment confronting itself and its own failure could come to very useful conclusions (very much the same conclusions that confrontations between community and college produce)—that this notion is not entirely foolish, may be suggested by the recognition on the part of the conference of the importance to the total educational scene of institutions which have a nonelitist tradition— black colleges, Indian colleges, Chicano-influenced institutions. This recognition came both from the establishment panel and from Mr. Wilcox's remarks in his comments on the conference, though he had not seen the transcript of the panel discussion when he wrote his comments. One conclusion: we are still able to do some reasoning together for the common profit. A similar coincidence between establishment position and community position may be seen on a great many other points. American higher education knows what it ought to do in many cases. It just hasn't done it. I say this descriptively, not aggressively.

American higher education has always been elitist; its faculties are still so, from Harvard to the latest community college trying to emulate either Harvard or its midwife, the local land-grant university. What the white establishment must see is that its collegiate way of life constitutes a style of life which has lost its content because the institutions out of which it grew are dead. (The situation is very well described by Alistair Cooke's article on Harvard in the *Manchester Guardian*, an article which describes Harvard after its 1969 SDS strike as a great brontosaurus of style with a small center of institutional purpose.) That this is the case for higher education generally and that the case can be otherwise is a matter described by Mr. Arrowsmith in his proposal for a university of the public interest, a street university. Such a university and similar sorts of institutions are proposed in other forms by other speakers: Mr. DeCarlo, Mr. DeMott, Mr. Powell.

The old "democratic institution," in whose hands lay the creation of whatever partial democracy we have had in the past, was surely the state normal school. We have often felt that analogous schools for our time could come into existence. If the liberal arts colleges became good teaching centers, everyone would know about teaching and learning; everyone would respect heterogeneity of culture and make an effort to teach, to relate, in terms of the cultural style and "history" represented by that *other*, that "thou," which is the student. But the liberal arts colleges have not so become. The last decade of NSF and Office of Education activity—the curriculum reform movement, the Title XI institutes, the regional labs, and now the TTT—has been directed toward stopping the war between colleges of education and colleges of arts and sciences. Yet the war goes on and children suffer, particularly children in locked-out communities.

Once in our history the democratic normal schools provided all of the training in teaching and in the liberal arts such as it was. Their functions were taken over by the teachers' colleges, many of which followed the Bagley plan and included liberal arts training in their curriculum. Columbia Teachers College was among these. But once the arts and sciences colleges had been defeated in their efforts to preserve higher education as an old style Ivy League sort of preserve, once the teachers' colleges were converted into state universities, what happened was that the democratization of education on the horizon—over 50 percent of our high school graduates beginning college though not staying long—went ahead while the foreground was ignored where one-fourth of our people remained functional illiterates, about one-fourth dropped out before finishing high school, and culture after culture was smashed on the iceberg of "curriculum standards," "structured curricula," College Boards. They were crushed by centralized educational authority controlled by WASP hierarchies, and by the research and scholarship establishment.

The liberal arts colleges, with the dawning of the fourth revolution, must find a new democratic purpose; and it is hard to see how that purpose will be all that different from that of the old normal schools, though teaching styles, and curricula, and the level of profundity will assuredly be different.

Colleges of education and liberal arts colleges surely must be

xlvi Introduction

merged as centers of liberal knowledge.[10] They must come together as an institution or as a series of small institutions to work on the democratic education of America. In any case, that notion is suggested in William Arrowsmith's paper; it is hinted at in papers by Richard Foster (his "new institution"), Benjamin DeMott, Paul Olson, and others. Even B. Othanel Smith, who speaks of a discipline which may be called "knowledge about acquiring knowledge" and of technological devices for studying this area and for learning to master it (i.e., to become a teacher), is speaking of an area which could be regarded as an application of various aspects of cognitive psychology. It does not matter which dies—the old arts college or the college of education; both are dead so far as American education is concerned. What matters is that the war cease and democratic education begin.

None of the sectors of education (colleges, schools, communities) can do it alone and no device (team teaching, modular scheduling, new calendars, or short hair) can do anything but divert us from the main question, which is how to produce better teachers. Unless the power structure is involved in reallocating power, buying and selling manpower devices and educational devices or bringing the sectors of American education together will be in vain. Unless we understand freedom, unless we can imagine the way into the other man's institution, we cannot educate. The guildhall which carries the shingle "Education" and the guildhall which carries the shingle "Liberal Arts" ought to come to be the guildhall "Liberalizing Education" or "Democratic Education."

The conclusions of individual members of the conference, which may lead to action on individual campuses, are to be found in the material which follows. The book is divided into seven sections: (I) "Give," (II) "Sympathize," (III) "Control," (IV) "The Education of

[10] I wrote to the speakers at the conference conveying my own conviction on this score before the conference:

> Furthermore, I believe that the essentials of pedagogy (banned from the liberal arts), when examined, have to do with substantive areas dealing with communication and behavior for fathers, artists, and businessmen as well as for teachers. Interestingly enough, the liberal arts deans themselves invariably hire and fire many if not most of the people in teacher education; to put it another way, at another level, it is an accepted fact that anywhere from 75 to 100 percent of the courses taken by an undergraduate who expects to become a teacher are in the liberal arts. Somewhere there is something more here than meets the eye. Ultimately, I suppose, we are asking why the liberal arts and teacher education are not essentially one and the same thing.

This letter was dated April 13, 1970.

Teachers and the University of Public Interest," (V) "Report from the Black and Brown Communities," (VI) "The Jesuit and the Trappist," and (VII) "Rapping about the University." Mr. Arrowsmith's section and the comment on his speech seemed to concern primarily how people, overcoming their hubris, can *give to* one another in education. Mr. DeMott's seemed to be concerned with how they could *sympathize with* one another in a meaningful way; Mr. DeCarlo's section seemed to concern primarily how man has *controlled* man narrowly, hierarchically, and destructively, and how his esthetic sense—his sense of the beauty of things—could become a new controlling force in his life and in education. The remaining sections are self-explanatory dialogue and comment.

Eliot speaks in *The Waste Land* of the fall of academic civilizations, with a sense very like that which we felt at Phoenix as campuses erupted in the wake of the Cambodian invasion:

> What is the city over the mountains
> Cracks and reforms and bursts in the violet air
> Falling towers
> Jerusalem Athens Alexandria
> Vienna London
> Unreal

He also speaks in the same section, as the rain which will bring new growth descends, of how new civilizations are built:

> Da
> Datta
> Da
> Dyadhvam
> Da
> Damyata
> Datta
> Dayadhvam
> Damyata[11]

It may not be accidental that, in the midst of the Cambodian invasion and the campus strikes, when the apocalypse was seemingly upon us, those who were discussing whatever is liberal in education should turn to such themes: giving, sympathizing, and controlling.

---

[11] "*Datta, dayadhvam, damyata*: Give, sympathize, control. The fable of the meaning of the Thunder is found in the Brihadaranyaka—Upanishad, 5, 1. A translation is found in Deussen's *Sechzig Upanishads des Veda*, p. 489."

The primary thrust of this section is the significance of man's capacity to develop a hubris which keeps him from seeing the "other"—a hubris which manifests itself in bad teaching as well as in the death of the sense of tragedy. Hubris is whatever excludes. The speakers are Mr. William Arrowsmith, classicist formerly from the University of Texas, and Mr. Timothy Healy, vice-chancellor of the City University of New York. Mr. Arrowsmith's speech, called "The Future of Teaching," given to the American Council on Education meeting in New Orleans in 1966, is included as the third piece in this section.

I
GIVE: *DATTA*

Datta, dayadhvam, damyata

WILLIAM ARROWSMITH

Teaching and the Liberal Arts: Notes Toward an Old Frontier

"All mapmakers," says Saul Bellow's wise old Sammler, "should place the Mississippi in the same location, and avoid originality. It may be boring, but one has to know where he is."

The Indians usually knew where they were before we uprooted them from themselves and from the land. They stood simply on the earth of their convictions, resisting as stubbornly as they could the outrageous benevolence of government policies and the gospel greed of the land-hungry whites. Exploitation, we have been told, cannot be seen as such by those who do it; it must be mystified and viewed as benevolence. It was in this spirit that the government tried a century ago to persuade, or otherwise compel, the Shoshones of Utah and Wyoming to renounce their ancient Earthmother, sell their arable land to the invaders, and retire to semideserts where— such was the white man's mystifying logic—they would learn the art of farming under conditions that doomed them to failure. The Indian agent explained his progressive proposals, and the tribe debated them. Then Chief Washakie rose to summarize. Mustering what little English he had, he said tersely but effectively, "God damn a potato!"—and with these "winged words" he sat down, adjourning the council. He meant, of course, that buffalo hunters had better things to do than grub for tubers like a lot of Irishmen or Paiutes. But that was not all. He also meant what Smohalla, the great prophet of the Columbia, said in answer to the same demands: "It is a bad word that comes from Washington always.... You ask me to cut grass and make hay and sell it and be rich like the white man. But how dare I cut my Mother's hair? Shall I take a knife [i.e., a plow] and tear my Mother's breast? Then when I die, she will not take me to her bosom to rest. My young men shall never work. Men who work cannot dream, and wisdom comes in dreams."

Aristocratic words. Too aristocratic for the whites, who characteristically mistook the disdain for drudgery as nothing more than Indian shiftlessness. But they are much more than contempt for menial labor. Behind these words of Washakie and Smohalla lies all of Indian life, the very heart of Indian culture. They are statements of the spirit, and the spirit's priorities, and they spring from a natural piety that merely practical or vulgar men could never hope to understand. Washakie, I suppose, had nothing against potatoes. He was a prudent man, a chief, and even Shoshones must eat. But there are some things a man, a true man, will not eat, even if he starves for his refusal. To the Indian the dream was the bearer of his identity, his name, just as it also conferred his citizenship—his membership in the great community outside himself to which he was forever linked, to the friendly dead, to the genius of the place, the Great Spirit overhead, the powers of nature, and all those things which we should now view as the voices of our unconscious and our past. In the dream he encountered the Other—something he recognized as kin to himself, but larger and unmistakably there. For it he felt the awe and aspiration of the limited for the unlimited. And in the dream he found a self by transcending himself.

I do not mystify. The young Indian on the verge of manhood waits, tense with promise, in the wilderness. He does not eat or sleep or drink. Because he invokes a higher power, he purifies himself; he is all aspiration. The dream comes like a revelation, inward yet also outward. It suddenly speaks his name, tells him who he is and what his ripening powers are—the grace of the otter, the badger's courage, the gravity of the elk. It makes him a man among men. The dream seals the maturing powers of the dreamer with the tutelary welcome of the larger world, the great chorus of the others. And what is true of the boy's vigil is also true for his people, whose sachems and shamans dream the great collective dreams of the tribe's fate, just as the Greek seer understood the voice of the oracular earth and the gods in it. Everything the Indian meant by his humanity and its fulfillment, every link with the great world of the others, was violated and annulled by that stupid word from Washington. And the word got the answer it deserved: "God damn a potato!"

1

There, my Mississippi is on the map. Education is a spiritual affair, a matter of fulfillment, a fatal business. An old and familiar text, it might seem, dressed up in topical Indian guise. Perhaps. The same convictions can be found in Plato, or Nietzsche, or Emerson, or in any ordinary commencement address. It is boring, but it is true. And perhaps it is not boring at all. But it is where we begin. "The mind of this country," said Emerson, a contemporary of Smohalla, "being taught to aim at low objects, feeds on itself. Young men of the fairest promise . . . are hindered from action by the disgust which the principles on which business is managed inspire, and turn drudges or die of disgust. . . . Our culture has truckled to the times. It is not manworthy. If the vast and spiritual are omitted, so are the practical and the moral. It does not make us brave or free. We teach boys to be such men as they are. We do not teach them to aspire to be all they can. We do not give them a training as if we believed in their noble nature. . . .We aim to make accountants, engineers, but not to make able, earnest, great-hearted men."[1] Smohalla and Washakie tell the same miserable story, but they tell it more forcefully, from the viewpoint of the victims who suffered the arrogance and inhumanity of the failed education Emerson describes. For Emerson the failure is mostly a matter of low ends, of making spiritual aspiration subservient to merely practical purposes. There is no hint in his words, as there is in Smohalla's, of the critical role played in education by the external community, the great world of "other" powers the youth encounters in his vigil. For Emerson, as for Nietzsche, it is a matter of individual aspiration which needs to find cultural accommodation. The individual is isolated in his heroic individualism, and his transcendence is a matter of imposing his will upon himself and the world.

This tradition of intense individualism and voluntarism, blended with and compounded by ideas of Manifest Destiny and the all-American "melting-pot," is the source of that arrogance and solipsism, that mindless assumption of white superiority, that Smohalla so resented. The conviction of cultural superiority was itself simply

[1] Ralph Waldo Emerson, "Education."

6 ◫ *Liberal Arts and Teacher Education*

a national expression of the individual's immersion in his own will.[2] Multiplied and magnified, the individual's egotism became the nation-state, but not a society, which implies a concord of discrete individuals, a civic sense of the "other." A society is precisely what we could not manage to create; citizenship was merely self-assimilation. And the evidence is all around us: will and isolation turned intolerant and violent; an absent-minded rage to expunge all difference, to annihilate the "other." The result is that syndrome of disease whose deadliest, most prevalent form is racism. Yet this racism, as ruthless or merely mindless acculturation, is still our standard educational practice. I think, for instance, of my own state of Texas, where Spanish-speaking children must go on strike in order to speak Spanish on their own schoolgrounds. Or of our unspeakable—our divine—arrogance in Vietnam.[3] Or of the Alaskan Eskimos, who by means of *Dick and Jane*—an instrument more lethal than the carbine—are being compelled to deny their own immemorial, working culture for one which has proven a miserable failure in suburban America. My point, however, is not to recite malpractices that are now notorious, but to point out the epidemic range and symptoms of the disease.

What cannot be tolerated, what must be always shunned, is the direct experience of difference, the naked, unassimilated encounter with the "other." When schoolchildren study foreign countries, it is not China or Pakistan or Chile they study, but Switzerland, Norway, or France—that is, the always assimilable, the not-so-strange. The practice is defended on grounds of pedagogical necessity, but its real purpose is to evade encounter by domesticating the alien texture of reality.[4] It is the same with the past as it is with the world.

---

[2] Cf. Austin Warren, *The New England Conscience*, p. 54: "Much of the falsity of the Protestant ethics lies in just what—whether in its popular or philosophic form—it has prided itself on: its concern with self and subjectivity. Concern with *my* motives, *my* intentions, *my* conscience is always in danger of becoming more concerned with me than with *the whole, vast, other world*. Egoism—refined subjectivity—is morally more dangerous, partly because more subtle, than plain frank egotism of selfishness" (emphasis added).

[3] The attitude of the soldiers who massacred Vietnamese civilians at My Lai is revealingly summarized in the words of William Doherty of Charlie Company: "It was pretty disgusting, but it was a different feeling. If they had been Americans, I might have felt different. I never really understood those people." Cf. Seymour M. Hersh, *My Lai 4: A Report on the Massacre and Its Aftermath*, (New York, 1970), pp. 89 ff.

[4] Hersh (*My Lai 4*, pp. 7 ff.) again is pat to the point: "In 1968 the Army's efforts to educate GIs on the rights of prisoners consisted of two hours of instruction a

Programs in the humanities are anemic because humanists mindlessly view the past not as a great source of "otherness"—what we no longer have, the skills we have lost and need now, what we never knew we lacked—but as cultural reinforcement for the present. The past justifies the present; we teach students, not how we might become different or better, but merely how we became what we are. In the schools and universities the languages are being "phased out," apparently because their central educational purpose—the access they provide to alternate ways of being human, and hence to our undiscovered selves—is no longer understood.[5] In the schools condescension and stultifying benevolence prevail: we teach *Mid-*

year.... The average GI's ignorance of Vietnamese customs was appalling, but even more appalling was the fact that the Army's efforts to give the men some kind of understanding of what they would be faced with were minimal. The Vietnam-bound soldiers were given... only one or two lectures on the country and its people while in training.... A Canadian nurse described how GIs assigned to pacification projects would often complain that the Vietnamese didn't care about their own children. They would say that the mothers tried to leave them behind when they were being evacuated. 'Saw it with my own eyes,' one GI said. 'A woman hopped up on the chopper after seeing her baby down on the ground. When I picked it up and handed it to her, she shouted and pointed to the ground and wouldn't take the baby from me.' The GI didn't know that a peasant woman in Quang Ngai believes it is unlucky to carry a baby across a threshold, and so she always sets the baby down, steps across, and then reaches back and picks it up. Another GI claimed that 'you can't help these dinks. They like to live like pigs in hovels, and even when you build them new houses, they won't live in them.' What *he* didn't know, however, was that according to the custom in that area, married women had to live in houses with full, double-sloped roofs. The new GI-built units had attached, single-slope corrugated tin-roofed huts. Since most of the peasant women were married, they refused to move into them.... Even worse than the misunderstandings were the deliberate cruelties and implicit assumptions of superiority on the part of the Americans.

[5] This misunderstanding, I should add, is not solely the work of scientists and engineers. Their rejection of university language study is in most cases simply a sensible rejection of the argument too often used by language instructors in favor of languages—that is, utility. For most scientists, etc., language study really isn't *professionally* very useful; important discoveries are very quickly translated, and English is now the scientific lingua franca. Why, then, spend years studying a language to no practical purpose? The fact is that the defenders of language study have failed to make the proper case. The study of languages—and literatures—is a liberal art, a "humanity," because mastery of a language and its literature gives us an indispensable purchase and perspective on ourselves and our own culture. The rigorous, close, disciplined study of difference is both liberating and civilizing. The humanistic case has not been made, I believe, because the scholars have abandoned the teaching of the languages (*and*, it seems, the literatures) to Berlitzers and audio-technicians. And in general they seem to prefer trying to make facsimile Frenchmen (or Italians, Germans, etc.) out of Americans to making sensitive and civilized and understanding Americans through the study of French (or Italian, German, etc.).

summer Night's Dream or As You Like It or even Macbeth (all of them badly for the most part), but not Hamlet or Lear; and the reason is not only their "difficulty" but our desire to spare the young the brush with the terrible, with the uncontrollably tragic. And so we puerilize them; we deprive them of the encounters, literary and human, which might educate them, and we then wonder why this process does not produce compassionate or greathearted men. Even youth culture, with its declared affinity for minorities and the outcast, is all too often hostile or indifferent to any curriculum or study that does not reinforce or reiterate its cardinal perceptions. No less than the "straight" culture, it excludes whatever it cannot cope with or somehow assimilate to itself. It is a closed, not an open, culture.[6]

A classicist would call this disease simply *hybris*. Inaccurately translated "pride," *hybris* has a constant aura of violence or violation. It suggests processes that have gotten out of hand, the luxuriance of things spilling over their natural limits, violating the physical space or the rights of others, their very right to exist. It is a denial, an annihilation, of the "other"; a violation of nature and natural law. Thus in fifth-century Attic law *hybris* means "rape"; imperialism is simply *hybris* on a grand political scale. A garden which is "lush" is said to have *hybris*—which means a discontented garden, a garden with megalomania, aspiring to be a jungle. Finally, there is a positive form of *hybris*—the metaphysical discontent of the hero, the obdurate, cross-grained perversity needed to accomplish great tasks. The opposite of *hybris* is *sophrosynē*. This means, not "moderation," but "the skill of mortality"—the self-knowledge of the man who knows that he is doomed, who accepts his limitations. He has encountered "the other," whether as god or man, and he therefore treats other men with the compassion his own doom claims from them. Now, in the Greek view, *hybris* can be met in only two ways. First, by the actual experience of disaster, the bitter tragic doom that teaches the man of *hybris* who he really is, his miserable anonymity

---

[6] This at least was the dispiriting conclusion I drew from a conference in which students at an experimental college were designing their own curriculum. What I found depressing was the almost routine exclusion of everything not already contained or implicit in peer-group culture. Norman O. Brown but not Plato; Hesse but not Leopardi or Goethe; Ramakrishna but not Iqbal; Cleaver but not Ibn-Khaldun, etc. Independent work presumably left the door open for curiosity; but curiosity was not much in evidence, especially where the past or the rigorous was concerned. If nobody called Homer a "honky" author, nobody thought he was worth reading. And the sciences, the law—those great humanistic structures—were not even mentioned.

and transience and nothingness. The second way is by education, which teaches *sophrosyne* through the tragic spectacle of doomed *hybris*. I believe that the essential social purpose of Greek tragedy—which was deliberately subsidized by the state for the instruction, not the amusement, of the people—was to educate a proud people, a people prone to *hybris*, in *sophrosyne*. Euripides in his *Trojan Women*, for instance, is visibly trying to elicit and to strengthen in his audience the feeling of compassion and humanity so achingly absent in the play and in Athenian foreign policy.

Hybris, then: an expansive, sometimes aggressive, sometimes mindless, solipsism, in which the assertion of self is a godlike denial of the other. Immured in folds of self-sufficiency, the man of racist *hybris* is almost unreachable; almost, it seems, unteachable. He can kill with something like negligence—with the barbarous but bland irritability of the massacres at My Lai and Wounded Knee. You can recognize his features in Ortega y Gasset's description of modern "mass man," the new man who claims to rule the world:

> Heir to an ample and generous past—generous both in ideals and in activities—the new commonalty has been spoiled by the world around it. To spoil means to put no limit on caprice. . . . The young child exposed to this regime has no experience of its own limits. By reason of the removal of all external restraint . . . he comes actually to believe that *he is the only one who exists*, and gets used to not considering others. . . . Whereas in past times life for the average man meant finding all around him difficulties, dangers, wants, limitations of his destiny, the new world appears as a sphere of practically limitless possibilities. . . . If the traditional sentiment whispered, "To live is to feel oneself limited, and therefore to have to count with that which limits us," the newest voice shouts: "To live is to meet with no limitation whatever and, consequently, to abandon oneself calmly to oneself. Practically nothing is impossible, nothing is dangerous, and, in principle, nobody is superior to anybody." Ingenuously, without any need of being vain, as the most natural thing in the world, he will consider and confirm as good everything he finds within himself: opinions, appetites, preferences, tastes. And why not, if . . . nothing and nobody force him to realize that he is a second-class man, subject to many limitations . . . ?[7]

[7] José Ortega y Gasset, *The Revolt of the Masses* (New York, 1957), pp. 58–62.

The ancient world knew mass man, too; but as a universal phenomenon, he is essentially modern. And no wonder. We have maximized *hybris*. Anything is now possible, and the possible is always desirable. It is that simple. There is no saving skill, no *sophrosynē*, no natural piety available to resist it with, or school it. What was once a chronic and dangerous human tendency, is now an almost certain fate. If only we could find or set a limit to our unimpeded wills, if we could only encounter the other, whether god or man.... But America is no longer a country where the "other" is to be encountered. We have brushes, but few encounters. The past is being systematically erased; the earth has few powers we respect. As for other men, other men in their tangible conditions, they are almost all unapproachably isolated. "No man is an island, entire of himself," said John Donne, who could not have imagined *this* America. Even the stages of human life have lost their continuity, their old sequence and proximity. Young and old simply fail to meet any more. Therefore they cannot qualify each other, cannot compose a sense or arc of common humanity. Florida, like Phoenix, is one vast geriatric spa, rabid with fear and hatred of the young, feeding on its own desperate isolation. The public schools, the high schools, are peergroup prisons, patrolled by armed adults and terrified teachers. Everywhere ghettos. Old and young, rich and poor, black and white, living and dead—not sensible pluralisms, but segregated parts of a once common life, fragments of a single condition! If there are encounters, they occur at the barriers, and they are violent or cold. And meanwhile in Washington the elected warlocks and warlords turn human differences into antagonistic blocs, chanting of unity but exploiting divisiveness in an orgy of bad faith. Never a healing word. "It is a bad word that comes from Washington always...." And as the encounters grow rarer and colder, as the "other" disappears from embrace and sight, the demonologies become more virulent and explosive. Outside the prison enclosure any evil can be believed of anybody, because there is nobody human there. Inside the barrier reef, the coral *hybris* grows.

As it swells, it takes its toll of the psyche, the inward man, fragmenting him like the world outside. And we suddenly discover in ourselves the shambles R. D. Laing has described so vividly: "Bodies half-dead; genitals dissociated from the heart; heart severed from head; head dissociated from genitals. Without inner unity, with just enough sense of continuity to clutch at identity—the current idolatry. Torn—body, mind, and spirit—by inner contradictions, pulled in different directions. Man cut off from his own mind, cut off equally from his own body—a half-crazed creature in a mad world!"[8]

Hybris nearly incorrigible, nearly hopeless! What then can educators do? Are we doomed to go on toiling forever behind, like Homer's goddesses of healing Prayer, in the wake of Ruin, trying in vain to undo the desolation and the hurt? Perhaps that is our modest, monumental job, the most we can do. There are many—an increasing number—who believe our crisis is so vast and so complex, and our margin of time so pathetically short, that we must turn all our energies to politics. I share their fears. If ever we desperately needed real political vision and leadership, the time is now. But there is not the slightest sign of either anywhere. And even if we had vision and leadership, we would still need educators who believed in the value and goodness of what they do, who still see their work as a necessary task of the spirit. Our permanent business is human fulfillment and the liberation of the mind—the great project of creating a larger humanity or simply preserving what human skills we still possess. The opportunities, the contexts, exist. The hunger for true education is everywhere. The schools and colleges are one of the last places in the society where real encounters can occur; here youth and adult, past and present, rich and poor, still meet. Here there is still a hope of making a self in collaboration with others. This is why the failure of education is so utterly killing—because the amplest and most generous expectations are still focused there, the last high hopes of the species.

2

There, my Mississippi is on the map. If we have maximized hybris, how can we enable and enlarge sophrosynē?

Clearly, by making those reforms it lies in our power to make. Not everything is possible. Politics is one thing, education another. And formal education is an awkward instrument for effecting major political change. What it can do, however, is to shape the sensibility of the age—its hopes, its aspiration, its maturing consciousness of human life and meaning—and to that degree radically affect the form of any future culture, including its political life. A truly liberal

[8] R. D. Laing, The Politics of Experience (New York 1967), p. 55.

education does not politicize; it has almost nothing to do with revolution or reaction, and its relevance is moral and metaphysical, not political. It liberates because it sets us free to become ourselves, to realize ourselves; it frees us to learn, slowly and painfully perhaps, our limitations and our powers, and to recognize our real modalities, undeafened by the overwhelming Muzak of the social and political enterprise. Liberally educated, we are free to become political at last, without risk of being captured and possessed by our politics. And this freedom, this ripeness of self, is the indispensable element in all true teaching, simply because it speaks so compellingly to those who hunger to be free—that is, presumably, to all men.

All liberal education assumes this hope, this hunger to be better in both teacher and taught. Every serious student hopes to be changed, to become better, by being educated. On this pivot everything turns. Nothing can be created from nothing, and you can only increase your student's virtue—or knowledge, or skill, or *sophrosynē*, or whatever—by assuming he has enough virtue to want more. He may lack it, but he *wants* it—and this wanting, this discontent, is the sign you are looking for. It is incipient virtue, or humanity, itself. As Nietzsche said, "The man who despises himself still honors the despiser within." Men are educable in direct proportion to their conviction of being imperfect, unfinished, base, unrealized; gods need neither education nor degrees. The teacher educates by being the man he is, by the power and beauty of his knowledge, as that knowledge is expressed in his conduct or being or understanding. He has no other authority. And the intrusion of any extraneous authority is a profanation of education. Men *want* education because they want to perfect their humanity. The creation of a joint humanity, the collaboration of teacher and student in the making of a self, is the aim of the enterprise.

Formal education, I am convinced, cannot improve, cannot set us free, until we recognize—and act on our recognition—that the liberal arts and teacher education are one and the same thing. Only when the liberal arts colleges renounce their servile professionalism and devote themselves seriously—that is, with *all* their resources—to the education of teachers, will public education ever become the instrument of a great human and democratic culture.

The stakes are high. The most revolutionary risk ever run by this country was its decision—an act of positive, heroic *hybris*—to dedicate itself to universal education. True, no such decision was ever actually taken; it was a decision reached by indirection and degrees, by incremental drift. Yet the drift was implicit in the national character—an evident *daimon* from the beginning. From the beginning we were aiming to make all men spiritually as well as socially and politically free. Only one other society in the history of mankind has taken a similar course, and that was Athens, which in the fifth century B.C. deliberately tried, by means of a curriculum of poetry and drama, to democratize a great aristocratic *ethos* and to impose on every citizen the burden of heroic *arete*. Ultimately that effort was a failure, but it was one of the most brilliant failures of human history.

Our own commitment to universal education is now in real jeopardy. On the one hand, it has been betrayed by an insidious elitism—the elitism of the learned professions—which has made liberal education the servant of merely professional ends and disavowed the needs of those students who lack scholarly or professional interests. On the other side, it has been betrayed by a class of pseudoprofessionals who, by means of their own illiteracy, have turned the public schools into nurseries of a massive illiteracy—an illiteracy which, in combination with that national *hybris* I see everywhere, now threatens to destroy the republic.

"No amount of reflection," wrote R. P. Blackmur with remarkable prescience fifteen years ago,

> has deflected me from the conclusion that the special problem of the humanities in our generation . . . is to struggle against the growth of the new illiteracy and the new intellectual proletariat, together with the curious side-consequence of these, the new and increasing distrust of the audience by public and quasi-public institutions. All three of these are the results of the appearance, in combination, of mass societies and universal education. . . . We deal not with ignorance but with deformities of knowledge. . . . The old illiteracy was inability to read; as the old literacy involved the habit of reading. The new illiteracy represents those who have been given the tool of reading without being given either the means or skill to read well or the material that ought to be read. The habit of reading in the new illiteracy is not limited to, but is everywhere supplied by, a press almost as illiterate as itself. It is in this way that opinion, instead of knowledge, has come to determine action; the inflammable opinion of the new illiterate is mistaken for the will

of the people, so that arson becomes a chief political instrument.[9]

Against *hybris*, *sophrosynē*; against the new illiteracy, a new literacy; against the arson of deformed knowledge, a renewal of the liberal arts. To educate a nation: it is the incomparable priority of the age. And it requires active mind at the top of its bent, flexible intelligence, a positive appetite for complexity and sympathy, and, most important of all, an openness to these terrible times in which we no longer know how to act in the confusion of being human. Youth culture, for all its quick compassion and its generous humanity, is not enough; it has no heart for the long haul, and it is increasingly anti-intellectual. Nor are the traditional liberal arts, with their impoverished parish of reality and their decorative scholars, any longer adequate. We simply cannot survive if we go on puerilizing and barbarizing the young with a hollow technical mockery of true knowledge. The humanist's *hybris* is his distrust of the audience, his habit, in Blackmur's phrase, of believing that the audience is not up to what he has to say and therefore ending up inferior to the potential response of his audience. We deny the student's hunger to be more than he is when we tell him he is not ready for Homer or *Lear*. And the consequence of this stultification, multiplied millions of times, is an illiterate electorate, militant *hybris*, and a racist society.

In an illiterate society the teacher's literacy may be the only literacy in sight; the teacher's *sophrosynē* may be the only approachable evidence of achieved humanity. Without the liberally educated man, as witness and seal of what he is, education will become more and more a mug's game, a trade school, a vulgar racket for privileged illiterates. Professionalism, scrappy or fastidious, will not do. Vulgarization deforms both student and citizen.

My *first* proposal is simplicity itself. Let the liberal arts colleges take as their primary function—their highest priority—the training of teachers—teachers for the primary and secondary schools. Six years ago James Conant, in *The Education of American Teachers*, made his valuable proposal that the liberal arts colleges should have the right to train and certify teachers. His unspoken purpose was to challenge the colleges of education to reform themselves; to make them recruit better students and to educate them better; to put

---

[9] R. P. Blackmur, "Toward a Modus Vivendi," in *The Lion and the Honeycomb* (New York, 1955), pp. 6–7.

content and rigor back into their programs. The threat of competition was the spur. But the suggestion was met by the colleges with small enthusiasm and token programs. A few colleges responded, and the M.A.T. programs were a notable step forward.[10] Yet no really serious or massive effort has yet been made, or even considered, by any leading university. This is not surprising since the universities long ago renounced the training of schoolteachers for the greater prestige of pure research and graduate instruction. The disdain academicians felt for the training of teachers was wholly in keeping with their own headlong professionalization. Later, not content with writing off the lower schools, they effectively renounced all undergraduate instruction which could not be accommodated to their professional routines. As for the liberal arts colleges, they were snobbishly skeptical of programs which might detract from their major effort, the preparation of students for graduate schools. The training of teachers, in both colleges and universities, was simply not then regarded as a serious intellectual operation. But if Conant were to renew his proposal now, it would meet, I believe, with a very different response.

The decisive fact is the satisfaction *this* generation might find in teaching the very young. Their complaints of their own education apply after all with even greater force to the primary and secondary students. Here, in the terrible bleakness of the schools—not merely ghetto schools, but almost all schools—is where the generous, lively talents of this generation might really flourish. *Here*, if anywhere, is where the future will be created or destroyed. Here is where we will change ourselves or not at all. Generosity of spirit is crucial. But so is bright, clear, nimble, trained intelligence. Teachers have for too long been recruited from the ranks of the not-too-bright, and then stultified by their education. If the material rewards are poor, this should hardly matter to a generation that has largely turned its back on business and the comforts and certainties of

---

[10] In general, the M.A.T. programs were a very distinct improvement. Almost for the first time, the anti-intellectualism of the colleges of education encountered the tougher, trained intelligence of the hard academic disciplines. Nonetheless, the M.A.T. programs were clearly a halfway house, a means whereby colleges could satisfy their consciences without seriously disturbing the regular academic programs. They were also prohibitively expensive, since they added a fifth academic year and wrote off as pretty much inviolable the four years of the education degree. And simply because they were a modest and halfway measure, they failed to provide any real competitive challenge to the colleges of education.

American affluence. What is needed now is a signal, a strong one, from a major university or college. The response, I am convinced, would be almost overwhelming.

As for the liberal arts colleges and the universities, they would have much to gain and little to lose. The most obvious gain would be the integrity of undergraduate education. At present the greatest threat comes from unimpeded professionalism—the *hybris* of learned disciplines, flourishing for their own sake. The classicist, say, who thinks his educational function is to recruit future classicists from among his students and washes his hands of the rest, is an unimpeded professional. Colleges are full of them, and departments exist for them. But the only corrective to unimpeded professionalism is a *positive impediment*—that is, a larger educational mission. This, it seems to me, is what the training of teachers might provide. What should a teacher know? Why should the young—that is, the future —be entrusted to him? What experience should he have? Nobody knows the answers to these questions, but they are the critical questions; they ask us to think about the *sort* of men we think we are educating. And it is this question which is now everywhere begged or answered in clichés, to the detriment of education. In the training of teachers, I believe, we have the only feasible modern version of a true liberal education, both broad *and* concentrated. Teacher means, moreover: *What do we want to be? What would we be if we could?*

3

I am not sanguine about the survival of the official, formal humanities, the liberal arts curriculum as it exists now in American universities. It will persist, of course: an imposing academic husk, respected and even revered. And there will still, I hope, be a place for its nobler scholars. But the real spirit of the liberal arts will vanish— is already vanishing—elsewhere, into the arts and the professions and perhaps the sciences, to reappear as an *ethos* rather than a discipline or subject matter. And everywhere the sensibility of the excluded non-Western world and the cultures of poverty is pressing for a place in the sun—a development which should stimulate and challenge and perhaps reinvigorate the traditional liberal arts.

The loss of the official humanities does not, I think, greatly matter. The texts and curriculum go underground, to reappear in new guises; the texts may change, but the spirit persists. What matters is that this new humanistic *ethos* should find congenial ground for growing. The greatest obstacle is still the vanity and stupidity of the established disciplines: moribund but as monstrously *there* as a dying whale. Disestablishment is what they deserve ("After such knowledge, what forgiveness?"), and disestablishment is their almost certain fate.

The liberal arts have not yet suffered the last of their humiliations. The groundswell of public opinion that condones neglect of students in the name of mostly worthless research is still building. It will end by compelling drastic revision of educational priorities. Neither conscience nor economy can tolerate a system that, in order to produce a tiny elite of professional scholars, stultifies thousands of potential teachers and perhaps millions of students, that makes the past and the great liberal arts merely decorative culture. It is just possible that poverty may bring the humanists to their senses; to a valid sense of the difference between curriculum and culture. Who hasn't heard professors of English heatedly argue that Melville and even Faulkner could not be really read without their mediation? Monstrous! What is still actively alive in the culture is deadened or destroyed by being curricularized before its time. Common ground —common culture—enclosed by a scholar or critic is lost ground. Losses surround us everywhere. After ten years of being worked up into courses and syllabi, black studies will be as useless to black pride as the Renaissance is useless to contemporary Italians. A few years of genteel poverty might encourage concentration on essentials, but one wonders why poverty should work when the threat of extinction has failed.

Paradoxically, the greatest present hope of liberal education, now a nearly desperate enterprise at all levels, is the crisis of all the social—not the academic—professions. The unnamable convulsion of our society—the convulsion for which we have no words, no skills, no styles of coping—has brought all professional certainties into dispute and even anarchy. We simply do not know whom to train for what contingencies or society, in what numbers, or how. Professional establishments have served us badly, and we confront chaos with the pat and selfish routines of professional classes incapable, in numbers and vigor and humanity, of coping. The consequence has been, at the point of contact between society and the professions, to create demands which will profoundly affect the academic disciplines. The most immediate result is a growing demand for the collapsing of all structural barriers between the professions and the disciplines, for doing away with the separate colleges of law, medicine, art, architecture, and communications, and merging them in new ways with the arts and sciences. And the reason is simple necessity.

We have integrated problems and disintegrated skills. And the alienation of knowledge and the liberal arts from the crisis of the professions is no longer a tolerable luxury. If the liberal arts attempt to maintain their traditional aloofness, their devotion to pure research and contemplation, their subject matters will simply be appropriated. The professions have no alternative; they are too close to society, to the convulsive chaos around us, to escape responsibility for change, for rational and humane action. The professions, I am suggesting, have encountered the "other"; a new humanism is already taking shape among younger professionals in response to the desperation of those who depend upon the professions. And because the professions cannot do without the arts of knowledge and the liberal arts, their encounter will eventually spread to education too.

The liberal arts may be radically changed in the process. It is their liberating and humanizing functions, not their curriculum, that are permanent. But it is from *outside* that reform will come. Not through existing disciplines where old routines and professional interests make fresh response nearly impossible. Rather from the world of the professions, from the public schools, from the communities, from the sciences, from all those encounters between crumbling ethical codes and the necessity to act *now*, even at the risk of having to improvise your values as you go. If conscientious, the lawyer faces the obsolescence of his statutes, of the very assumptions of law perhaps; the doctor is trapped in an agony of choice for which his traditional code provides only uncertain and inadequate answers. Whether they like it or not, the professions are doomed to the agony of value, to metaphysical danger, to a leap of faith. From these encounters may emerge a sense of someone *there*, of conscience and care. This sense of care then comes to the university, where professionals are trained, in quest of company, solutions, validations, help. But help is not to be expected from academic humanists, nor is it forthcoming. It comes, if at all, from the professions themselves, which thereby take on the burden of reforming themselves, humanizing themselves, adjusting to these new problematics of value. And the consequence, profession by profession, is an involvement in choice and purpose which slowly, gropingly, uncertainly improvises a new *ethos*, an attitude toward the use of professional skills arrived at by hunch and instinct and maturing meditation. In this new community of amateurs lies, I am convinced, the future of the liberal arts.

This community is of course much larger than the immediate professional community. It includes all those who feel, however incoherently, that the great task of the times is to create a new breed of professional as well as new institutional forms—above all, new schools and universities—to cope with the problems of scale and value imposed by the new mass society. The formal humanism of the old university failed because it could not connect its theory with its practice; because it pretended to be only discipline, it lost its power as *ethos*. Behind all demands for new educational institutions is the notion of the liberal arts as an attitude everywhere informing an *engaged* intellect; the very engagement, it is hoped, will sharpen and define the emergent mission. Where these demands have not been merely demands for direct political action, their effect is to make of schools and universities a secular church. They are spiritual demands and should be recognized as such.

An example. A year or so ago the chairman of the board of regents of the University of Texas authorized the chopping down of a dozen magnificent live oaks in order to make room for a culvert. Resisted by droves of student Druids perched in the doomed trees, the chairman himself, for all the world like a Texas Xerxes, cheered on the bulldozers with idiot glee. But he miscalculated: his opposition was not merely outraged students, but a sudden, large, angry coalition of townspeople, faculty, and students. He had failed to observe a critical fact: the feeling for the environment is an extremely potent form of feeling, a force that will soon, it seems, be chartering universities and even churches. And the reason is that unmistakably religious and scientific feelings find here something like respectable scientific status. Beneath all the talk of ecosystems lies a new intimation of natural law, a muddled but powerful feeling of kinship with the life of earth and a new reverence for the cosmos. Of a fresh *sophrosynē*. So too, in student revolt, one senses the presence, beneath all the hokum, of religious feelings that have, as yet, no institutional home or focus.

The demand for a new reformed university is potent because the intent behind the demands is to make education the home of those orphaned religious feelings. The sudden felt antagonism between society and its schools conceals, I believe, the ancient quarrel between secular and spiritual institutions. Certainly the universities are being asked to assume tasks that once belonged to family and church, but which those institutions now lack the intellect—and also the moral courage—to perform. And this suggests that the major problem for the liberal arts in our time may be to recognize and redefine, in study and conduct, the metaphysical and religious ground of our motives and meanings. I write, I should explain, as a secular intellectual. These are not for me easy or comforting conclusions. But I am driven to them by events and pressures I cannot otherwise explain.

We cannot yet say whether the effort to create a new university (or new schools)—that is, structures in which a new humanism might be defined and embodied—will succeed. The obstacles are formidable. But so are the stakes. It would be a disaster if, in the struggle over the university, either the radicals or the conservatives won a clear-cut victory. If the university and schools are politicized according to radical doctrine, they will forfeit their potential as spiritual institutions and become merely another set of (probably impotent) political lobbies.

4

My *second* proposal is therefore that we deliberately set about creating what I have elsewhere called a "university of the public interest."[11] By this I mean a university dedicated to the advocacy of just those public interests—in education, in health, in population control, in social justice, in the environment—that are now endangered by organized greed, professional mindlessness, miseducation, and policies of "benign neglect." In short, a modern Socratic university for a mass society, an organization of concerned professionals determined to apply their skills as effectively as possible, and to educate their students by enlisting their efforts in the same mission. By "Socratic" I mean to suggest both power of mind and the conscience of knowledge. A university of the public interest would educate by the power and example of its advocacy; because it addressed itself, with the full power of active mind, to the public's sense

[11] Cf. "Idea of a New University" in *Center Magazine*, March–April, 1970.

of justice, compassion, beauty, in the hope of thereby eliciting or strengthening the moral skills, the literacy, that now seem paralyzed or lost. Lost because unaddressed; because daily diminished; made illiterate by half-truths and politic lies, by deliberate arson, by being always addressed in terms of its basest, least generous powers. A teacher appeals to the powers he hopes to enlarge. The spirit must be visible or it will not be believed. And in a mass society the individual tends to become invisible; this is why we need spiritual institutions and concerted commitment.

Creating a university of the public interest means above all to reform the major professions. The nation has no future worth thinking about unless we can produce, swiftly and in quantity, a different kind of professional: a lawyer whose client is the public interest, an architect who is more than the cagey flunky of his client, an engineer sensitive to other factors than cost. The problem is not talent. Talent abounds. What is lacking are institutions that demand or permit a talented man's best work, that encourage gifted men to exercise their compassion and conscience. Professional education is now in a ferment of reform. But the pace needs quickening. And this can best be done, I believe, by chartering the university itself as a corporation for the public interest. It would provide, for instance, an institutional shelter for the public-interest lawyer, or a base for systematic criticism of professional performance in the society at large: the work of architects, the projects of engineers. It would attempt to publish a national newspaper. It would actively sponsor and protect the economic and cultural interests of those minorities too small or weak to help themselves. That is, the university would house and train the conscience of the professions, and proceed to give that conscience tangible and active expression. It would also seek to provide the public education, and the ramifying reforms, which programs affecting the public interest must have.

I assume that the public interest will be served by such projects, and that such service should best be pluralistic. An orthodoxy of benevolence would be intolerable. The educational benefits, I would argue, are extraordinary. First, a context in which knowledge, applied in a spirit of service, could be made moral; in which skills and values could be enlarged and refined by significant use. Second, an overriding mission in terms of which men might pool specialized skills, simply because there is no other way of getting their task done; in short, a context in which interdisciplinary work would occur naturally, as it now does not. Third, the community such collaboration might create—the community we do not have. Fourth, the possibility of recruiting generous human energies which now have almost nowhere to go—energies which, turned rancid and frustrated, make education impossible. Finally, the hope of restoring the authority of reason and intelligence by virtue of their *visible* pertinence to the task in hand.

The purport of this proposal is to make the university a third force in American life—a force that is neither government nor industry, but rather a new form of spiritual institution. I offer no apology for the phrase. No great society has yet managed to survive without powerful spiritual institutions, whether subversive or established. They are made up of men who, in Chapman's words, sound a certain note: "They hold a tuning-fork and sound A, and everybody knows it really is A, though the time-honored pitch is G flat. The community cannot get that A out of its head. Nothing can prevent an upward tendency in the popular tone so long as the real A is kept sounding." It was the intent of the founding fathers that family and church should speak for the spirit in American life. They could not have foreseen the dreadful eclipse of both those institutions, nor the ominous concentrations of wealth—and hence of political power—in recent years. To some degree the spirit survived in the courts and the foundations; but Congress has now emasculated the foundations, and the courts have been gutted. The spirit is not in good health or odor. Many think it a myth. And with good reason. Unselfishness in American life is unincorporated; it has no coherent party or program, no normalized institutional home. And the absence is as tangible as the absence of God. Indeed, the demands now being made of the university are, I believe, as unappeasable as they are because they are unrecognized demands of the spirit. The university is being asked to act as a spiritual institution. But because nobody believes in spiritual institutions, the demands come disguised as intransigent political demands.

The critical problem is to make the university a *potent* institution of the spirit. Otherwise it will not have the kind of influence needed, in a mass society, to affect the quality of life. The difficulty is transcending old habits. So long as the university community believes its true constituency is the classroom, it is doomed to the custody of increasingly dissatisfied and ungrateful students. Our schools and universities now have a mandate to educate everybody. But we cannot confine all the young to institutions. And the consequence is that the classroom becomes the country. But you can't educate a country by classroom techniques, by formal instruction. You educate rather as an artist does, by what you say and do, by rational persuasion; or, like a pre-Socratic, by embodiment and example. You address your audience without condescension, with the fineness and complexity reality requires; you refuse to collaborate in extending the new illiteracy. That is, the university shows, *as an institution*, what men might be if they were *free* to be what they wanted. It liberates because it *practices* the liberal arts. It embodies conscience because it trains conscientious professionals; compassion, because only compassion could explain its strange and generous behavior, and so on. Its potency derives not only from the spirit, but from its institutional elan, the energy and modernity of its action.

A university of the public interest is not, I believe, a visionary project. It is already emerging everywhere around us, in random experiments and programs, the shape of the future institution looming unmistakably behind the confusion and frustration and anger. Abortive as the efforts to reform education have been, the efforts take a common direction, and it is important to name it. Otherwise we are apt to miss what is positive and see only anarchy and trouble. We are on the verge of creating, here in America, a great new social and educational institution, a new form of the university and perhaps the school too, adapted to the needs of a new society and the agony of our present condition.

5

Let me close, and come full circle, with the words of still another Indian. The speaker is Chief Seattle; the occasion is his response to the demand of the whites that he and his tribe retire to a small reservation on Puget Sound. Seattle's statement is one of the very greatest of American speeches—all radiant *sophrosynē*, a tragic charity that includes even the white oppressors in the range of its understanding. You have to go the *Iliad*, to that supreme moment in the final book when Achilles speaks to Priam across every conceivable gulf of condition—age, culture, and fortune—to find anything quite like it. To us, now, Seattle speaks as a voice of that great community of the "others," which all education hopes to knit into our lives, until listening to it and heeding it become conduct and a second, larger, nature. Seattle is a great teacher. Listen:

Brothers: That sky above us has pitied our fathers for many hundreds of years. To us it looks unchanging, but it may change. Today it is fair. Tomorrow it may be covered with cloud.

My words are like the stars. They do not set. What Seattle says, the great chief in Washington can count on as surely as our white brothers can count on the return of the seasons.

The White Chief's son says his father sends words of friendship and good will. This is kind of him, since we know he has little need of our friendship in return. His people are many, like the grass that covers the plains. My people are few, like the trees scattered by the storms on the grasslands.

The great—and good, I believe—White Chief sends us word that he wants to buy our land. But he will reserve us enough so that we can live comfortably. This seems generous, since the red man no longer has rights he need respect. It may also be wise, since we no longer need a large country. Once my people covered this land like a flood tide moving with the wind across the shell-littered flats. But that time is gone, and with it the greatness of tribes now almost forgotten.

But I will not mourn the passing of my people. Nor do I blame our white brothers for causing it. We too were perhaps partly to blame. When our young men grow angry at some wrong, real or imagined, they make their faces ugly with black paint. Their hearts too are ugly and black. They are hard and their cruelty knows no limits. And our old men cannot restrain them.

Let us hope that the wars between the red man and his white brothers will never come again. We would have everything to lose and nothing to gain. Young men view revenge as gain, even when they lose their own lives. But the old men who stay behind in time of war, mothers with sons to lose—they know better.

Our great father in Washington—for he must be our father now as well as yours, since George has moved his boundary northward—our great and good father sends us word by his son, who is surely a great chief among his people, that he will protect us if we do what he wants. His brave soldiers will be a strong wall for my people, and his great warships will fill our harbors. Then our ancient enemies to the north—the Haidas and Tsimshians—will no longer frighten our women and old men. Then he will be our father and we will be his children.

But can that ever be? Your God loves your people and hates mine. He puts his strong arm around the white man and leads him by the hand, as a father leads his little boy. He has abandoned his red children. He makes your people stronger every day. Soon they will flood all the land. But my people are an ebb tide, we will never return. No, the white man's God cannot love his red children or he would protect them. Now we are orphans. There is no one to help us.

So how can we be brothers? How can your father be our father, and make us prosper and send us dreams of future greatness? Your God is prejudiced. He came to the white man. We never saw him, never even heard his voice. He gave the white man laws, but he had no word for his red children whose numbers once filled this land as the stars filled the sky.

No, we are two separate races, and we must stay separate. There is little in common between us.

To us the ashes of our fathers are sacred. Their graves are holy ground. But you are wanderers, you leave your fathers' graves behind you, and you do not care.

Your religion was written on tables of stone by the iron finger of an angry God, so you would not forget it. The red man could never understand it or remember it. Our religion is the ways of our forefathers, the dreams of our old men, sent them by the Great Spirit, and the visions of our sachems. And it is written in the hearts of our people.

Your dead forget you and the country of their birth as soon as they go beyond the grave and walk among the stars. They are quickly forgotten and they never return. Our dead never forget this beautiful earth. It is their mother. They always love and remember her rivers, her great mountains, her valleys. They long for the living, who are lonely too and who long for the dead. And their spirits often return to visit and console us.

No, day and night cannot live together.

The red man has always retreated before the advancing white man, as the mist on the mountain slopes runs before the morning sun.

So your offer seems fair, and I think my people will accept it and go to the reservation you offer them. We will live apart, and in peace. For the words of the Great White Chief are like the words of nature speaking to my people out of great darkness—a darkness that gathers around us like the night fog moving inland from the sea.

It matters little where we pass the rest of our days. They are not many. The Indians' night will be dark. No bright star shines on his horizons. The wind is sad. Fate hunts the red man down. Wherever he goes, he will hear the approaching steps of his destroyer, and prepare to die, like the wounded doe who hears the steps of the hunter.

A few more moons, a few more winters, and none of the

children of the great tribes that once lived in this wide earth that roam now in small bands in the woods will be left to mourn the graves of a people once as powerful and as hopeful as yours.

But why should I mourn the passing of my people? Tribes are made of men, nothing more. Men come and go, like the waves of the sea. A tear, a prayer to the Great Spirit, a dirge, and they are gone from our longing eyes forever. Even the white man, whose God walked and talked with him as friend to friend, cannot be exempt from the common destiny.

We may be brothers after all. We shall see.

We will consider your offer. When we have decided, we will let you know. Should we accept, I here and now make this condition: we will never be denied the right to visit, at any time, the graves of our fathers and our friends.

Every part of this earth is sacred to my people. Every hillside, every valley, every clearing and wood, is holy in the memory and experience of my people. Even those unspeaking stones along the shore are loud with events and memories in the life of my people. The ground beneath your feet responds more lovingly to our steps than yours, because it is the ashes of our grandfathers. Our bare feet know the kindred touch. The earth is rich with the lives of our kin.

The young men, the mothers, and girls, the little children who once lived and were happy here, still love these lonely places. And at evening the forests are dark with the presence of the dead. When the last red man has vanished from this earth, and his memory is only a story among the whites, these shores will still swarm with the invisible dead of my people. And when your children's children think they are alone in the fields, the forests, the shops, the highways, or the quiet of the woods, they will not be alone. There is no place in this country where a man can be alone. At night when the streets of your towns and cities are quiet, and you think they are empty, they will throng with the returning spirits that once thronged them, and that still love these places. The white man will never be alone.

So let him be just and deal kindly with my people. The dead have power too.[12]

[12] Seattle's speech was delivered, in 1856, in his native Duwamish before an audience which included Isaac Stevens, governor of Washington Territory. It was translated on the spot by a Dr. Henry Smith of Seattle, who later published a highly "improved" version of Seattle's speech in the *Seattle Star* (October 29, 1877). Nonetheless, the speech in Smith's version evidently followed the original closely. The version printed here is my "translation" of Henry Smith's Victorian English. What I have done is simply to remove verbal flourishes and obvious Victorian poeticisms; the various embellishments which successive editors gradually intruded into Seattle's speech as reported by Smith have also been removed.

TIMOTHY HEALY

The Liberal Arts, Open Admissions, and the Training of Teachers

When I left New York this morning, of the City University's colleges two were absolutely peaceful—they are brand new and have as yet no students; three were in relative calm—they are upper-division or graduate schools; twelve were under siege; two had been taken; and we hadn't heard from one. On the average we're in splendid shape.

Following Professor Arrowsmith is difficult. Any kind of negative reaction is precluded by respect and affection for the man. And although I have some worries about what a national newspaper put out by all us intellectuals would look like, his lonely battle against the corruption of our profession is one I would be proud to carry a spear in. So this evening I would like to follow several of his ideas and make them fit into a precise time and place—now and New York.

He quoted a haunting phrase, and before dinner the pair of us got together and decided that while the sources of our quotes were very different, the drift of them was much the same. One of his chiefs says, "Wisdom comes in dreams," and I have always thought that of all the dreams invented by Western man, or any kind of man, the dream of liberal education is the best. I am haunted by lines spoken by a character whom, given my shape, it's highly appropriate to quote, Caliban in *The Tempest*. One of the loveliest of his speeches begins:

> Be not afeard; the isle is full of noises,
> Sounds and sweet airs, that give delight, and hurt not.
> Sometimes a thousand twangling instruments
> Will hum about mine ears; and sometime voices,
> That, if I then had waked after long sleep,
> Will make me sleep again; and then, in dreaming,
> The clouds methought would open, and show riches
> Ready to drop upon me; that, when I waked,
> I cried to dream again.

Those words have always seemed to me to be a description of what a liberal arts college was all about. In the days when I could still talk to freshmen, I used to tell them that when it was all over they, like Caliban, would "cry to dream again." So I would like to talk first about the world of the liberal arts. And I would like to locate them in that strange, complex, beautiful, tough, dirty, grim, dangerous, agonized city from which I come. I say this not in any disappreciation of Boston, or Chicago, or Los Angeles, but simply because what I know is New York, and as one of the few natives who still live in it, I love to talk of it.

I would also like to talk about New York because I want to dissociate myself from "the bad word that comes from Washington." There are at least half a dozen ways in which the City University of New York wants to distinguish itself from the word from Washington. Let me give one or two examples. The word from Washington is that the wave of the future is the community college. The City University has eight community colleges, and they are better than anything within long-range missile distance of us. But we are coming to the conclusion that they may very well contain within themselves the seeds of their own destruction. There is in each of them an almost quintessential drift toward senior college status. This is the way the faculty mind works and at the end of two years this is the way the student mind works. There is a steady effort to make technical and scientific courses more difficult, since ultimately the prestige of the community college will depend upon the number of its students who transfer into senior college programs. There is the natural yen of the student to wrestle only with familiar devils (thus for all his denials aping his elders); he would just as soon continue his education where he started it. Finally there is the thrust of the city itself, demanding ever more and more fully trained citizens to make it work. As if that argument were not enough, there's one that works in the other direction. We are faced with the total collapse of the secondary system that feeds us. The only new form that exists on the landscape is the "middle college." And the community college is the perfect base for the middle college. So either way you look at it, in our great cities, the two-year-college idea may have a very limited life span.

Another area where the City University is beginning to differ sharply from official wisdom is in the world of teacher education. As one reads the literature, and also as one considers the facts, it becomes more and more obvious that something is disastrously wrong with our undergraduate teacher training. There is of course one school that says we should return to the isolated teacher-education college, and reinstitute the normal schools. On the basic ground that it is seldom possible to return to the past, I tend to think this option will be of limited value. There is another voice in the land crying somewhat loudly that all undergraduate teacher education as we now know it ought simply to be scrapped. In my own opinion this voice may prevail.

Let me give you the reasons why by way of an analogy. The pride and joy of the public secondary system in New York City is its academic diploma. In order to understand this strange and beautiful creation, let us imagine a large hospital situation which manages to grind out the following statistics. Forty percent of the patients for whom the hospital has responsibility die before they reach it or before treatment begins; another 48 percent die during treatment or immediately after it; 12 percent survive treatment and thus by a curious kind of therapy are called "cured," but all who deal with them have to acknowledge that they are in very seriously weak shape, and are likely to die in the relatively near future. Obviously any hospital that managed to collect such statistics about itself would not last long. But if you transfer the same figures, 40, 48, and 12 percent, to the educational enterprise in secondary schools in the New York City area, you have a fairly accurate map of what happens to most black or Puerto Rican youngsters. The odds on graduating with an academic diploma are 12 to 88. None of us may really have much of a solution. All of us have a ghastly problem.

One of the consequences of the awful statistics with which we live is that the City University of New York is (perhaps against its will and despite its "better judgment") becoming at least partially what Professor Arrowsmith calls a university of the public interest. There is talk in the air today of the shift from mass to universal higher education, and it is always talked of as an impossible dream. Even mass higher education may have been something of a dream in 1847 when the Free Academy was founded for some 96 students. The Free Academy has grown into the City University, and the 96 students have come up to almost 200,000. At the beginning it may have been a dream, but at the moment it is very much a fact. There are other facts, however, to worry us. In every one of our major cities it is now established that the young man or woman who at sixteen or seventeen is not prepared to take on some postsecondary education might just as well be declared a permanent alien in the century in which he lives. In New York City alone we are declaring some 40,000 young people a year out of the twentieth century. And if sometime within the next two decades they don't burn our precious city down about the ears, then they are bigger fools than we thought they were. We as citizens cannot allow our city to strangle its own young, and for that reason at least one university of the public interest has embarked upon a policy which will be known to history as "open admissions."

Open admissions means that every student graduating from a secondary school in New York City this coming June will be admitted to some part of the City University, as far as possible according to his preference, and with a serious effort made to get him into a college and a program appropriate to his needs and desires. I put the term *open admissions* in verbal quotes a few minutes ago, because there are some severe limitations to it.

First of all, we are coping only with the class of June, 1970. Secondly, we are coping only with those who graduate. (Neither I nor anybody else is under any illusions as to what a diploma from a high school in the City of New York may mean. Our current guess is that some 10,000 to 12,000 of the 35,000 freshmen we will take in will need serious, not to say massive, remedial help in reading, mathematics, and English composition.) Thus open admissions excludes all those who do not have a diploma, and excludes as well those who took a diploma before this June.

The assignment of students to senior and junior colleges is of course the critical issue even in this reduced understanding of open admissions. Again in rough terms, we will assign to the senior colleges of the system those students who have an 80 percent average or stand in the upper half of their high school class. At this point it might be fair to remark that we are thus in a curious position of saying we trust absolutely nothing that comes from the public high school system, but on the other hand we are treating the final grade-point average a student achieves and his rank in class as laws of nature. The illogic doesn't escape us. But as Professor Arrowsmith says, you have to put the Mississippi someplace.

We are laboring under one other mandate which is of capital importance. This mandate comes to us from the board of higher education which ordered the university so to admit its students that it achieved some real racial balance in each unit. Our goal is approximately a 30 percent mix of minority students in each institution. The danger in any such kind of admissions policy is that institutions will adapt themselves to the geographical area in which they lie. Another danger is that we can end up shunting all of our black and Puerto Rican students into the community colleges and thus really run a two-track system: the fast senior college track for white middle-class kids, and the slower community college track for black and Puerto Rican students. The university has decided it will not do this. The one movable card in our hand is the SEEK Program. Since it is geographically based, it can be used to make certain that each of our colleges comes close to the racial distribution which exists in our feeder high schools. We undoubtedly will not succeed at this totally. We will also, however, not run a segregated community college system.

One last note needs to be added. There was no euphoria as the university began this program. Everyone connected with it has the cold and sobering realization that in large part it is bound to fail. Some of the reasons for the percentage of failure which we know we will have I will talk of later. But one essential statistic needs to be gotten on the table immediately. Let us presuppose that our total success ratio (that means the number of youngsters who ultimately receive a degree) is only 20 to 30 percent. All of us hope that it will be far higher. And all of us will work to make it so. But in this world there are very few guarantees. The statistic that is important is that the 20 or 30 percent is not to be compared to some lower figure, but to zero.

There were of course enormous objections to the whole idea of open admissions. Some of these were the kind of objections that could not be answered. The black and Puerto Rican community considered the whole thing a vast hoax. Were I either at eighteen or

32 Liberal Arts and Teacher Education

eighty a member of the black and Puerto Rican community, I would also consider that any proposal coming from the established educational authorities in the city was a vast hoax. Nothing that we say will be believed, nor should it be. In fact it will be the better part of the decade before these communities will believe even in what we do.

Another community objection came from the Jewish community in New York, and this was an even more difficult one. At just the time when, thanks to student disruptions, many observers saw a wave of anti-Semitism sweeping through the admissions offices in the nation's prestige colleges, the open admissions plan of the university was read as the imposition of a quota system on higher education. Thus for every student included under the quota some non-quota student would be excluded. Once again there is no psychological way of meeting this objection. The Board of Higher Education decided that every student who would normally have been admitted under previous admissions canons was still to be admitted. We will have to wait for the fact of what we are doing to overcome the thoroughly understandable psychological reaction against it.

The major argument against open admissions was of course the argument drawn from "standards." Despite the fact that the very logic of the situation forces one to admit that a university's standards are really determined not by what it takes in but by what it puts out, this controversy raged loud and long. There are a variety of reasons for not yielding on this point.

All of our cherished predictors (the handicap statistics in our admissions office, the way we, like our coaches, tell ourselves that we will not take on anybody who isn't preprofessional the moment he comes to us) are highly fallible instruments. It is true that you can get a fairly good idea of what a student will do in college by looking at his high school performance. It is also true that fully a quarter of those admitted in highly selected white colleges with college board scores over 700 will have "C" averages by the time they finish.

One final argument is thrown at us again and again, and it too concerns standards. It usually takes the form of the question, What do we know about the purposes of these students who will come to us in such crowds next year? There really is only one answer to that question, and that is neither I nor anyone else working for the university is God. We are the judge of no man's purpose. In addition, we can add the human fact that all purpose alters in fulfillment. How many of us here tonight would settle for higher education as we knew and understood it as freshmen or as sophomores? In fact, how many of us would settle for it as we knew it all those years ago as graduate students?

There is a fair question about the purpose of the university and of the city, and that is quite clear. Next year City University will probably be the only place in the city of New York where there is a shared experience among different racial and ethnic groups. The experience may be differently entered upon, but at least its place is common, its subject is common, and it may as time goes on develop some commonality of life styles. There is much to be said for bringing men together and giving them something to care about until the magic time comes when they learn to care for each other.

The greatest single argument against open admissions, and the one for which there really isn't an answer, is that by beginning compensatory and remedial education at the age of eighteen you are probably quadrupling its expense. What can be done in the high schools for one dollar is going to cost us four dollars, because a nineteen-year-old needs clothes, he needs dates, he needs to buy a beer, he needs money, and he needs a certain amount of pride. If the youngster comes from the inner ghettos itself, he will also need funds to support his children. This kind of massive public support really cannot last. Ultimately doing things the most expensive way is going to catch up with us, and that of course brings me back to teacher education and the high schools. The place where a boy or a girl learns to read and write ought not to be college.

There are of course some problems which cannot be laid at the door of the high school. No teacher-education program is going to enable a teacher to deal effectively with drug addiction. That's a police problem and sooner or later the city police are going to have to try to solve it. Since the disease has now spread to the comfortable white suburbs where we keep our children, the solution may actually be forthcoming. Another thing that no teacher can deal with is malnutrition. In the City College SEEK Program, fully 30 percent of the dropouts do so for reasons of health. In the richest city in the world the most frequent health reason given is malnutrition. Finally, the teacher-training institution cannot cope with the lack of qualified black and Puerto Rican applicants. Sooner or later something drastic is going to have to be done to find teachers and counselors for our elementary and secondary schools who declare by their very physical presence that they share the problems, the life style, and the imaginative patterns of the youngsters they are teaching. I have a sneaking suspicion the Irish said the same thing when they took over the public school system sixty years ago. And I'm pretty sure that they didn't smile when they said it.

In talking about high schools I am very much afraid that I will sound patronizing. Let me put myself on the same hook with any possible victim I may snag. The City University of New York trains 50 percent of the teachers for the school system in New York. So whatever blame is to be distributed must in large part fall upon us. Nor can we hide behind the usual excuse that state education authorities force us to train teachers in ways we would not normally use. I'm afraid that is a dodge. We have a rather absolute grip on the tenderest portion of the state education department's anatomy. They will certify what we produce because they have to. That 50 percent is simply not going to be produced from any other source. Columbia, Fordham, and NYU together can hardly scratch the surface. So if the City University is in control of the flow itself, it is also in control of the calibration of that flow.

But even leaving those disclaimers apart, there are still some very serious questions that have to be raised. I think the wisest living American in teacher education is Dean Harry Rivlin. He raises a major problem with his remark that we train teachers for Manhattan, Kansas, and Manhattan, New York, in exactly the same way. One of our major problems is that most of those teachers are white, and consequently we cannot provide an ethnic mix in the faculty which corresponds both to the reality of the city and to the life styles of the students who are being taught. New York is using an entrenched and cumbersome bureaucracy to face the skirmish troops sent out by its local communities, and sooner or later the communities are going to have to win for the oldest and simplest of reasons: they are indeed the people. Someone has to start taking Charles Weingartner (he is, after all, one of our own faculty members) seriously and ask when we're going to stop talking about teaching and begin talking about learning. There is an element of sheer mindless traditionalism which has almost ecclesiastical overtones in all of our primary and secondary schooling. Lord knows there's enough of it in colleges, but by the time the students come to us they are able either to laugh it off, or shrug it off, or, just as they say, "off it." It might remain a possibility, at least in a speculative world, that the principal thrust of our teacher-training institutions ought not to be to train new teachers but to retrain old ones. The schools could conceivably do a much better job of handling the novices.

I certainly did not come all this way to pontificate to those whose livelihood depends upon the training of teachers. If there is a fence, I am afraid I stand by training and my past on the other side of it. But perhaps the other side has the clearest view of what the stakes are. And let us for a moment come back to Professor Arrowsmith's Indians who talked about the priorities of the spirit, for education is indeed a spiritual affair. Let me just briefly sketch two of the major stakes. The first, the most threatening, and from where I sit, the most pressing, is the viability of our cities. As the cities are run now, torn between poor (largely black) and rich (largely white), they really are verging on the unworkable. I'm not talking about the issue of ecology, which I think was raised as a smoke screen to obscure other issues. Technical problems admit to technical solutions and ought to receive them as quickly as possible. But I am talking about the life style of those who walk the city streets. New York faces one-quarter of its citizens who have no share in it, no stake in its welfare, and who cannot for that reason have any love for it. Open admissions is aimed to look at that quarter of the city's citizens and give them a share in the city, give them something to care about in the city. If all this sounds defensive, it might be best to admit flatly that it is. The fear of hell has kept a lot of Christians honest.

There is another stake. Whitehead commented that any society that doesn't change its symbols every fifty years is doomed. In the youth of our ghetto, not because they are young but because they are outside of our society, we have locked up a whole new American imagination. We have a different way of seeing our past, of seeing our institutions, of seeing ourselves. As long as we who are professionally engaged in education are willing to settle for anything that loses us that new imagination, we are indubitably the poorer. If you look at what could happen in our great cities, at the opportunity that we have to weave a new speech, to reach a new vision, to revel in new perceptions, new metaphors, and new symbols in our national life, if you see this possibility and watch us missing it, you feel like crying with Samson, "Oh, dark, dark, dark amidst the blaze of noon."

I'll finish, as Professor Arrowsmith did, on a quote, but this time from an older chief. It is from Thomas More, and it's one I find I need more and more as I get older and older. It was written in a letter to the regent masters at the University of Oxford. "God made plants for their simplicity, animals for their innocence, but he made man, us, to serve him wittily in the tangle of his mind." We are bound to get lost in the tangle. Let us for the next three days at least try to use some of our wits.

WILLIAM ARROWSMITH

The Future of Teaching[1]

During the Roman Saturnalia even slaves were permitted to speak freely, even about slavery. I am here in this American carnival city to speak, I suppose, for the classroom teacher, and I claim, o decani praesidesque, the ancient privilege of immunity for saying almost exactly what I think. I expect to be discounted as either innocent or impertinent, but that hardly matters. "So long as a man is trying to tell the truth," wrote John Jay Chapman, "his remarks will contain a margin which others will regard as mystifying and irritating exaggeration. It is this very margin of controversy that does the work. No explosion follows a lie."[2]

Let me say immediately that I am concerned here with only one kind of teaching, and I am eager to talk about it because it is the kind of teaching with which this meeting is apparently least concerned. I mean the ancient, crucial, high art of teaching, the kind of teaching which alone can claim to be called educational, an essential element in all noble human culture, and hence a task of infinitely more importance than research scholarship. With the teacher as transmitter or conductor of knowledge, as servant or partner of research, I have no concern. He is useful and necessary and, because he does the bulk of university teaching, it is important that his job be effectively performed and intelligently evaluated. But so long as the

---

[1] Text of keynote address, meeting of American Council on Education, New Orleans, Louisiana, October 13, 1966.
[2] *Practical Agitation* (New York, 1909), p. 51.

teacher is viewed as merely a diffuser of knowledge or a high popularizer, his position will necessarily be a modest and even menial one. And precisely this, I think, is the prevalent view of the teacher's function, the view overwhelmingly assumed even among those who want to redress the balance in favor of the teacher. Is it any wonder, then, that the teacher enjoys no honor? For if the teacher stands to the scholar as the pianist to the composer, there can be no question of parity; teaching of this kind is necessary but secondary. So too is the comparatively subtler and more difficult kind of teaching that is concerned with scholarly methodology and the crucial "skeletal" skills of creative research. Only when large demands are made of the teacher, when we ask him to assume a primary role as educator in his own right, will it be possible to restore dignity to teaching. Teaching, I repeat, is not honored among us either because its function is grossly misconceived or its cultural value not understood. The reason is the overwhelming positivism of our technocratic society and the arrogance of scholarship. Behind the disregard for the teacher lies the transparent sickness of the humanities in the university and in American life generally. Indeed, nothing more vividly illustrates the myopia of academic humanism than its failure to realize that the fate of any true culture is revealed in the value it sets upon the teacher and the way it defines him. "*The advancement of learning at the expense of man*," writes Nietzsche, "is the most pernicious thing in the world. The stunted man is a backward step for humanity; he casts his *shadow* over all time to come. It debases conviction, the natural purpose of the particular field of learning; learning itself is finally destroyed. It is advanced, true, but its effect on life is nil or immoral."[3]

What matters, then, is the kind of context that we can create for teaching and the largeness of the demands made upon the teacher. Certainly he will have no function or honor worthy of the name until we are prepared to make the purpose of education what it always was—the molding of men rather than the production of knowledge. It is my hope that education in this sense will not be driven from the university by the knowledge-technicians. But this higher form of teaching does not die merely because the university will not practice it. Its future is always assured since human beings and human culture cannot do without it. And if the university does not educate, others will. Education will pass, as it is passing now, to the artist, to the

[3] *Wir Philologen*, p. 175.

intellectual, to the gurus of the mass media, the charismatic charlatans and sages, and the whole immense range of secular and religious street-corner fakes and saints. The context counts. Socrates took to the streets, but so does every demagogue or fraud. By virtue of its traditions and pretensions the university is, I believe, a not inappropriate place for education to occur. But we will not transform the university milieu nor create teachers by the meretricious device of offering prizes or bribes or "teaching sabbaticals" or building a favorable "image." At present the universities are as uncongenial to teaching as the Mojave Desert to a clutch of Druid priests. If you want to restore a Druid priesthood, you cannot do it by offering prizes for Druid-of-the-year. If you want Druids, you must grow forests. There is no other way of setting about it.

I am suggesting what will doubtless seem paradox or treason—that there is no *necessary* link between scholarship and education, nor between research and culture, and that in actual practice scholarship is no longer a significant educational force. Scholars, to be sure, are unprecedentedly powerful, but their power is professional and technocratic; as educators they have been eagerly disqualifying themselves for more than a century, and their disqualification is now nearly total. The scholar has disowned the student—that is, the student who is not a potential scholar—and the student has reasonably retaliated by abandoning the scholar. This, I believe, is the only natural reading of what I take to be a momentous event—the secession of the student from the institutions of higher learning on the grounds that they no longer educate and are therefore, in his word, *irrelevant*. By making education the slave of scholarship, the university has renounced its responsibility to human culture and its old, proud claim to possess, as educator and molder of men, an *ecumenical* function. It has disowned, in short, what teaching has always meant: a care and concern for the future of man, a Platonic love of the species, not for what it is, but what it might be. It is a momentous refusal. I do not exaggerate. When the president of Cornell seriously proposes that the university should abandon liberal education so that specialization can begin with matriculation —and when he advocates this in order to *reconcile* the conflicting claims of research and teaching![4]—it should be obvious even to the skeptical that education is being strangled in its citadel, and strangled furthermore on behalf of the crassest technocracy. I find it very

[4] James A. Perkins, *The University in Transition* (Princeton, 1966), pp. 43–45.

difficult to imagine the rationalization of these salaried wardens of a great, ecumenical tradition, who apparently view themselves and the institutions they administer as mere servants of national and professional interests. A hundred years ago Nietzsche denounced the subservience of German universities to an inhuman scholarly technology and the interest of the Reich: "The entire system of higher education has lost what matters most: the end as well as the means to the end. That education, that *Bildung* is itself an end—and not the state—this has been forgotten. Educators are needed who have themselves been educated, not the learned louts whom the universities today offer our youth. Educators are lacking... hence the decline of German culture."[5] And what has happened in Germany is now an American story.

We too lack educators—by which I mean Socratic *teachers*, visible embodiments of the *realized* humanity of our aspirations, intelligence, skill, scholarship; men ripened or ripening into realization, as Socrates at the close of the *Symposium* comes to be, and therefore personally guarantees, his own definition of love. Our universities and our society need this compelling embodiment, this exemplification of what we are all presumably at, as they have never needed it before. It is *men* we need, not programs. It is possible for a student to go from kindergarten to graduate school without ever encountering a *man*—a man who might for the first time give him the only profound motivation for learning, the hope of becoming a better man. Learning matters, of course; but it is the *means*, not the *end*, and the end must always be either radiantly visible, or profoundly implied, in the means. It is only in the teacher that the end is apparent; he can humanize because he possesses the human skills which give him the *power* to humanize others. If that power is not felt, nothing of any educational value can occur. The humanities stand or fall according to the human worth of the man who professes them. If undergraduates ever met teachers of this kind, then the inhuman professionalism of the graduate schools might have some plausibility; there would be an educational base. But nothing can be expected of a system in which men who have not themselves been educated presume to educate others. Our entire educational enterprise is in fact founded upon the wholly false premise that *at some prior stage* the essential educational work has been done. The whole structure is built on rotten foundations, and the routines of

[5] "What the Germans Lack," *Twilight of the Idols*, p. 5.

education have begun to threaten and destroy what they were intended to save. There is a very real sense, for instance, in which scholarship has become pernicious to literature; the humanities as presently taught are destructive of the past and therefore of the present.

I repeat: the teacher is both the end and the sanction of the education he gives. This is why it is completely reasonable that a student should expect a classicist to live classically. The man who teaches Shakespeare or Homer runs the supreme risk. This is surely as it should be. Charisma in a teacher is not a mystery or nimbus of personality, but radiant *exemplification* to which the student contributes a correspondingly radiant hunger for becoming. What is classic and past instructs us in our *potential size*, offers the greatest human scale against which to measure ourselves. The teacher, like his text, is thus the mediator between past and present, present and future, and he matters because there is no *human* mediator but him. He is the student's only evidence outside the text that a great humanity exists: upon his *impersonation* both his text and his student's human fate depend. For student and teacher alike, ripeness is all. The age of the student does not matter.

Men, not programs; *galvanizers*, not conductors. When students say that their education is irrelevant, they mean above all the absence of this man. Without him the whole enterprise is ashes, sheer phoniness. This is why students are so quick, and so right, to suspect a fatal hypocrisy in the teacher who lives without the slightest relation to what he knows, whose texts are wholly divorced from his life, from human life. What students want is not necessarily what they need; but in this case it is the students who are right and the universities which are wrong. The irony of the situation is enough to make strong men weep. Here, unmistakably, we have students concerned to ask the crucial questions—identity, meaning, right and wrong, the good life—and they get in response not bread but a stone. Here we have a generation blessedly capable of moral outrage, and it is the bitterest of anomalies that the humanities should be dying among students capable of moral outrage in a morally outrageous world. Almost without exception the response of the universities to this profound hunger for education, for compelling examples of human courage and compassionate intelligence, has been mean, parochial, uncomprehending, or cold. Above all, *cold*. The waste in sheer human incentive, in disappointment in matters where disappointment is destructive and fatal, is appalling. But what fills one with rage is the callousness of scholars, the incredible lack of human concern among humanists, the monumental indifference of the learned to human misery and need. Why, you ask, is teaching held in contempt? Because it has become contemptible by indifference. Teaching has been fatally trivialized by scholarship which has become trivial. What, I find myself wondering, would education be like if humanists and teachers had the courage of their traditions and dared to face their students as men in whom their studies and texts found worthy, or at least attempted, embodiment?

Such embodiment may be personal, rational, and contemplative, or activist and public. What matters is the integration of significant life and knowledge, of compassionate study and informed conduct. The teacher in this sense goes where the action is, where his example is most needed. Moreover, it is by going there that he can hope to recover the great, complex power of the text whose custodian he is. The point is important. We must at any cost find room in our universities for those who are capable of *living or acting upon a pure text*. Lacking such men, the student distrusts the teacher and the culture he represents; the culture is defeated in the teacher's failure. I am not suggesting that teachers must be heroes or great men, but they must understand greatness and desire it for themselves and others. Only so can they speak to the student's hunger for the same greatness. It is important, however, that our sense of human greatness find *varied* incarnation. One thing a student needs to know is how men cope with the vast, impersonal chaos of modern existence. For most of us this is a matter of daily improvisation. We no longer have the ability to cope together, with a collective style based upon a common set of values, pagan, say, or Christian—it is rather an individualistic *sauve qui peut*, requiring educated hunchwork, luck, imagination, skill, and the habit of hope. This present generation has experienced drastic change and it therefore has a drastic need for significant styles of coping, present and past and as varied as possible. What is wanted is a repertory of convincing, visible, and powerful life-styles. And this the university should, as *alma mater*, be able and happy to provide. It takes all kinds of men to make a *university*—not scholars only.

For the scholar's example is no longer adequate to educate, though at its best it may belong among the higher styles. His comparative security, his cosy enclave of learning with its narrow departmental limits, and his murderous preference for a single mode of the mind—the discursive or methodological, do not call it "rational"—with its neat problems and solutions, his stunted humanity—all this strikes the student as irrelevant and even repugnant. What he wants is models of committed integrity, as whole as they can be in a time of fragmented men. Admittedly such models are hard to find, and integrated men are not to be expected. Hence it is essential that a student be confronted with as many *different*, vivid modes as we can muster; from these he may be able to infer the great, crucial idea of all true education—the single, many-sided transformation of himself, the *man* he wants to be. These men are hard to find because nobody is concerned to find them. And meanwhile our universities are making them rarer.

One point should be made. When I say that scholarship no longer educates, I am not thereby joining what Professor Bell calls the "apocalyptic" faction against the exponents of order and reason. But I also believe that the true stature of reason is no longer visible in technical scholarship, and that the academic sense of order is inadequate because it is not related to the real chaos of existence. Finally it is order and not instinctual anarchy that we want, and when I speak of a style of life, I mean by style *controlled* passion, not the free play of instinct. It is because reason and order have been so diminished in the university that we require a repertory of models before we set about constructing a curriculum. The days of the syllabus are gone forever; we are not yet ready for a viable curriculum. General education has failed, not because of its curricular inadequacy (though it *is* inadequate), but because men of general intelligence are not available to teach it. It has ended up therefore in the hands of specialists who always betrayed it in practice. If I had a campus to play with, my first step would be to plant there, at any price, the six or seven charismatic teachers of my acquaintance; their collective *areté* would, I am convinced, create a curriculum that would truly, explosively, educate. But it is these men we must have, regardless of their pedigrees—prophets, poets, apocalyptics, scientists, scholars, intellectuals, men who sprawl across departmental boundaries, who will not toe the line, individuals as large as life, irrepressible, troublesome and—exemplary. Either we must make scholarship whole and ripe and human again, or we must import into the university every conceivable variety of active, shaping, seminal humanity we can find.

At present the latter course is probably the more practicable. By usurping the whole job of education and by claiming to represent the whole mind or the only part of the mind that matters, scholarship has had the effect of destroying what education, generously defined, might provide—the basis of a common culture. We have provided men with skills they cannot meaningfully use, and by so doing we have *alienated* the laymen of any coherent future culture. R. P. Blackmur comes pat to my point: "What we have, with respect to the old forms of our culture, is the disappearance of the man who, by his education, his tradition, and his own responsive life, was the layman to all the forms of his society. The mind no longer feels omniform or that it knows its own interest. We have a society of priests or experts who are strangely alien to the great mass movements which they presumably express or control."[6] In the profession of the teacher lies one of the few correctives to the alienation which technical scholarship has conferred upon us, since, like the artist, the teacher offers cultural skills in living and loving use.

But teaching will not easily recover its great, lost function. The forces arrayed—I will not say *against* teaching, but *for* research—are formidable indeed, composing a gigantic scholarly cartel. At its base is the department, the matrix of university power, protected from above by the graduate deans and administrators, who are more and more drawn from the research professoriat and therefore share its aims and ambitions. National structure is provided by the great foundations and the learned societies which form the American Council of Learned Societies. And now there is the new National Endowment for the Humanities, whose depressingly conventional initial programs (*inter alia*, a grant for papyrological studies and historical bibliography) look as though they might have been designed by an unprogrammed computer in collaboration with a retired professor of Coptic. Even the Woodrow Wilson Foundation, designed "to attract men and women to the profession of college teaching," now seems to be tailoring its standards more and more to the pinched professionalism of the graduate schools. There is also the Cartter report;[7] intended to assess the quality of graduate programs on the basis of *informed* opinion, it will almost inevitably have the effect of stifling innovation, if only because informed schol-

---

[6] *The Lion and the Honeycomb* (New York, 1955), p. 189.

[7] Allan M. Cartter, *An Assessment of Quality in Graduate Education* (American Council on Education, 1966).

arly opinion is unadventurous and tyrannous as well as profoundly snobbish. My argument is this: at every level the forces making for scholarly conformity are immense, and the rewards of conformity high. If these forces are not directly hostile to teaching, they are certainly profoundly indifferent.

My point is not merely negative. If there is to be reform within the existing institutional framework, it must be radical. Teaching will not be restored by tinkering with the curriculum, by minor structural changes, or modest innovations in graduate degree programs. I offer the following observations as instances only; to my mind they represent the kind of profound structural reform that must precede real change. I believe they are practicable, but I offer them nonetheless with considerable pessimism, in the doubt that there is presently enough energy and leadership in the American university for it to be reformed from within.

Administration and Innovation

Innovation, experiment, reform—these are crucial, and the pity is that, apart from a few noteworthy experiments, there is so little real innovation. Wherever one looks, there is the same vacuum of leadership, the same failure of nerve. For this I believe administrators must shoulder the blame, or most of it. It is idle to expect anything from the faculties, who are caught both in the hideous jungle of academic bureaucracy and their own professional lethargy. Nor can one look to the providential intervention of the foundations; they can perhaps fund imagination and courage, but they cannot, apparently, provide it. It is above all to local institutions—the colleges, the universities—that one must turn. They are funded by communities—states, alumni, student fees—and they therefore have a responsibility to the community that supports them, but above all to that general culture that I have identified with the ideal role of the teacher. But if community and faculty support is to be enlisted (and community tyranny to be avoided), there must be something more than mere management by administrators; there must be leadership, which means a sense of the whole endeavor. Chairmen of departments and deans have constituencies to represent; only the presidents and provosts can speak on behalf of the whole enterprise.

I believe that administrators fail to make anything like full, or imaginative, use of their power. As an ex-chairman I understand that administrators are not omnipotent, that hypocrisy and evasion go with the job. But I am not prepared to believe that presidents are powerless; too many instances of abuse of power convince me to the contrary. It is the margin of freedom that matters, and it is only with the failure of administrators to use this margin that I find fault. What is stunning is the universal torpor, the apparent dedication to the principle of *laisser aller*. If presidents are too harassed to provide leadership, what has happened to the provosts? Why are the deans so subservient to the departments, so supinely deferential to the research professoriat? Why don't administrators take the stump on behalf of their policies? There is, I suspect, only one answer, and it is not powerlessness, but lack of policies and ideas, and a long habit of prostration before success. A man cannot stump for programs he doesn't have, and this is why so many administrators talk such dreary rubbish. They have, quite literally, nothing to say. Alternatively, they are the prisoners of their origins, the professoriat from which they emerge and whose assumptions and aims they share. Hence they conceive of their task as the encouragement of the status quo and, when confronted with the crisis of education, claim, like Clark Kerr, that chaos is positively good for us, or, like President Perkins, that we can reconcile teaching and scholarship by the simple device of abandoning liberal education.

THE COLLEGES

I can think of no more conspicuous failure of leadership than in the liberal arts colleges. With a few notable exceptions, the record of the college is one of failure, at least if judged by its own claims. Whatever else it may be, Socratic it is not, neither in faculty nor style nor results. This I take to be a matter of fact. Certainly it is hard to imagine a more damningly documented indictment of the liberal arts college than that of the Jacob study,[8] with its bleak conclusion that, apart from three or four colleges, the effect of college teaching on student values is simply nil, zero, and that what small change occurs comes from the student subculture. The conclusion is the more devastating because it is precisely on the claim to *teach* that the American college stakes its case. Here—in low student-teacher ratios, in college plans, tutorials, etc.—it has

[8] Philip E. Jacob, *Changing Values in College: An Exploratory Study of the Impact of College Teaching* (New York, 1957).

spent its money and ingenuity, and it is here that its failure has been spectacular. Why?

In my opinion, the colleges have failed as teaching institutions because they have been subverted from within. They have recruited their faculties heavily from the major graduate institutions, and these recruits have inevitably altered the tone and finally the function of the colleges. There has doubtless been pressure from the graduate schools, but for the most part the colleges have consented to the process. And they are now in the ludicrous position of proudly claiming on the one hand that seventy-odd percent of their graduates go on to graduate or professional schools, and on the other of complaining that they are being turned into prep schools for graduate study. Gentility and snobbery have played a large part in this subversion, as well as the hunger for academic respectability which is now firmly linked to the business of research. Instead of cleaving to their Socratic pretensions and traditions, the colleges have tended instead to become petty universities, differing from the universities only in a slightly higher regard for the teacher and a corresponding tolerance of the student. If the wealthier colleges have managed to recruit able faculty, the poor colleges have fared badly, recruiting second- and third-rate Ph.D.s, who for their part regard the college as an academic boondocks and lust for the day when they can return to the urban Edens of research. In the meantime they teach the only thing they know—technical expertise—and thereby both corrupt their students and refuse their Socratic opportunities. The colleges, in short, have yoked themselves to Pharaoh's chariot, and if they regret their loss of function, they have only themselves to blame. A handful of small colleges have dared to break the bond of snobbery and respectability that binds the college to the university, and they have done so simply by daring to profess the values they assert and finding teachers who profess them too.

Organizational energy and intelligence are crucial if the liberal arts college is to escape subordination to graduate education. I am of course in violent disagreement with those who believe that "the selective liberal arts colleges of the future . . . must become first-rate preparatory colleges for graduate education."[9] If we believe that the liberal traditions of the colleges are viable and that the college may have a higher function than feeding professional schools, then we

[9] Allan M. Cartter, "University Teaching and Excellence," *Educational Record*, Spring, 1966, p. 297.

must see about saving it. If I am right, the trouble with the colleges is that they recruit their faculties from uncongenial sources; the well is poisoned. By imitating the universities, the colleges have everything to lose and nothing to gain; neither their funds nor their human resources are adequate to the competition. My solution is dramatically simple. Let the colleges go into business on their own, *against* the graduate universities; let them form their own league, as it were, and train the kind of man they cannot expect to recruit from the universities. I am aware that such federations are in the air, and perhaps already exist; but I am emphatically *not* suggesting federation on the principle of beating the graduate schools at their own game. It should be a *different game altogether*, designed to produce men who do not think it beneath their dignity to educate others; men in whom the general civilized intelligence survives; humanists with a concern for men; scholars convinced that the world needs humane knowledge as never before. Ideally, I think, it would seek to *involve* its students in the real world, and it would surely seek real association with the vocations and professions. But its primary purpose would be to produce truly educated graduates as well as teachers to whom it could reasonably entrust the crucial task of providing models for those who wanted to become civilized men instead of scholars. I also believe that a formidable but generous enterprise helps to summon large behavior into being, and that the immense task of building institutions worthy of his love and learning might do much to create the kind of man who is missing. Enterprises which require humanity are the first prerequisite for a greater humanity. Men must *use* themselves significantly in order to grow. That is the law of all education, all growth. Why not apply it *to education?* We need new or renewed institutions; in the act of renewing them we may renew ourselves.

Such institutions would surely not lack for students. Those who desire further study but have no wish to be processed as professors are, I am convinced, far more numerous than is commonly suspected. The country is rich; leisure is available; educational expectations are rising. Far too many graduates of our colleges and universities feel, moreover, that they never got an education, and it is these who go on to graduate school in the hope of getting what they failed to get as undergraduates. It is graduate *education* they want, not graduate *training*. This is why dissatisfaction with the graduate schools is so keen. There is simply *no option* available on the graduate level;

everything is geared to professional training. And among those disenchanted with graduate school are precisely those from whom the colleges should in fact be recruiting their faculties—those students who are not averse to learning but who demand that it be given relevance and embodiment. It seems a cruel shame that such talent should go to waste or find no meaningful fulfillment at a time when it is so terribly needed. We are not so rich in the *higher* human resources that this source can be so tragically wasted.

Are there enough men to staff more than three or four such experimental "graduate" centers in the liberal arts? Probably not. But what matters is that there should be at least a handful of colleges in this country which dare to resist the conformity imposed by the research cartel and to distinguish themselves by putting the teacher—and therefore the humanities—squarely at the center of the curriculum. Two or three such places would, I am convinced, reinvigorate, perhaps even revolutionize, American education simply by providing convincing examples of the daring and diversity we need. The logical place for them to be established is either upon the existing base of the better liberal arts colleges, or as a new "higher college" created by a group of colleges acting in concert. Only by some such device, by striking at the source of the trouble, can the traditional role of the college be protected and expanded. It would be a staggering loss if the only institution of higher education still committed to liberal education—that is, to the creation of civilized men, the indispensable and large-minded amateur who is the layman to any coherent or general culture—should be subverted by the demand for professionals and technicians.

The Universities

Teaching is notoriously worse off in the universities than in the colleges. Not only is the university traditionally more committed to pure research, but it is particularly vulnerable to the pressures that have eroded the teacher's status. Vast numbers of students, huge classes, intense competition for federal funds and therefore for distinguished research professors, political and professional pressures—all these have operated to downgrade and even discredit teaching. But even in the university it is the creative use of the margin of freedom that matters. Something has been done, for instance, to give the multiversity a human scale—through honors programs, emphasis on individual work, residential colleges, and so on. But helpful as these reforms are, they have not succeeded in changing the imbalance. And this, I believe, is because none of the reforms really touches the nub of the problem. And that is the structure of the university itself, the way in which its physical organization determines its policies and precludes change and reform. Certainly no real change in the status of teaching can possibly occur without a radical change in the present power structure of the university.

Perhaps this is impossible, but I am not convinced that this is so. At present the heart of university power is the department. It is this departmental power that now so vehemently promotes research and is hostile or indifferent to teaching. It is at the departmental level that teaching evaluation is subverted, since chairmen apparently equate research and teaching; it is there that publish-or-perish policies are really promulgated; that the pressure for reduced teaching loads derives; from there that graduate deans are recruited; that the demand for early specialization arises, as well as the jealous specialism that fragments the curriculum into warring factions. Put a mild and gentle man of broad learning into a department chairmanship, and within two years he will either be murdered by his colleagues or become an aggressive and vindictive *mafioso* of the crassest specialism. The process can no more be resisted than the ravages of time. It is inexorable and destructive; and it is the remorseless tragedy of university politics.

This is why it is so imperative that some rival to it, some countervailing, antidepartmental force be created. Research is dominant now because teaching has no effective representation, no normalized political place or power, within the structure of the university. The departments are theoretically composed of teachers, or teacher-scholars, but actually they have been wholly captured by the research professoriat. The research scholar has *everything*—the departments, the powerful committees, the learned societies, the federal funds, the deanships, and the presidencies—and if he chooses to say that he finds teaching distasteful and unworthy of his abilities, who will say him Nay? Who speaks for teaching here? Clearly nobody, except perhaps the students. If teaching is to survive within the modern university on terms of something like parity with research, it must somehow acquire institutional power. The teacher, like the scholar, must have a base, a position, a budget, students, an honored and normalized function. He cannot meaningfully exist in any other way. This, I am convinced, is simple political realism.

The obvious vehicle for such a countervailing force would be the so-called university professorship. For though this professorship is still an uncertain novelty, occupying a still undefined institutional position, it has usually come into existence because enterprising administrators felt the need for countering the effects of extreme departmental specialism. Thus while the university professor may retain a departmental base, his appointment is a "university" one insofar as it cuts across departmental and even college lines. This "horizontal" professor has of course aroused the jealousies of departments, and they have frequently responded by cutting off the new professor's access to students. What is now needed, I believe, is a deliberate effort to expand and consolidate the university professorship with the hope of eventually creating a new professoriat of such power that it can challenge the supremacy of the research departments. I have no illusion that this will be an easy task, but the precedent exists and the principle has been established. It would seem folly not to follow it up. Clearly the problems of defining the relations of two such professoriats to each other and to the administration and students would be of exceptional and maddening difficulty, but I doubt they are insoluble. So far as function is concerned, it would seem natural to assign to the university professorship all those tasks at which the departments have proven themselves incompetent—the courses in general education, humanities, interdisciplinary programs, supervision of the teacher-oriented degree programs, etc.—perhaps even the formal responsibility for evaluating teaching throughout the university. But its overall concern would be with teaching, and with the training of teachers. It would therefore, I hope, display that broad spectrum of high and varied human skills that can significantly claim to be called *educational*, every conceivable great style of human existence and mode of mind side by side—the prophetic, the rational, the political, the apocalyptic, the scientific, the artistic. There would of course be an honored place in it for scholars, too, but only for scholars whose scholarship *educates*. I suspect this proposal will strike most of my audience as fantastic, but so, when you think about it, is the present state of affairs—a vast educational enterprise built entirely upon a caste of learned men whose learning has no relevance to the young and even seems to alienate the young from both education and culture. It is a vision of madness accomplished.

Pluralism

My argument would not be complete without a word about pluralism. Educators never tire of saying that ours is a pluralistic system and that pluralism is good since it accords with the nature of American society. I share this view, but my fear is that, where higher education is concerned, we are rapidly junking pluralism for monolithic uniformity. One can understand why this is happening, but it seems to me the process must now be resolutely opposed. If education is to become, as perhaps it must in part, an "instrument of national policy," then we must have also institutions that still perform an *ecumenical* function, that speak for man rather than for the state or the nation. Professional training at the graduate level is now corrupting all higher education by ruthlessly expelling from the curriculum everything that does not conform to professional utility. By so doing it is forcing the student—who may want to be more than merely a professor—into the streets and out of the culture. The student becomes marginal simply out of opposition to the elite which has expelled him. Alternatively, he responds by violent and often unintelligent assertions of those very values, especially freedom, which the university seems to have abandoned. His attempts at heroism thus become merely anarchic; he loses the skills of educated heroism, even while claiming to assert them. What we must have, unless we are prepared to abandon our fates to parochial technicians, is precisely the pluralism to which we are committed. We need *options, choices, alternatives*; we need to honor the diversity of human skills and needs. We simply cannot afford, except at the cost of everything, to permit the range of realization to be narrowed to one small mode of the mind, and that a mode which seems to be incapable of compassion for any other mode, which seems, in fact, to have lost respect for humanity.

One final point. I expect to be told that I am actually meeting the problem of research and teaching not by reconciling them but by divorcing them altogether. That is my intention, and one which I am prepared to risk, since the only likely alternative is to make teaching the lackey of scholarship. I think we have reached the point at which slogans like "scholar-teacher" merely darken counsel; there may have been a time when that was a viable ideal, and doubtless some exceptionally gifted men still incarnate it. But by and large its vogue passes on to the professor the two functions which the university has inherited and which it cannot meaningfully reconcile. The realities of educational practice make it starkly apparent that no reconciliation can now occur except at the expense of teaching. And I am not prepared to incur that expense if it can humanly be avoided. This is why I urge you to consider freshly the wisdom of separating teaching and research. It is my conviction that significant teaching and fresh energy in academic institutions may eventually make scholarship human again, and that an invigorated scholarship will once again accept the burden of teaching as the source of its vigor and the test of its wisdom.

II
SYMPATHIZE: *DAYADHVAM*

> I had three friends.
> One asked me to sleep on the mat.
> One asked me to sleep on the ground.
> One asked me to sleep on his breast.
> I saw myself carried on a river.
> I saw the king of the river and
>   the king of the sun.
> There in that country I saw palm trees
>   so weighed down with fruit,
> That the limbs bent under the fruit,
>   and the fruit killed it.
>
>   YORUBA

The following section tends to center around the claim on sympathy, on love, on understanding which the liberal arts are supposed to make. The central speech, by Benjamin DeMott, "The Liberal Arts and the War against Stone Men," sets up an emblematic personification of the man who does not understand unless he sees: the stone man. The remaining speeches by Charles Wilson, "Some Additional Aspects of the War against Stone Men"; Paul Olson, "The Condition of Being at Home in the World"; Richard Foster, "Stone Men, Accountability, and the Evolution of Teachers of Teachers"; and Charles Leyba, "Stone Men and the Neo-Dantesque Hell of Environment," speak of ways in which the stone in the stone man can be broken so that the man of flesh and blood can come out of the idol or mummy.

BENJAMIN DEMOTT

The Liberal Arts and the War against Stone Men

Forgive me the absence of a graceful start. There is so much to say and so much to defend that I'm put in mind of Lincoln's remark to the fat lady who sat on his stovepipe hat—"Madam," he said, "I could have told you it wouldn't fit." What needs to be said here won't fit either—not into the time and maybe not into the situation.

Forgive me also the obvious, implicit, perhaps simplistic faith that teaching counts, that at this moment the teacher is a central being, that we have to think of him not with old-style piety or fondness or good-natured amusement, but instead with unprecedented intensity. I believe—best for me to say it bluntly—that it's extremely doubtful anyone but this man can do what must be done if American society is to survive.

And forgive me too the tendency to ride for the widest horizon. "My work in the specialized subject of the visual pigment of the eye," says George Wald, is like "a narrow window through which at a distance one can see only a crack of light. As one comes closer the view grows wider and wider until finally through this same window one is looking at the universe." Like many another comment by the great teacher and Nobel laureate, this one is dense with implications for the subject before us. For the moment, though, take it in its easiest dimension—as a remark about the way in which quality of focus, not the area surveyed, determines the size of a subject. It is perfectly possible to talk about relationships between the liberal arts and teacher preparation in a manner that confines the subject to pedagogical turf—that is, to a comparison of the merits of potential liberal arts contributions with those of other existing models of learning and teaching. But it's no less possible to come closer to the issue, whereupon the relationship between liberal arts and teacher preparation is perceived more spaciously, as part of a landscape extending beyond the schoolyard to the social realities of the general culture. It's possible, as I say, to do that—and also risky, of course, like all large views, all attempts at "looking at the universe."

My assumption is that the full range of considerations affecting teacher training can't be brought into decent view unless this risk is run. We can and should consider pedagogical trends as things in themselves. We can and should ask which assumptions about effective teaching are gaining favor at present and which are losing favor. But we must also concern ourselves with social needs: we need to know the probable impact of these needs and troubles on the work of teaching, as part of the whole work of society, in the immediate future. Only with that knowledge in hand can we judge among the instruments and organizations of learning that put themselves forth as plausible, useful means of training tomorrow's teachers.

We gain a sliver of information bearing on both matters—pedagogical trends and social needs—by glancing briefly at the efforts of educational institutions to speak to the present ecological crisis. No public event except the war has had comparable impact on academies. And none has restored to life as many ailing—and admirable—pedagogical causes. The focus on survival has underlined pedagogical themes endlessly teased and deprecated by the knowing in the recent past.

Professor Barry Commoner argues that "you can't look at turbidity in a stream intelligently without having some knowledge about the banks of the stream and the forest that's growing twenty-five yards away." The *New York Times* environmental correspondent recently observed, after surveying developments in college and university ecology action centers, that awareness of this truth is encouraging the replacement of "the closed-shop compartmentalization of the traditional disciplines—such as biology, chemistry, physics, botany, and geology—[with] an eclectic approach."

Support for interdisciplinary work has in turn nourished the cause of "experiential education"—studies that move out from classroom and library situations into the field, confronting the social and political (as well as natural) intricacies of immediate experience. And a result of both impulses has been the reanimation of an educational ideal that until lately had almost ceased surfacing even in commencement oratory—the Whole Man, the scholar-citizen determined not only to know but to connect his knowledge with the moral imperatives of community concern. Doubtless the dignity and interconnectedness of these themes should always have been taken seriously. But they weren't, as we well know, and the rehabilitation of these themes stands high among the significant, visible, public consequences of the environmental revolution thus far.

But the point of speaking of that revolution isn't to give it high marks for recovering buried educational treasure. It's merely to draw attention to the truth that the most exciting and most potent teaching styles or methodologies now appearing are interdisciplinary, experiential, and community-oriented. The styles in question may or may not become a norm, but there's rising force behind them. And—here is the point that matters—the force stems not alone from the emergency character of ecological issues—and not alone from internal developments within the special world of pedagogy itself. It is traceable as well to a taste that preceded the discovery of the abuse of nature: the taste both of younger teachers and students alike for "open experience," ways of thinking that ventilate problems and situations with general air, that acknowledge the interdisciplinary character of events in daily life, that drive hard for the human meanings in any natural, historical, or cultural event.

But let me repeat myself: ruminations about current tastes, fashions, and the like are a shade too remote—even though ecology is on their borders—from the context in which thinking about teaching should now take place. The easygoing assumption that leisure persists, that there is time for new pedagogical treats and pleasures and styles to come to notice, that lives and whole societies are not hanging in the balance, that we're in position to fiddle and diddle over our choices—this understanding of our situation is false. The dominant force in the contemporary world—namely, the crisis of violence—erupts everywhere, with no notice; it is ferociously impatient with gentlemanly fiddling; it should be the center of thinking about education now.

True enough, we're encouraged to believe that the crisis is momentary, that there's no reason to allow it to press its weight heavily on decisions about whether or not to replace, say, the idea of teaching "subjects" with the idea of inquiring into complex human situations. In the face of bombings, student protest, crippling strikes, in the face of the rage and anguish of left-out minorities, in the midst of the most exacerbated period of human relations of this century—we're told that confident, right-minded men will kindly accept the reassurances offered by the Authorities. The authorities promise to find the actual criminals—bombers, bank burners, disrupters—find them, catch them, sock it to them good in a California blood bath. (Let it come down, says Governor Reagan.) They will simultaneously run a national speakout against violence and disruption—the White House, Walter Cronkite, everybody on the networks in the act. And they will also dig into the nitty-gritty—the serious preventive side: security guards at the elevator banks, I.D. cards for everybody (temporary workers to top executives), double locks on the washrooms, doubled "infiltrational personnel" on the police forces, beefed-up bomb squads nationwide, withdrawals of federal scholarship funds from protesters, glass boxes for trial disrupters, etc.

But the truth is that reassurance of this sort—given the problems of this age—is thin beyond belief. The present moment, long in the making, fierce in its complications, resists formulaic handling—explodes it in fact. The problems at the core haven't as yet been named in terms that show us the right uses of our best practical and intellectual energy either in or out of schools. And the very act of naming them, clarifying them to ourselves, requires, over and above a series of bold initiatives by government and the media, the creation of a wholly new language for discourse on exacerbated public issues, and a wholly new center for the life of the American classroom.

Why is this our need? What is wrong with our present style of talk? There's no mystery about this: Americans numbering in the millions are passionately conscious of corruption, pollution, and meretriciousness in the national life, determined to cry damnation down on it, enraged by other people's obliviousness to evil. The millions in question, some young, some old, have listened hard to challenges thrown down before their imperturbable neighbors by dozens of writers—challenges like these from Professor Commager:

> Who are you . . . to counsel reason and moderation? Is it reason and moderation you have displayed in your policies toward Vietnam? Who are you to deplore violence, you who have poured more bombs on Vietnam than were rained on either

Germany or Japan during the last war? Who are you to plead the cause of law and order, you who are even now waging a lawless war with lawless weapons? Who are you to counsel patience, you who have displayed so little patience with Communist China, and who were so impatient to plunge into Santo Domingo with your Marines before there was any evidence of danger there? Who are you to counsel judiciousness, you who launched the Bay of Pigs attack on a sovereign nation, and who were prepared to condemn the world to a nuclear war at the time of missile crisis? Who are you to deplore with such anguish the flouting of civil laws, you who have flouted the provisions of the 14th and 15th Amendments for a century?

People young and old in significant numbers have heard these questions, have posed a hundred others lighting up hypocrisy and meanness, and as they hear their own voices and others similarly pitched, it's incomprehensible to them that any of their countrymen can hold good opinions of themselves, live at peace with themselves, without hurling body and mind against the machine of contemporary "is-ness."

Yet, despite this fury, this positive certainty on the left, the same sense of incomprehensibility rules the minds of the other side. The case is that neither party, neither the protesters nor the famous silent majority, has in its possession the crudest means of escaping their locked-in worlds—their singleness and one-sidedness, their iron habit of referring every difference between themselves and others to fixed, impersonal, historical categories of absolute virtue and vice. Neither party has been educated in its lifetime to press for knowledge of the genesis of understandings, attitudes, opinions differing from its own.—This man speaks my tongue, knows my institutions, claims to respect heroes of the past who are heroes to me. He's no damned foreigner. Yet he's sealed off from me, blind to the causes and provocations that rouse my fury: he doesn't think these things matter. How could he have arrived at such a view? What conditioning can our differences be traced to? What must I know about his assumptions and past, what must he know about mine in turn, in order for us to conceive of the possibility of arguing? If we could believe in that possibility, we might also come to concede there are alternatives for us both besides contriving each other's instant destruction with stolen dynamite in secret cellars. Or looting stores. Or speaking always of pigs. Or raging at the guaranteed annual income. Or transforming courtrooms into variety shows.

But how can we begin to believe? On the one hand, children and grownups alike hear the commonplaces of mockery and hate and polarization from elected public leaders as well as from student radical groups. On the other, they're offered the familiar American rhetoric of unity and melting pot and sameness, a pretense that major differences don't exist, that shared community concern is all. The rules of a unity game are passed down from above—in terms that may have seemed honorable and plausible (forward together) when invented, but that are now worsening differences by denying them. And the public school insists on telling the same story. Nowhere can "we" or "they" see a road out from blankness and self-righteousness. Yet until such a road is begun—until modest, slow, molecular, definitive, social work, explicit acts of imagination, are set in course—chatter about reconciliation can't be other than self-deceit, and the possibility of sustaining order and justice even on a limited scale decreases.

Where and how can such roads be planned and built? Only, I believe, in settings where the preoccupation is not with immediacies of negotiation, confrontation and demand; only where there is still time for education of the imagination. The task of the school at this moment is to step into the breach created by the refusal of public leaders and media alike to begin work on the job of clarifying openly and patiently the roots of contemporary division. For the foreseeable future the soundest test of pedagogical, as well as political, integrity and competence must become aptness at moving men on from the jail of the single perspective, skill at imagining ways of combating the trivialization of difference in American society. But it is in the school, not in the political arena, that the chances of effecting such movement are best. The aim need not be to cease teaching history, geography, math, sentence structure; the aim must be to cease teaching them as systems closing upon themselves. The aim is so to conceive subject matter and the activities of classrooms as to allow both to contribute to the creation of human beings who are proof against stereotypes, whether of hippies, crackers, greasers, longhairs, or skinheads—human beings in the habit of pressing constantly for openings through which sympathetic comprehension of how the "opposing views" came into being may become feasible. The new school, the necessary American place of learning, must be conceived as a kind of gym for the exercise of the constructive imagination.

Now it will be said that the kind of education I am speaking of is unaffordable: we cannot rear a generation bare of number facts, spelling facts, particulars of knowledge. I believe assent to these dogmas of "fact" is—we may as well face this too—intellectually irresponsible. An invaluable American writer, Charles Horton Cooley, laid it down years ago that:

> the imaginations which people have of one another are the *solid facts* of society.... I do not mean merely that society should be studied by the imagination—that is true of all investigations in their higher reaches—but that the *object* of study is primarily an imaginative idea or group of ideas in the mind, that we have to imagine imaginations. The intimate grasp of any social fact will be found to require that we divine what men think of one another. Charity, for instance [we call it welfare] is not understood without imagining what ideas giver and recipient have of each other; to grasp homicide we must, for one thing, conceive how the offender thinks of his victim and of the administrators of the law; the relation between the employing and hand-laboring classes is first of all a matter of personal attitude which we must apprehend by sympathy with both, and so on.

Nor did Cooley stop here—with a mere definition of an appropriate area of inquiry. He went on to assert that the quality of imaginative sympathies is the surest measure of the degree of human growth and fulfillment: "One's range of sympathy is a measure of his personality, indicating how much or how little of a man he is." He was certain beyond doubt that those who deprecated this sympathy, shrugged it off with prattle about sensitivity, missed its richly complicated nature and meaning:

> [Sympathy] is in no way a special faculty but a function of the whole mind to which every special faculty contributes, so that what a person is and what he can understand or enter into through the life of others are very much the same thing. We often hear people described as sympathetic who have little mental power, but are of a sensitive, impressionable, quickly responsive type of mind. The sympathy of such a mind always has some defect corresponding to its lack of character and of

constructive force. A strong, deep, understanding of other people implies mental energy and stability; it is a work of persistent, cumulative imagination.

Let me hurry to say that my mention of Cooley and the native American tradition that understands the nurture of the imagination to be a key to general human growth doesn't imply belief that the tradition is more than a minority affair, far removed from dominant group sentiment. The weight of the wider culture presses continually toward feats of objectification—objectification of labor (the assembly line, time study), of love (sex research), of desire (image making, consumer research), of skills (SATs). At its center stands the conviction that fulfillment is deliverance into an objective function—a job, a title, a carpet, an income, a pool, somebody else's respect. I, the free American, am free to "find my own place," my "social niche," my "professional slot." I go forth from myself, I go places, ranch house to White House, dropout to Ph.D., twelve dollars weekly to a hundred a day. And up the line, where I have it made, I am more interested in a man's behavior than in his inner life, I believe man's first duty is to adjust himself to his environment and to majority opinion, I doubt that anybody can feel his way into the innermost being of another person, I don't give a damn about inward truths.

Men thus educated are, as Sartre said, "attracted by the durability of stone. They want to be massive and impenetrable. . . . They want to exist all at once and right away. They do not want acquired opinions, they want them to be innate; since they are afraid of reasoning [and imagining], they want to adopt a mode of life in which reasoning and research play but a subordinate role, in which one never seeks but that which one has already found. . . . If you insist too much, they close up, they point out with one superb word that the time to argue has passed."

And as needs to be added, such men are more and more commonly being found not just among so-called extremists—they are coming to abound in the middle. Their common assumption is that the structure of American life needs no transforming, the nation can continue more or less as it is. Their common response, when they hear a Gaylord Nelson or a George Harrar calling for a new environmental ethic, or when they hear a Senator Muskie speaking out against the culture of greed, is to utter the derisive word. *They cannot believe we are in a serious jam.* They blink away the rage and frustration and impotence seething around them. They insist that a school is a school is a school—which is to say, a place into which things as they are must never be permitted to make their way. It is wrong to allow such men to usurp the title of "disciplinarians," or "preservers of standards": the standards of learning they endorse are in fact not worthy of serious respect, and the "skills" they prize are in truth at once less than intellectual and less than humane. They have ridden human-ness down in the name of objective consciousness and ego gratification, and it is time they met serious challenge.

It is one thing to say all this, to assert the absolute need for an end to the domination of education by people of the kind just described, and another to specify means of meeting that need. We have no instrument ready to hand, no organization of learning that's perfectly suited to the task of teacher preparation conceived in the terms I've been using. Certainly the kitsch new gospel of relevance, with its manic obliviousness to all experience except Now is useless. Certainly the graduate professional schools are less than hopeful: preoccupied with the classic problems and interiorized difficulties of individual disciplines and professions, they've been disinclined to resee the so-called subject matter areas, uninterested in adapting materials from them for use in training imaginations. And certainly the teachers' colleges in their turn are also wanting. Preoccupied with education as a kind of free-floating entity, complete with its local philosophy, psychology, history, grammar, and the like, they have addressed subject matter areas far too timidly, awed by "progressions" and "pyramids" and "ascending levels of difficulty" laid out by the graduate centers. Characteristically the student teacher who learns in his ed psych course of the wisdom of teaching pupils, not subjects, etc., simultaneously learns in subject matter courses the current word on the causes of the Civil War—a word it's assumed he will pass on, intact, sanctified, in good time. The task of perceiving conflict—any conflict—afresh, making it matter, knowing it from within, discovering its substantive realities in human response, cannot appear in this context as significant work.

The liberal arts organization of learning, on the other hand, does hold out some serious promise, in my opinion. The reasons this is so are two in number. First, since many who study in liberal arts institutions look toward graduate specialization, these institutions have been obliged to maintain relatively high levels of conversancy with the living world of learning—the world in which argument about human and natural history is carried on with high conviction, energy, certainty of its importance. Teachers trained in this context are likely to be discouraged from the easy assumption that developing human powers of imagination is a task that can be entered upon without substantive knowledge, or with an ignorant disposition to believe relevant means recent, etc. The second reason is that, because it has long functioned as the introducer of the disciplines to high school graduates, the liberal arts institution has some consciousness of problems in connecting the world of learning with life: it knows—at its best—that ingenuity is required.

One can overestimate the extent of this consciousness, admittedly. Who among us is unacquainted with feeble "basic courses" in literature—the "humanities course" in tragedy, for instance, which is one long experience of closure, containment, disciplinary shibboleth. Tragedy is held to be momentous in such an enterprise because it belongs to the history of tragedy, or to the development of a literary form, or to some other body of literary knowledge composing an objective tradition. And the difference between tragedy studied on these terms, and the terms the critic Hazlitt specified when he defended the study of tragedy as essential to liberal learning, brings sane men close to tears. Tragedy matters, Hazlitt claimed, not because it's part of the history of lit, but because it "substitutes imaginary sympathy for mere selfishness ... gives us a high and permanent interest, beyond ourselves, in humanity as such ... raises the great, the remote, and the possible to an equality with the real, the little and the near ... makes man a partaker with his kind ... subdues and softens the stubbornness of his will ... teaches him that there are and have been others like himself, by showing him as in a glass what they have felt, thought and done ... opens the chambers of the human heart."

But while professionalization and the refusal to turn out toward life situations and life needs have touched the liberal arts, they have not yet hardened them past the point of redemption. Men and women like those here today could be instrumental in helping the liberal arts retain their flexibility, and adapt themselves to imaginative gaps existing within communities. It's doubtful indeed, in my view, that there is a more promising context for the training of teachers available today, a facility better suited to the transformation of inert "bodies of knowledge" into active settings for the nurture of men capable of "imagining imaginations."

I do not want to end, of course, by lobbying for this or that educational instrument. Nor do I want to end without acknowledging that my remarks plainly do not meet head-on the question how to develop conceptual skills and expertise at manipulative operations among those seeking upward mobility after generations of deprivation. And neither do they address the problem of appropriate kinds of teaching materials: what exactly do teachers use in class? What books are read? What media are employed? What matters are discussed? What exactly is "acted out?" Dissatisfaction with my remarks is inevitable on this score, if no other, and it's far from certain that in the time allowed for interaction I can provide adequately concrete examples, proposals, teaching strategies.

But as everyone knows, to give a talk is to make a choice—and my choice rests on assumptions that are, good or bad, at least fully expressible. I assume—let me spell it out fully—that our nation has tended, as Toqueville said, to make light of differences in its ranks, has considered that if all men were free to choose what they wanted, all men would choose the same things, has rooted its very belief in individualism in a sense of ultimate human sameness. I assume, further, that we live in a time—say it once more—when this fundamental sense or intuition of unity quakes and wavers inside us: we sustain a notion of community now only by dint of hard, ceaseless, molecular, definitive, imaginative labor. I assume that, because we have not been giving ourselves to this labor, we are in fact in an extremely difficult situation, one requiring us to open ourselves up to each other *now*, *swiftly*, aiming at penetration, complexity, honesty, working our way down from self-righteousness, lifting up a little from hate. And finally I assume that subjects as well as children, human knowledge and thought as well as human character, would be the better—meaning richer, truer, closer to the insides of life—if we were to succeed in reconstructing the learning and teaching community as an arena in which men come to know each other from within. There is a beautiful passage in Emerson celebrating the people of a country different from his own for their "solidarity, or responsibleness, and trust in each other." The people in question are notable for the extraordinary "communicableness of [their] knowledge and ideas," and for a "great ability . . . poured into the general mind [enabling] each of them at a pinch [to] stand in the shoes of the other.... The laborer is a possible lord. The lord is a possible basket-maker." Emerson claims that "an electric touch by any of their national ideas melts [these people] into one family, and brings the hoards of power which they individually are always hiving into use and play for all." I believe the key national idea that draws men close in this fashion, that melts men out of stoniness, is the idea of a penetrating, comprehensive, imaginative sympathy. And I believe it is time we moved that idea closer to the center of the American educational enterprise.

CHARLES Z. WILSON

Some Additional Aspects of the War against Stone Men

Dr. DeMott's paper is extremely stimulating even though I am not in full accord with some of his views. It is clear to me that contributions from the liberal arts to teacher training *can be* extensive if we accept the fact that educational reforms in both the liberal arts and teacher education must be geared to the social and cultural needs of today's society. Schools of education have failed because they have promoted a kind of professionalism among faculty and students that has stifled interaction, except in the most artificial sense, between teachers and community groups. Like many of our professional schools, schools of education have lost sight of their *raison d'être*, which is to serve and to stimulate problem solving.

The failings of professional schools may in part be attributed to their reluctance to depart from the research, the scholarly aloofness, that has characterized the basic disciplines of the liberal arts. Faculty and students of professional schools have sought security in the halls of the liberal arts; their tests of success have been unduly biased toward traditional measures of scholarship, while the pragmatic considerations necessary to solving problems have been largely ignored. I am not as sanguine as Dr. DeMott about the likelihood of the liberal arts having a major impact on the training of teachers. I am convinced there are stone men at every level of our society—in our schools, in our universities, and even in our liberal arts colleges. We must fight a number of battles against stone men before the liberal arts will be free to undertake the educational missions defined by the current needs in teacher training.

Stone Men—An Alternative View

Dr. DeMott's concept of the stone men has its origin in the writings of Sartre. I would like to depart somewhat from his view with the full understanding that I am perhaps distorting Dr. DeMott's eloquent message. On any given day, any one of us can be a stone man. "One never seeks but that which one has already found" describes a rational man. For the rational man as much as any other is burdened by human frailties—he fears uncertainty, takes comfort in his own past experiences, and finds change threatening. He is human. Social scientists have avoided recognizing the stone-man mentality in their midst by creating caricatures—the "economic man," the "political man," and so on. These are men who presumably know their best interests, and by serving their individual interests, they always serve the interests of society. They, of course, are a myth.

The stone man is real! In his book, *Models of Man*, Herbert A. Simon discusses at length the rationality of man in the face of conflict and complex problem solving. Simon describes for me the essence of the stone man with his concept of *bounded rationality:*

> The capacity of the human mind for formulating and solving complex problems is very small compared with the size of the problems whose solution is required for objectively rational behavior in the real world—or even for a reasonable approximation to such objective rationality.[1]

Men act and behave on the basis of highly simplified views of real situations. The stone man is a product of the limits of human perception.

The stone man, therefore, is a man whose presence permeates our society. To say there are stoney men in the liberal arts is to say that we must face some realities about the capacities of the liberal arts to adapt and change. I suggest that because all men are to some extent made of stone, the following battles must be fought:

1. Liberal arts colleges as academic organizations must become responsive to change and innovations at the level required to serve the needs of teacher training.

---

[1] Herbert A. Simon, *Models of Man* (New York, 1957), p. 198.

2. The social sciences must be reoriented toward social problem solving.
3. If the liberal arts are to become creative in teacher training, they must establish direct working relationships with communities outside the university.

Let me elaborate on these contentions.

Organizational Change

Because men are bounded in their rationality, it should not be surprising that professors and scholars in the liberal arts find security in departmental identification and in approaches to teaching and learning which were successful in the past. Organizations, however, can increase the capacity of men to solve problems. If the liberal arts are to make a major contribution to teacher training, college organizations must be responsive to the tensions resulting from movements toward change and responsive also to the knowledge demands of education. The college organization should operate to help participants with new problems, encourage the search for new solutions, find ways of inviting and giving access to new participants, and facilitate the process of change.

The track record of the liberal arts in recent years is a source of concern when one speaks of educational change. Consider the following cases:

Case 1. Last year, a dozen student activists at UCLA became enthusiastic over the development of curricula around "self-directed learning." The title, of course, carries the message. Students, young adults, we must recall, have to struggle against considerable odds to influence and shape their learning experience. Nevertheless, these students organized, prepared a proposal for $100,000, and received funding. That project failed because my colleagues and I behaved as if we were men of stone, unable to meet change creatively: the rules of the University prohibit students from being principal investigators and assuming full fiscal and programmatic responsibilities for grants. We did not change those rules! Students, like any other adults, want to control their projects and be instrumental in bringing about change through their efforts; we would not give the students this control, and created, by denying the students control, a distrust and dissonance that permeated the entire project. Faculty found it difficult to teach and participate in a "student thing" because of the risk of "retarding" their careers.

In general, innovative student programs get little response from the traditional liberal arts organization. Consider the student-developed experimental colleges. *Where are they today?* How many such programs were nurtured by our liberal arts organizations.

Case 2. Another case is the coming of age of ethnic programs at our major universities. More than three years ago, black students forced us to recognize the fact that institutions of higher education have neglected and, in some instances, misrepresented the cultural and social contributions of black Americans. In this struggle for recognition, some students lost their lives; others suffered serious injuries and received psychological scars that will follow them the rest of their lives. Today, Mexican-Americans, Asian-Americans, and American Indians are raising the same questions with the same amount of determination to be heard. The response of the university has been dismal. *I know of no major university in this country with a first-rate ethnic program even in the embryonic state.*

Ethnic studies offer opportunities for the liberal arts to innovate and give new directions to higher education. Many minority students have a pragmatic bent; they seek knowledge to solve problems and to influence the world around them. The liberal arts as an academic organization could benefit from the interdisciplinary push that minority students seek through relevant curricula. Alternative mixtures of classroom and field educational experiences in courses can open avenues for relating to communities external to the university or college.

It doesn't take much imagination to project how innovations such as "self-directed" learning and ethnically focused programs could stimulate the major disciplines of the liberal arts. One result that could be extremely useful in serving the needs of teacher training is the development of an empirically sound body of knowledge about the social and cultural aspects of ghettos and barrios.

To repeat my argument, the capacity of the liberal arts to liberate men's minds is beyond question. However, the ability of liberal arts colleges or educational organizations to free men from the rational boundaries that characterize stone men is *not* beyond question. Thus, before raising our expectations for contributions from the liberal arts to teacher education, we must consider their serious restrictions.

Social Sciences and Problem Solving

The current experiences of teachers suggest that adequate empirical knowledge about the social, political, and economic forces at large in urban communities and about how these forces shape the educational needs of students and adults is not available from the social sciences as they have developed up to now. The limits to our knowledge are agonizingly apparent in matters of public policy. Our national leadership prescribes directions for education on the basis of concepts and frameworks that make no pretense of reflecting the realities of the social and cultural needs of our society.

Recently David C. McClelland and David G. Winter[2] suggested that economic development in less developed countries could be accelerated by a method of psychological education for potential entrepreneurs, men who have a high achievement-need.

One question which is raised by this study is, To what extent can black or Mexican-American youths increase their success in regular educational programs by taking similar psychological training courses? By teaching students to establish realistic goals and successfully achieve them, can we accelerate and increase success in their formal schooling? If such were the case, perhaps an alternative education system would be appropriate for the ghetto or the barrio. Yet our national leaders speak uniformly of only one style of learning.

To develop a basis for reforming education, we need many more interdisciplinary efforts. I am not very optimistic about the prospects of reorienting the social sciences without some real battles. Social scientists especially have been encouraged through past success to remain apart and aloof, to maintain jealously their own turf.

Liberal Arts and the Community

Finally, I think the war against stone men must be extended to include battles for more direct interaction between the liberal arts and the community. It is not clear that the liberal arts can serve the needs of teacher training without establishing direct working relationships with community groups along clearly defined lines. One solution to this problem lies in a new model of research and service for

[2] David C. McClelland and David G. Winter, *Motivating Economic Achievement* (New York, 1969).

disciplines seeking to work with communities in activities such as teacher training.

A case in point is the Pico-Union community project of Los Angeles. The Pico-Union Neighborhood Council is an organization which represents a population of Mexican-Americans, American Indians, blacks, and newly arrived immigrants from Latin American countries. Two years ago, representatives of the council, with the support of students and several key staff members of the Urban Affairs Department of University Extension, came to my office for help. They wanted assistance in developing the means of maintaining control over the planning and redevelopment of their neighborhood. While we have been successful on many fronts in cooperative efforts in this project, one of the most exciting features has been the development of a model for combining research and service that has led several social scientists participating in a problem-solving capacity on the council's task forces to evolve new research/action programs in the Pico-Union area. With financial support from the Community Redevelopment Agency, our researchers trained neighborhood workers to serve as interviewers and analysts and then employed them to collect data which would facilitate analysis and planning in their community. We found through mutual effort a framework for advancing the research and empirical foundations for policy and at the same time providing through such efforts a service to the community. I maintain that the liberal arts must search for models such as this that will permit them to obtain a much broader understanding of the educational problems of the community.

In summary, our war is against the limited perception of men, the limited capacity to deal with complex problems such as those facing education. I have described three of the battles that need to be fought if we are to make the liberal arts effective in teacher training. They are the battles:

1. To increase the responsiveness of the liberal arts college to change;
2. To reorient the social sciences toward social problem solving; and
3. To establish direct relations between the liberal arts and the community.

PAUL OLSON

The Condition of being at Home in the World

These are uncivil surroundings, the videotaping lights in one's eyes, you (the audience) rendered invisible. It is a difficult situation in which to consider the art of teaching things humane, liberal, and liberating. Given this context, given the current crisis of the country (the Cambodian invasion), consideration of that art may be impossible. The time, the place, even the setting, are right for subjectivity; so, in order to speak at all, I want to speak first about myself. Then I will talk about Ben DeMott's argument and about what I think should be done to the liberal arts.

I want to speak first about myself because I feel that in the process of working for the reform of the education of teachers, I have partly become Ben DeMott's stone man. I have worked for almost ten years with the Nebraska Curriculum Center, and then with the Tri-University Project,[1] trying to create, out of the materials at my disposal, genuinely free and liberal education. I have recently resigned my position as director of these projects because I saw developing in myself the love of objectification and the movement toward inflexibility which I was hoping to root out of others. The movement in myself came, in part, out of the hatred and fear that I encountered in the educational establishment; it also came out of the indifference that I encountered in those of my colleagues in the liberal arts

[1] The Tri-University Project was the original project funded by the Bureau of Elementary and Secondary Education for training the teachers of teachers. The project is now funded through the Bureau of Education Personnel Development.

colleges who didn't give a damn about education. But most of all it came out of me. It came out of me because I lacked sufficient inner resources and sufficient moral force to speak with authority to the situation to which I addressed myself. I saw myself becoming uncivil to my children while I was trying to help the nation with its elementary education; I saw myself becoming indecent to my colleagues while I was trying to learn decency to black people, Indian people, Chicano people, and to those people who have professional commitments different from mine.

I would hope that out of this new direction I am taking something civil will come. I said in my letter of resignation to my staff that I was "tired of sitting among the noise and denying the voice." With Yeats I will have to lie down "where all the ladders start / In the foul rag and bone shop of the heart." What I don't have, indeed what all of us miss, is that moral authority which would permit us to say anything really meaningful about how decent human communities ought to be constructed. In the process of trying to develop that moral authority, we destroy; if moral authority fails to come spontaneously, if it fails to come from within, and from within the structure of the situation in which we find ourselves, what we tend to do is to project—with a fierceness which equals that of the military —our visions of what other communities ought to be like. What I found within myself was the hubris that Dr. Arrowsmith has described. And upon reflection what I have begun to worry about in our discussions is that the hubris we discover seems always to be someone else's hubris. The stoniness is always someone else's stone.

Let me talk briefly to what I believe to be the main point of Dr. DeMott's paper. Ben DeMott, it seems to me, is trying to restore, and rightly so, a sense of what the liberal arts are about in the Western university. That is, he conceives of the liberal arts as enabling men to live in an imaginatively flexible universe—as empowering them to be free of themselves and of the immediate constraints imposed by the time and by the space they occupy. Ben's argument as I see it, and perhaps I am unjust to him, is a reconstruction of Matthew Arnold's argument in *Culture and Anarchy*, that education is designed to widen imaginative sympathy. It is also a sort of recapitulation of Keats's argument that the function of poetry is to provide "negative capability," the capacity to project oneself, as it were, into a variety of contradictory situations, and to sustain the contradictions without losing an understanding of any of them.[2] His argument may be seen as a restatement of Swift's argument in the *Fable of the Bees* that it is our function, as educated men, to be capable of gathering from the flowers given us by other cultures and men, such honey as contains the light of reason and the sweetness of civility. In a distant and veiled way, what has been said recalls Hugh of St. Victor's argument in the *Didascalicon* (Mr. DeMott may wish to disown me at this point) to the effect that the function of education is to make men more at home with love—to make us better lovers, in the medieval sense of the word. When the "liberal education" which we know was first established in the twelfth-century schools of Paris, its study—as described by Hugh of St. Victor and John of Salisbury—was fundamentally the study of things and the study of words: the study of things as created by the Creator and therefore inducing us to love him better, and the study of words as telling us the nature of our fellow man and therefore inducing us to love them better.[3]

One can see a kind of continuity as existing from Hugh of St. Victor's argument, to Matthew Arnold's argument, to Ben's argument—a continuity with respect to what the liberal arts are all about. What we have lost since the time of Hugh is a mandate (we *live* in a civilization which has very little in the way of a mandate); what I look for, and miss, in Ben's argument, is its mandate. Sympathy is not a mandate; it is a prelude to love; but it does not, of necessity, imply that one will go to the wall for somebody else or love him in any fundamental or meaningful sense.

Let me give you an example of what I mean when I say this: I am presently teaching a black literature course in the Tri-University Project. In that course, we—black and white together—explore the

---

[2] The *Letters of John Keats*, ed. Maurice Buxton Forman (London, 1952), p. 71.
[3] The study of words was also seen as enabling people better to understand biblical words; cf. D. W. Robertson, "Some Medieval Literary Terminology, with Special Reference to Chretien de Troyes," *Studies in Philology*, XLVIII (1951), pp. 677–83. The notion that "speaking together" and the study of speaking together are aspects of what makes a man both human and humane is expressed in Giles of Rome's *De Regimine Principum* and in Aristotle's *Politics*. Such Aristotelian notions may, in part, underlie the medieval institution of having frequent "parlements" to determine the direction of institutions and the development of the great English institution of parliament itself. Sir John Fortescue's *De Natura Legis Naturae* and his *De Laudibus Legum Angliae* are instructive in this regard. A very good history of the early development of the liberal arts is contained in Philippe Aries, *Centuries of Childhood* (New York, 1962), pp. 145–63.

relationship among ourselves and between ourselves and our pasts: Africa and Europe, slave and slaver, ghetto and ghettoizer. We are at present examining, in Frederick Law Olmstead's *The Cotton Kingdom*, a number of the metaphors which appear in many of the writers who concern themselves with the antebellum South: the black man as child; the black man as beast of burden; the black man as wild beast; the black man as gargoyle (that is, as a person without a soul). All of these metaphors appear to be as ancient as our country. We also look at other metaphors which are collateral with these metaphors in the writings and perceptions of eighteenth- and nineteenth-century writers: if the black man is said to be a child, then the white man is compared to a father; if the black man is a beast, then the white man is almost invariably a tamer; if the black man is a half-souled gargoyle, then the white man is a fully-souled man; if the black man is pictured as created to be a beast of burden, then the weight of European technological civilization is often pictured as what is most worth his bearing. So the old metaphors go.

What we find, of course, is that in our own talk and in our own behavior, these metaphors, perspectives, and ways of seeing appear constantly. They appear in me—reflected implicitly, subtly—in my behavior. They appear in the behavior and perceptions of my classes. We know what is there—what traditions and historical relations make us see one another as we do. That is what sympathy is, understanding the other's perspective and history. But it is not enough. Though we look at the personal genesis of these metaphors as they have come to be embodied in our behavior, though we look at their use in the economy of passion that is our country today, what we find is that we—black and white—*continue to act these metaphors out*. And recognizing that we act them out does not make us more loving. There are very few people in that black-white group with which I work who would go to the wall for one another. At the end of last year, after a very similar kind of study—in a very intense literary group—we held a summary discussion, and one of the things all of us recognized was that we who had studied together, with a small project for a year, in quite intense circumstances, did not care for each other in any very fundamental sense.

I do not believe that the liberal arts can create decent human community. They can survey the grounds where community can be built, and perhaps they can draw a ground plan; but the liberal arts do not create loving human communities. A very interesting study by R. L. Lytton and J. F. Scott—a study which looks at the nature of neurosis in modern society and the way in which our social organization contributes to that neurosis—suggests that certain characteristics clearly define a healthy society, a society in which neurosis is not prevalent. What characterizes such a society is that change is slow and continuity is sustained by customs, traditions, attitudes (which is not to say that change is nonexistent, or that it is programmed). Healthy societies are societies in which no human activity stands alone: work is not separated from play; study (*gnosis*) is at one with work (*praxis*); the activity of youth is not set off from the activity of age. No one stands alone for one moment. Youth and age, home and business, the religious and the secular are together. The important groups are small.[4]

It is clear from Lytton and Scott's description that the societies which exhibit all of these characteristics are small-group societies. The authors point, for example, to the society described by George Homans in *English Villagers of the Thirteenth Century*[5] and to some modern non-Western societies. It is not accidental that Mr. Arrowsmith spoke of American Indian society when he looked in recent civilizations for that health which arises out of the tragic sense, the sense of hubris recognized and known for what it is. Such societies know that they cannot do everything with machines, and that the ghost is more important than the machine.

What we must create now, and what, perhaps, we are in the process of creating, are the equivalents—the metaphysical or physical equivalents—of small-group societies in a technological context. We are beginning to see little movements in the direction of our taking responsibility for one another, little movements in the direction of rootedness, in the direction of putting work and play and youth and age back together. I speak of Bettelheim's book on the kibbutz and what the kibbutz movement in Israel has done to restore the sense of small-group community between youth and age;[6] I speak of Urie Bronfenbrenner's recent book on the education of children in the Soviet Union;[7] I speak most of all of the black power and red power

---

[4] *The Community Factor in Modern Technology* (UNESCO, 1952), p. 15; cf. J. D. Van Den Berg, *The Changing Nature of Man* (New York, 1961), pp. 161–65.

[5] Cambridge, Mass., 1941, passim.

[6] *Children of the Dream: Communal Child Rearing and American Education* (New York, 1969); cf. Professor Bettelheim's more recent articles and statements in a variety of magazines.

[7] With J. C. Condry, Jr., *Two Worlds of Childhood: U.S. and U.S.S.R.* (New York, 1970).

movements as they are directed toward refocusing the attention of the adult members of the community on the child and toward making the community school a center in which people take responsibility for everything from breakfast to the curriculum.[8]

If we are to move our society toward realizing the humane things that Ben DeMott is talking about, it is the movement toward creating collegiate living communities, the movement toward creating artificial, admittedly phoney, small-group societies, which gives hope that sympathy may become health and even love in our many-cultured, cosmopolitan society.

To return to my black literature class and our reading of Olmstead: the form of our perception *is* important; how we see one another is important; but what is more important is the mandate which we feel once the perception is gained. That mandate is described in a passage from Ralph Ellison which puts together for me the issue of what the liberal arts have to say about the world in which we find ourselves. The passage does not mistake the relevant for the recent: what it does is to take the *Odyssey* and its ancient allegorical interpretations[9] and make these ours—incorporate them into our perceptions.

> We who struggle with form and with America should remember [the sea nymph's] advice to Menelaus when in the *Odyssey* he and his friends are seeking their way home. She tells him to seize her father, Proteus, and to hold him fast "however he may struggle and fight. He will turn into all sorts of shapes to try you," she says, "into all creatures that live and move upon the earth, into water, into blazing fire; but you must hold him fast and press him all the harder. When he is himself, and questions you in the same shape that he was when you saw him in his bed, let the old man go; and then, sir, ask which god it is who is angry, and how you shall make your way homewards over the fish-giving sea."
>
> For the novelist, Proteus stands for both America and the inheritance of illusion through which all men must fight to achieve reality; the offended god stands for our sins against those principles we all hold sacred. The way home we seek is that

---

[8] Ken Haskin's film of his work with the Morgan School is helpful here; it is available from EDC. The Morgan School is a community-monitored school in Washington, D.C.; Mr. Haskins was a principal of the school.

[9] Cf. Felix Buffière, *Les Mythes d'Homère et la pensée Grecque* (Paris, 1956), passim.

condition of man's being at home in the world, which is called love, and which we term democracy. Our task then is always to challenge the apparent forms of reality—that is, the fixed manners and values of the few, and to struggle with it until it reveals its mad, vari-implicated chaos, its false faces, and on until it surrenders its insight, its truth.[10]

What can the liberal arts do in the journey—in that journey toward love and toward that Ithaca which we call democracy? First of all, we can begin to create the conditions necessary to decent human communities in our own colleges. I am very impressed by the residential colleges. I also feel, after Lytton and Scott, that professors ought to be living in these colleges, and that their children ought to be there too.

Second, we can exhibit the kind of ruddiness and readiness for sacrifice necessary to civil man. I appreciated Dr. Arrowsmith's attack on the AAUP. The professional establishment in higher education in this country has dedicated itself fundamentally to crassness, to protecting itself from accountability. We cannot work in poverty communities unless we ourselves are willing to give a great deal of our lives and a lot of our resources to those communities—quietly, the left hand not knowing what the right hand does. We cannot create justice out of greed.

The third thing we can do is simply to care about the training of teachers. We can teach well ourselves, and we can place teachers-to-be in the best liberal arts classes, under the best teachers that we have available. Generally the "best" classes, or those putatively best, are reserved for those who, to all appearances, serve the social crisis least: over 50 percent of the teachers in America are trained at AAUP-rated C, D, and E institutions; 90 percent of the black teachers are trained at these institutions. American elementary and secondary teachers are recruited by higher education. Yet they are almost immediately partly set apart, because they are to be teachers, by the snobbishness of liberal arts people about the teaching profession. ("If they're not too bright, they can always go into teaching —particularly the girls.") Not surprisingly, American teachers are, according to the Coleman report, among the most provincial, the least socially concerned, the least bright, and the least intellectually autonomous of our students.[11]

[10] *Shadow and Act* (New York, 1966), pp. 113–14.
[11] *The Educational Professions* (U.S. Dept. of H.E.W., 1968), pp. 36–39.

Fourth, the liberal arts can open themselves up to evaluation. The schools can; the schools of education are beginning to ask questions about how they serve society. Why can't we?

Fifth, we can fight against the funding of stoniness. The Office of Education, particularly through ESEA, is a massive effort to fund stone men through the writing of behavioral objectives and the manipulation of people according to Skinnerian principles. The fundamental dedication of the Office of Education, as it has offered direction and given funds in the name of research and demonstration, is to an ideal of education which is based on a narrow conception of what behavior modification is and an exceedingly narrow conception of the nature of man. You cannot create a civil culture by shaping people in a self-conscious fashion and by following those Skinnerian principles which allow one to say to other men, not "I—Thou," but "I—It"; or "I manipulate you," not "We act together for the common good."

Sixth, we can insist that the institutions which we create be tempered to the pasts and the cultures of the people with whom we deal: Latin-American culture, the wonderfully various American Indian cultures; black cultures, including those of Yoruba and Dahomey, the Voudan culture of the Caribbean, the black culture of New Orleans, the "Winti" worship of Dutch Guiana,[12] soul religion in the United States, the religion and culture of ecstasy and of man's possession by a spirit outside himself.

Historically black culture is one which is social-contestive and one which makes use of the circle aesthetic.[13] The schools which white America has created for black Americans are schools which deny the social-contestive (as opposed to the individualistic), and which also deny the right of black children to become "men of words" in that circle which belongs to their own culture.

Seventh, we can demand that the liberal arts colleges indeed be liberal. What we are teaching presently in some parts of our liberal arts schools is how to be "Technological Men," or how to be

---

[12] Cf. Melville J. Herskovits, *The New World Negro* (Bloomington, Ind., 1966), pp. 280–302 and passim.

[13] Cf. Jahnheinz Jahn, *Muntu: The New African Culture* (New York, 1961), passim; cf. Roger D. Abrahams, "Can You Dig It?: Aspects of the African Esthetic in Afro-America," unpublished paper; Roger Abrahams has written widely on "ring play," ring worship, music, and the circle aesthetic in African and Afro-American culture. The film "Pizza, Pizza, Daddio" is an interesting exemplification of what I am referring to.

members of what Milovan Djilas has called the "New Class." I have been on the advisory committee of a distinguished English department which teaches literature from London, Boston, Paris, and New York. But it teaches almost no Chicano literature, no Indian literature, no Asian literature, and no African literature. It teaches no approach to the literary text other than a historical-critical approach similar to that of Professor Bredvold, teaching that approach sometimes narrowly and parochially, sometimes incredibly richly and broadly.[14] What is discouraging is that the often wonderfully brilliant graduate students of this same department do not wish to entertain the notion that a liberal, diverse community could truly exist in the department. To have had more than one approach, or to have studied other writers, I was told by one Ph.D. candidate, would have been to invite "chaos into the department." This attitude is not unusual in America's departments of English. One day festival will invade these workaday domains, and chaos will come.

Finally, liberal arts schools need to learn not to open CUNY to black kids, saying to them, "There you can elevate yourselves." Instead the schools—we ourselves—need to learn how to get to the point where the kids will be willing to let *us* into Harlem. The sources of our sanity do not lie in higher education: they lie in children; they lie in those populations which have been locked out; they lie in oppressed peoples. They lie in the rural areas. The kind of community that I am interested in creating is the kind of community where the children give as much education to adults as adults give to children.

I would like to read three poems to you, poems that children have written as their contribution to the community that I am a part of; they have educated me. They tell me, I think, that something new is coming. The first goes like this:

> Trees grow very big
> They drink up the sun proudly
> They wave their branches
> They sing to the happy wind
> As it passes through their boughs.
>
> (RICHARD SNYDER)

---

[14] Professor Bredvold was the author of *The Intellectual Milieu of John Dryden*, an examination of the history of seventeenth-century religious ideas. The approach is a rich one, but it by no means exhausts our capacity to deal in a scholarly fashion with the imaginative traditions of other ages and cultures.

The second poem is of mountains:

> The mountains have grass
> The flowers praise the mountains
> The grass sings to it
> Dirt helps the mountains to grow
> Mountains stay graceful for years.
>
> (RICHARD SNYDER)

The third concerns racism:

> Black kids are black
>   and play in the ghetto
> White kids are white
>   and play in the meadow
> Some Black people like it
>   and some people don't
> Some white people don't even care
>   and some never won't.
>
> (SIDNEY WHIGHAM)

On teaching:

> A teacher is someone who talks
> When no one is even interested.
>
> (TRACY PALMER)

"The way home which we seek is that condition of Man's being at home in the world which is called love, and which we term democracy."

RICHARD FOSTER

Stone Men, Accountability, and the Evolution of Teachers of Teachers

I have several reservations in trying to make this presentation a reaction to what I have heard thus far at this conference. My main reservation has to do with the whole question of what a school superintendent—who in most people's minds epitomizes this stone age and its stone men—is doing on this platform. What is a superintendent doing among such erudite people? I have one answer to that question. Perhaps another will suggest itself before I'm through talking.

In any case, whenever there has been a TTT meeting that Don Bigelow or his people have called and the public schools have not been represented, I appear at the next meeting to tell the assemblage that the last meeting, while perhaps interesting, was irrelevant—that it couldn't possibly be relevant to bring together two groups (liberal arts professors and professors of education) who don't know anything about what is going on in schools and let them talk to each other about what should be going on in the schools. One of Don's ways of preventing me from stating the same thing on each such occasion is to say, "OK, get on one of the panels." So here I am. A panelist—with a particular point of view.

I

Some persistent themes do seem to pervade all of the presentations I've heard here. I hear over and over that if you wait too long on anything that you have come to realize you should do, whether it is desegregation or the implementation of some other idea, you lose your commitment, you lose your credibility, you lose your relationship with people, you lose the love of people, you lose all kinds of trust. Then, with your options vastly reduced, you try to plunge ahead as best you can. The City University of New York is the best example I can cite from this conference: the only thing you can do is try open enrollment even though it seems destined to fail in five years. It seems to me that the national government works in accord with this particular policy: it waits too long, if it cares at all, to deal with the poor, to deal with the denied, to deal with war; and the only thing it can then come up with is ecology. New York and the national government seem to be following the same kind of general principle. Perhaps it isn't surprising, then, that I disagree with one thing Ben DeMott said. I think the notion that, somehow or other, it is going to be out of peace and reflection that the new ideas are going to come is nothing more than a cliché of thought. If what he says is true, I'm dead as an educational innovator. Yet I feel that living in Berkeley has been my salvation. Most of my life is spent in confrontation, and I think the most creative ideas come out of it.

Let me offer a simple example: we have a law in our state which says that if you pass out any material on public school grounds you have to have prior permission to do so from the principal. Our kids in Berkeley are very alive politically. They know the scene is real, and it's "right on" for them. As a result they had decided to put out an underground newspaper. It was called the *Packrat* and looked like the *Berkeley Barb* without advertising (and if you don't understand that, you're just not in the liberal arts). Now, they included in their first issue one word that seems to throw American culture in general. The first part of the word is usually preceded by "mother," but they left that prefix out. Well, they applied the word to the Vietnam war; and the principal, a very good principal, said to them in a very low-keyed way, "Hey, will you please cease and desist. You know there's a state law about that." And they looked up at him and said, "We really would like to, but we think the First Amendment to the Constitution supersedes the education code. Therefore, we will continue." The principal's interpretation required that he rightfully suspend seven of them, which he did.

When I met the students and their parents Monday morning, they made very clear what had taken place. And they wanted immediate action. I asked them if I might have twenty-four hours to talk with the staff and they said no. By negotiation and creativity I got twelve. And that's pretty good. If you get 50 percent of what you ask for in that kind of negotiation, you're in.

In my negotiations with the high school staff, I found that they, like most staffs, were stone men. They decided they couldn't move from their position because they had an education code. They forgot about the kind of people who created it. In our state, that's important. So I took the next step. I said, "OK, then you negotiate with me tonight as we meet with the kids." Well, the negotiation went on for two nights. I won't take you through the details but from the seven kids suspended we learned a good deal. Five of their parents were lawyers, including one who was a leading labor attorney in the Berkeley area; both the students and their parents had some reason to understand the law and the importance of the spirit of the law. By two o'clock in the morning of the second night of negotiations, we still had arrived at no decision. So one of the young men who had spent the entire day with me looked up at me and said, "Dr. Foster, punish me in any way you want, I can't give up any of my principles." I looked down at Dan with love, because I loved him, and I said, "Dan, you remind me of the Birch Society; I can't tell the difference." And he started to cry, a seventeen- or eighteen-year-old beautiful kid. I put my arm around him and I said, "You know, I truly love you, but somehow or other if we who love and who are liberal and open can't make it, there's no hope for America."

Dan sat for about five minutes. Then he called a caucus of the students. He said, "Parents stay out of it. Administrators stay out of it. Teachers and all you other unimportant people stay out of the way." And the kids went off into a side room and in forty-five minutes came up with a compromise—a respectable, legitimate, creative compromise with which we have been living during the rest of this year.

Out of that compromise has come a look at all the other kinds of things that we automatically do with kids in school. That negotiation has forced us as an institution to question such things as whether or not there should be prerequisites for any of the courses we offer; and, by the way, if you want to get an academic faculty uptight, just suggest that if a kid thinks he can handle trigonometry without algebra and geometry, then it's his risk and he ought to have a crack at it. You break the whole system wide open. "There's no question about it," the faculty say, "because prerequisites are the hallowed ground on which we stand. Prerequisites prove that what we say has some importance because there's something that had to come before it." (I will refrain from using my single word response, but will remind you of what Emerson said—that the language of the street was always more expressive than the language of the academy.)

II

A second thing I would like to talk about is the assumption of this conference that there's going to be a new alliance between the liberal arts college and the school of education; that somehow out of this bold alliance there's going to come a creative thrust toward some kind of change, a new energy that will bring these two groups closer together. There is one problem with the assumption: that problem is the fundamental lack of contact with reality of all of higher education. I was listening when Don Bigelow asked Bert Burns yesterday, "Is your campus still intact, Bert?" And Bert nodded that yes, it was when he had left it the day before. The situation in the public schools and on the urban scene in general is much more tenuous than that. My answer usually has to be, "Well, I called the office five minutes ago, and the system was intact." There's a world out there that's changing so rapidly and so consistently, as far as kids are concerned, that by the time you guys get together and talk, you'll be talking about the old world. I am suggesting that the marriage between the liberal arts and education will be announced but never consummated: there will be no birth, no real creation. Two groups will come together in a hybrid fashion—I could have said in a bastardly fashion—but nothing will come of it, no better teaching will come out of it.

III

With that as a background let me say what I'm trying to present. I'm saying that the fond notion that out of each of you is going to come some change is one I can't buy. Last night's comment, that assassins are waiting for you to come home from this meeting suggesting change, was much more believable. Those assassins who hold power back there—they're called deans, they're called academic senates, and they're called colleagues—they'll chop you off right at the knees just as you get started because your idea may break the stone in those stone men. We have evidence of this. We hired twelve of you to work for the National Task Force on Teaching the Disadvantaged up in New England. We said we'd pay you extra money if you'd just go into the public schools and teach. I guess it was nine out of the twelve who, at the end of the time they taught, said they would have to hide it from their colleagues because it was not held in high repute to be able to teach kids. They had to make sure their deans didn't know about it because they wouldn't get advancement if it were known that they were teaching kids. So I'm saying that I really don't have any faith in the model you've suggested for the schools or for you. I think it's a cop-out.

I do, however, have a suggestion as to what you might do. I suggest that you're going to have to develop a cohesive new power of your own, that you set up an alternative model of what you're going to do. Set up a situation in which you don't have all those messy people having power. I'm really saying that you should create, under the umbrella called the university, a new university that has something to do with love and kids and teaching, a university that has to do with the problems of America. Make sure that it has *goals* and that it has *instructional theory*—instructional theory in depth. And make it have *power*. I am suggesting that the only way to go is to set this new university in competition with the existing system. And it must be based on the idea that the affective and cognitive domains can never be separated except for research purposes, and it has to save kids, all kinds of kids. (Most of our schools fail about 50 percent of the poor kids. When you get to New York, as we learned last night, the failure rate reaches 88 percent. When you get to college it reaches 95 percent. I'm saying we are going to have to reverse these statistics.)

How are you going to do this? I want to suggest something that may sound crazy. I want to suggest that the professors—from assistant professors to full professors—who teach in this new school get their increases in salary in accord with their ability, and the abilities of the teachers whom they train, to relate to kids in teaching situations. The research will still get done, but now it will be a part of the relation to the student; for the professors will receive salary advancements on a five-year delayed program. They will be paid a basic salary and then we will look at their creations—the teachers—five years later. If the teachers they have trained provide creative, loving support to kids who need that kind of help, then we will pay their professors a bonus as we do with an insurance salesman who gets his premiums on a delayed basis.

I'm saying that as long as we are kept fat and healthy in the present moment and experience no sense of accountability for what's out there five years from now, we won't change: we won't change without pressure, we're made of stone. As soon as colleges and universities are made to know that the payment is out there, as soon as they know that what's happening to kids out in the school is going to determine the professor's reward, they'll become human. They'll care what happens; and you won't worry so much about those academic deans and colleagues who'll be waiting for you to come home, waiting to shear you of any new ideas you might have brought back with you.

CHARLES LEYBA

Stone Men and the Neo-Dantesque Hell of Environment

I

I would like to talk a little bit under the rubric "Notes from My Early Childhood."

By the time I was old enough to be aware that I had to go to school, I could see that the world was firmly in the grips of white people; I felt that there was, economically and intellectually, nothing left for me and for my people. I accepted unquestioningly the propaganda that told me that I came from a dumb and dirty minority. It is easy enough to account for my feeling. Look, for instance, at Ted Parsons's dissertation, in which he studies about the Mexican-American student and the teacher. He asked the white students to answer a question which went roughly this way: "Who would you label dumb?" About 80 percent of the white students answered, "Mexican-American students." When he asked the question "Who do you label smart?" about 80 percent of the white children answered, "White kids." "Now," he said, "Let's question the Mexican-American children on the same points." The Mexican-American children responded 70 percent of the time, "We think the Mexican-American kid is dumb, and that the Anglo is smart."

The ball game is over when one thinks this way, but this is how Mexican-American children have come to think. We, as Mexican-Americans, have an awesome respect for knowledge: we do not deride it, we do not hate it; we have a storied and fabled love of the person who is learned, but our respect has gotten so out of hand that we are afraid of approaching learning or the learned person at all. Mr. Parsons came to a further finding. In his research, he had Mexican-American children continually arrive at school with fairly new clothing; then he asked teachers what children they would label dirty: they answered 80 percent of the time by labeling children from the Mexican-American minority dirty, though during that time he carefully made sure that the Mexican-American children's shoes were polished, their clothes washed, ironed, and creased.

What was left to us in early childhood was for us to be happy; we became a happy people, made love, and passed on, as our heritage to you, a minority that is today 50 percent below the age of eighteen (50 percent of the Mexican-American community is below the age of eighteen). We are not very sure how many of us are around because the census people decided that they would not count us last time. They did put a little dotted line where it said "Other." So if one is Mexican-American and not too scared to admit it, one may write it in. Many of the Mexican-Americans will not write it in: there are a half-million "illegals" in Los Angeles County. Do you think they're going to answer the census? Are you kidding? They'll fade into the woodwork and come back out when the census man is gone.

I was told in school that it was dumb, really dumb, to speak two languages. Whenever I spoke in Spanish, the teacher got paranoid and said, "Hey, you're telling secrets. You stand up here and tell the rest of us what you're talking about." But there are some expressions in Spanish that are so beautiful that they make you salivate; you must say them in Spanish to know their beauty. For example, to talk about love in English is to sound like the burping of a forty-five caliber machine gun; to speak of it in Spanish is almost to be disrobed by the word.

What did the schoolteacher teach me about myself? What did she teach me about the heroes in *our* history? The Mexican-American minority has, in the classic sense of the word, an ancient history. Our heroes belong to the Southwest, they belong to Mexico, they belong to the Aztec and Mayan civilizations; they cross the Atlantic and can be found in Spain and France. But the schools did not teach me anything about these heroes and their societies. They taught me instead about George Washington's blood; they taught me nothing about the blood of Indians, the blood of Frenchmen, and the blood of Spaniards, about all that has been given me which makes me proud and about all that has been given me which contributes to my defects.

II

These are the perceptions of childhood. After childhood comes the long period when I was in the womb of the liberal arts colleges. I graduated from a liberal arts college; I didn't have teaching credentials because I couldn't afford them. I went out to teach with a provisional credential. They gave me X number of years to acquire a standard credential; they put me in the classroom; I taught. Who prepared me to teach? The liberal artist prepared me to teach. And what did I do? Because I have learned the myths of the liberal arts college well, I considered my subject matter a sacred trust: I knew its well-vocabularied incantations, incantations which were intelligible only to the middle class, intelligible to those people who already knew the incantations. I didn't have to teach the middle-class children. Those who smiled and knew what I was talking about made me feel, "Hey, that's a good student! I'll talk to him after school; I'll talk to her after school." And those who didn't already know the incantations—children who did not come from middle-class homes—I labeled as "the dumb insensate mob," those who weren't eager about my eagerness. I was a product of the liberal arts; I allowed only the coterie in; I was, like my college professors, *the professor* who considered his subject matter an academic hymen to be kept forever inviolate.

During the days of my first teaching, the district officials used to come in occasionally and administer the Iowa Test to my students (I was in a school now that was half black and half "anglo"). The officials would tell me and my colleagues in this school: "Look, the Iowa Test indicates that you really have two student bodies here: you've got a bimodal distribution. You've got the college prep kids and then you've got the 'other.'" It made us feel good to know that we were liberal artists, feeding into such great liberal arts institutions as UCLA. UCLA rates the top ten high schools in the city. If we were not rated among the top ten, we had to find some reason for our bad rating. One year when we fell out of the top ten, UCLA said, "You've got two student bodies; you've got the college prep body, with which you're doing a beautiful job. Their curve skewed in the right direction; then you've got the other student body, and that other body is just screwed."

What was it that woke me up? Our department chairman came to us one day and said, "If you are teaching any of the beginning language courses, you must flunk 60 percent of your kids." "Why?" "Because if they don't start taking language in junior high school, then we know they're really disadvantaged; we offer beginning language at the senior high school because at the senior high school we must democratically offer the opportunity to start even to the 'disadvantaged.' But you will find that the disadvantaged kids are going to want to take a course only so that they can go back into their disadvantaged neighborhood and say, 'Hey, I'm taking a college prep course.' These kids are just social climbers. Clean them out." When my chairman told me to do that, it occurred to me that something was wrong. The low-income kids whom I was teaching may not have wanted to take the language: they may have been very mistaken about their ability to take the language; nonetheless, we have to take as authentic the evidence of their wanting to study that language given us by their registering for it.

III

I had to ask myself, "Why are these things happening?" And I saw that these things were happening for two reasons—because of the pressures created by two interests: the graduate school and American business. The graduate school has as its intermediate-level generals the major departments in the undergraduate colleges; these, in turn, have their first lieutenants the general education professors; and the general education professors have as their trench fighters schoolteachers who are prepared and sent out to teach by America's undergraduate colleges. The graduate school and American business have turned education into an interlocking fishladder requiring increasingly complex skills, skills that repel the normal minority person by the time he reaches the middle elementary school. The ecological system is a complete one; if the typical middle-class home is a furnished school, then the typical school is an unfurnished middle-class home; and the school leads directly upward into general education, the major, the graduate school, and over into American business or the vocationalized major department itself. Given this ecological system, the liberal arts colleges and the graduate schools are developing a three-tiered society: at the top level are the white, Anglo-Saxon, Protestant, Jewish, Oriental people—managers, technicians, owners of businesses; at the intermediate level are the black sociologists, the government workers, and so forth; and at the bottom level are my people, who plant ivy along the freeway, wash dishes, wait on tables, and make token appearances at conferences.

IV

As to a program of action to break this system: first, I would suggest that you go back next week and cut the general education program away from the major right away. Use it as a laboratory in the community. Have the general education professor go out and teach on site; let him teach young people who are college students to work as aides or whatever in the schools. Have him teach a combination of these young college students plus the high school students listening to them. They will make him relevant immediately. (Incidentally, from what I have heard up to this point, perhaps the quickest way to make liberal arts relevant right now would be for me to snap my fingers and take away 50 percent of your vocabulary. Then you might learn how to teach.)

Second, develop laboratory general education projects. Why is it necessary, for instance, that you teach *Hamlet* or *Macbeth* or something like that in a general education course? Why isn't it possible for you liberal arts people to teach children's literature for people who want to be elementary school teachers? Why don't you have your students write literature, and why don't you teach the art of writing literature for particular children and communities, an extremely practical art? *Hear educators!* I am asking your help to give the credential new meaning. I do not want you to yield up units to us in the form of "FTEs." (The FTE is academic property.) Like you, we once wanted the big ranch granted us by our dominant positions in the normal schools, but I as a representative of a college of education am not asking for that ranch now. I'm saying, "Let's work together." Let us work together to give the credential meaning by developing new conceptions of education. Presently, we pretend to prepare teachers by pushing them through an overly vocationalized and overly subject matter–oriented college experience. By emphasizing reading, we indirectly cut college out for many disadvantaged kids, saying to these disadvantaged kids, "You cannot be educated until you can read." But when a person reaches the age of sixteen or seventeen years and has not learned to read, most efforts to make him read will be failures; on the other hand, by that time the same 'illiterate' person may be ready for education in many other areas, and we should educate him in those areas. We should teach him the arts of reasoning clearly, of expressing himself well, of deciding the difference between honest and biased opinion; we should teach him the difference between opinion and certitude, between certitude and proof and evidence. Such training would cut down on all of our prejudices right away; it would help us to create an open culture.

We can create a genuinely open culture. Imagine, just imagine, what would happen if we could prepare young people who would come to know themselves during the first two to four years of college studies, young people who knew their own culture and who had an insight into their own psyches. Imagine sending three of these kids over to General Motors to get a job, kids who have bachelor's degrees in the subjects of reasoning, self-knowledge, and culture. First comes a white kid. The interviewer asks him, "What did you major in?" The white kid says, "Well, I majored in knowing my culture, and knowing all of this, I can discuss it beautifully. I know the difference between opinion and certitude and falsity, and yet, with all of this, I still know how to love." "I'm sorry, GM doesn't want you." The black person says, "This is what I learned: self-knowledge, pride, my culture, reasoning." The Mexican-American says, "I learned self-knowledge, pride, culture, reasoning." The General Motors interviewer says, "Who am I going to hire?" The interviewer could no longer discriminate. As things are at present, discrimination has been given justification in the most immovable variable we know—the deprived environment.[1] Religion may be wrong in teaching predestination, its predestination is no more fearful than our secular economic predestination, a predestination which condemns minorities to the neo-Dantian hell comprised by "minority status."

[1] Cf. the researches of J. McVicker Hunt and others who attribute academic difficulties of the children of poverty to environmental deprivation.

III
CONTROL: DAMYATA

"The Day of the sun has been my strength. The pale of the moon shall be my robe."

Waelpanne, speaking of what controlled him.

"I did not know then how much was ended. When I look back now from the high hill of my old age, I can see the butchered women and children lying heaped and scattered all along the crooked gulch as plain as when I saw them with eyes still young. And I can see that something else died there in the bloody mud, and was buried in the blizzard. A people's dream died there. It was a beautiful dream.

And I, to whom so great a vision was given in my youth—you see me now a pitiful old man who has done nothing, for the hoop is broken and scattered. There is no center any longer, and the sacred tree is dead."

Black Elk, Oglala Sioux medicine man, speaking of the first controlling of the Oglala Sioux through the massacre at Wounded Knee.

Mr. Charles DeCarlo speaks of the notion of managerial skills in our society and of the exclusion of the liberal spirit, of the sense of comedy and of tragedy, from present management. Mr. DeCarlo's former work was as a manager for IBM—doing computerized management tasks and teaching others how to do them; his present work is the presidency of Sarah Lawrence College. DeCarlo now looks to a new sort of ethos and a new sort of inner control. His presentation is followed by those of Mr. B. Othanel Smith, who speaks of the management of teaching; Mr. José Burruel, who speaks of how the Chicano community is managed—squeezed between the political forces destroying it and the irrelevance of the education provided it; and Mr. Bernard Watson, who observes some of the dangers which a liberal education poses—dangers that the young people in America will learn to ask questions which America is not willing to answer.

CHARLES DECARLO

The Liberal Arts: Antidote to Simplism

A friend of mine recently remarked that Albert Speer's memoirs, *Inside the Third Reich*, are a testament to the importance of the liberal arts and a diagram suggesting the nature and resolution of man's problems. Speer, the brilliant architect and technician who in his early thirties became a major power with Hitler and went on to become head of production in the German economy, must have appeared, at the height of his career, as the perfect example of a rational and successful manager. Yet it was only after the war and twenty years in prison, during which he was able to study philosophy, poetry, and history, that he emerged free and transformed, a liberally educated man. His book is a dialogue in memory between the older man, who has learned suffering and had time to question all things, and the young man, so full of energy, dreams, and certainty.

In a much more modest and symbolic way my own career, and those of many others in our managerial society, has paralleled this unhappy revelation in time. Perhaps the best introduction to my concerns about the liberal arts might be to start by describing a bit of my own career. After the war ended, I knocked about, was in doubt and confused. In today's terms I would probably have been called emotionally disturbed and alienated. In any case, since I had good grades in college, I was invited to teach. I did this, and taught mathematics while working on a doctoral degree under the GI bill. I also ran a small business in the background and made a rather good living. Unfortunately, I felt the academic career was a put-on. In my own restlessness I watched the faculty at close range worrying about textbooks, course credits; heard the "poor rogues talk of court news; who loses and who wins, who's in, who's out." I decided I couldn't possibly be a teacher. However, I was taught to finish what I started, so I did indeed complete the degree. I left and floated and then finally went into business. The merger of electronics and mathematics was just beginning and no one thought of mathematics as particularly practical. It took me—you won't believe this—nearly six months to convince IBM to hire me. After three years in the Navy and a similar period in graduate school, where every task was defined, the idea of moving freely as a salesman appealed to me. And so I started in IBM at the lowest level of sales. Out of my experience I think I can give you some truths that I have learned, truths that probably few people would admit. Like Albert Speer, I was largely educated *after* my technical training, educated by books and observation to realize that life was neither rational nor simple. It is in the light of that experience that I have entitled this paper "The Liberal Arts: Antidote to Simplism."

In going to work for IBM I went into an industry that was just getting under way. After preliminary training and field work in sales I joined a group in the designing and marketing of the first commercially produced large scientific computer. Our group rapidly expanded and, under the designation of applied science, we set out to apply computers and systems to the widest possible range of human activity.

It was then that I began to develop what I'd now almost call a disease of the mind, an overly rational attitude. I saw every problem as reducible to a series of relationships, relationships such that, if we had the data, we could build the analogue of the phenomena and, working with the analogue, we could inevitably make a series of deductions, draw a series of conclusions. I began to believe that there was an answer to everything. I saw, for example, the enormous power of human organization, and learned how to go about organizing work. I participated directly in the design of work, reducing to a pattern all types of functions, from the very top caliber engineering and scientific work right down to premium billing and insurance rate adjustment. In other words, I was busy taking the humanity out of work and replacing it with order.

After several years I was put in charge of product planning and engineering for the IBM line of large machines. One of the first things that happened in my new job was a visit from some teachers and engineering classes from various universities. They had come to ask, "What should we be teaching so that we can get the right people into your industry?" We couldn't convince them that what they wanted to teach had already been built in IBM and other laboratories—that it was virtually already out of date. I was just beginning to get a glimmer of the notion that what we really needed were bright people, not people trained with a certain technical curriculum. Later we had two days of meetings with engineering and business school deans. Those meetings were an absolute waste because the deans wanted to find specific things to teach and we wanted to tell them that we wanted *people* to work with.

The industry kept growing. I began to see more clearly how products are designed in this society. I remember visiting a large automobile company to learn how an automobile is designed. I believe you would have the same feeling I had after two or three days in Detroit—a feeling that you're in an unreal world. The whole design process seems backwards. Instead of starting with the goal of producing cheap, safe, and effective transportation, using sound engineering principles to satisfy that goal, the goal is to produce something with style which will sell to a particular and created market. Sound engineering principles are violated, and Ralph Nader is the ultimate result. The violation of good engineering principles and the goal of style remind one of Ahab, whose methods were sane but whose goal was mad.

Later I was put in charge of education and executive development, and I here saw the problem of trying to get people, particularly scientifically trained men, to manage other people. I began to understand the importance of tragedy and comedy and the drama that is inherent in life. I tried to introduce in training programs many kinds of liberalizing education, but too often it was too little and too late.

While in this job I had another experience that you'll be interested in. For about three years IBM cosponsored affairs called junior science symposia. An effort would be made to have the high schools send to these symposia the two hundred brightest kids. We'd match them up with physical scientists and mathematicians. The kids would present papers and then the senior scientists would present papers. In this way the kids would have an idea of what a real science conference is like. Some of the student papers represented pretty good scientific work. Now one of these conferences included two bright boys of about fourteen or fifteen, an army colonel, a teacher at West Point, and another man who was a physicist. One boy was a Jewish boy from the Bronx, and as we were having lunch, the discussion swung around to Hitler. This boy gave a very cold analysis of how Hitler's policies were quite understandable. That was a sort of blinding moment for me, because I suddenly realized that we had in industry's laboratories men who were thirty or forty who had obviously been bright, dedicated kids, men who were sort of the neighborhood genius at fourteen. But by the time these men were thirty, they had developed into just ordinary, decently good engineers, enormously lacking a dimension of humane understanding. What a horrible price to pay—to have these kids turned off humanity and intensified to technique so early in life—just so their parents could say, "Gee, see how little Johnny did his biology experiment," or "See how great he is!"

It was then that I began to see the arrogance of science and technology, particularly as we attempted to move from designing simple systems like the space program to tackling social problems. As you may know, it's no great, stunning intellectual achievement to be able to bring men back who are lost in space. In this case men are working with a beautifully meshed system of mechanics. Because the system is determined by Newtonian mechanics, it is possible ahead of time to simulate the system and to anticipate practically all conditions. The brilliance is demonstrated in the technology and engineering necessary to provide the enormous number of parts, the linkages and control systems. These along with engineering of rockets to throw the vehicle with sufficient energy to achieve orbital velocity present no major theoretical advance, but are the results of well planned grinding developments.

The space program, as brilliant as it looks, is really a rather minor intellectual achievement. It is also minor in part because our society was able to mount it *only* because it didn't get in the way of any other institution. The goals of the program were very simple, namely, to get men in space and to get them back: functions could be organized; companies and groups could be engaged on specific tasks to be integrated under one large overriding goal. Again the image of Ahab haunts us.

I become very upset when I see the approach to social problems that flowed from our space achievements—the notion that if we can put a man on the moon, then we can solve all the problems of New

York City. This notion is based on the idea that we can reduce any problem to a set of simpler elements and then recombine them and work that recombination as a solution.

The more technology progressed, the more depressed I became at how far we had gone, at how brilliant we had been in our own techniques, and how arrogantly we were trying to pursue human problems with mathematics and with the half man the scientist is. So I decided after a period of time to make a change. I, myself, was also changing; I guess if you're alive you have to change. In any case, as the business world got bigger around me and the social problems got more and more complicated, I decided that the time had come to leave business.

At this same time I began to think quite a bit about education, particularly after having been involved with IBM's huge education organization. We had been somewhat successful at everything from training forty-five-year-old plant workers in algebra and engineering principles to helping an executive managing 30,000 people to be a bit more human. I decided there was something important about education. I became aware of the truth in Kant's remark that man is the only being that needs education, that he can only become man with education, and that he becomes what education makes him. So I began to look back and realize that the very complexity of the field that I had been in was predicated on the belief that we could know everything about the world. Further, if we just kept probing deeper and deeper we'd know more and more until, ultimately, we'd have the answer. In other words, as long as I lived in a world of answer-prone people the search for *how* things worked, the demand to *use* the answers would keep me from asking the why, the questions.

I decided to leave IBM and go into some kind of educational life. I wanted to be with young people because I think young people have the most interesting problems in our society. So I ended up at Sarah Lawrence, a small, special place, intensely and intimately human.

You know, I think liberal education is *all* questions with only *some* answers. Questions are important because as you continuously reshape them you find out what the answers you have really mean. And the questions I come up with are the ones everyone who has had the benefit of a liberal education simply has in his blood: questions of man. His values, will they change? Why will they? Can he change? What's man's responsibility to man? What's involved in the idea of humanity? And why does man know he can die, and will, and can still endure? The liberal arts college where I now am, in fact every liberal arts college, should teach these questions and not answers.

I feel personally that if I can keep young people asking more questions when they leave college than when they enter, I'll consider myself to have been successful at Sarah Lawrence. And their questioning must be free. I suppose that that's what the word "liberalizing" means. But it also means to *be*, to be anxious, to know your end. This is difficult to live with, more so in an age when everyone is insecure and wanting certainty.

I contend not only that the liberal arts are important to us but that they are also affordable. The only laboratory we need for a liberal arts education is our human consciousness; the materials we can shape out of our personalities. We will continue to ask the same questions that have bothered everyone who has ever spoken a language. And one of these cardinal questions concerns the ideal balance of change and continuity.

A question that bugs me, and I'm sure bugs you, is why man fools himself about change. I'm convinced that man doesn't change at all, or that he changes so little that it is imperceptible. Out of his consciousness man has created something called technology, which now has begun to have an existence of its own. When the advances of technology change the world in accord with what we think we want to achieve, we find ourselves attending science and industry conferences proudly talking on how to "manage" technological change. When the achievements of technology get out of hand, when technology causes pollution or causes a population explosion, then the technologists get together to discuss what they are pleased to call the "problems of an advanced society." This may sound mystical, but I am convinced that once the material world is triggered by an idea, the world so created moves on its own—and poor man has to accommodate as best he can.

Now, the only way man can accommodate is to have some sense of where he has been and what might have been the intentions of his acts. That's why history is so important; that's why I can't understand the insistence on relevancy, on immediacy, on "nowness," which is so characteristic of our time. If you don't know where you've been, it's impossible even to get a fix on what might happen in the future.

I left the world of the exclusively *now* to come to the liberal arts, so perhaps I can lay it on the line from my own experience: we should separate the education of the human being from the training necessary for industry and the professions. It is pointless to use youth as a time of specialized training for work in IBM or in the medical profession or the law profession: there isn't one of those entities that can't do a better job of *training* than the liberal arts, no matter how complex the skill needed. But in response to vocational pressures much of the liberal arts curriculum has become so much garbage: the more professionalized the school, the more garbaged the curriculum. And the garbage is packaged as pseudo-knowing, as units that can be built like dominoes. I believe we must stop requiring that everything fit into exactly thirteen or sixteen weeks and that it all add up to some career-launching pad. The most gifted, and the most productive, people I've ever worked with are people who surmounted such education. This is an unfortuante commentary on the world and our method of preparing for it.

I do think the whole question of the liberal arts and teacher education is peculiarly important at this time; I do accept the notion that we're living in a time of discontinuity. I'm sure that these are really different times not probably so shockingly different as some would have us believe, but certainly different enough that we should make a reassessment of whether we need to change basic practices. The difference that strikes me most strongly, I suppose because it's antithetical to my own values, is the rejection by so many people today of reason and discourse as a means of organizing themselves and accommodating themselves to life. For example, Richard Rylan, a young graduate of Harvard, wrote in defense of terrorism:

> I've only learned two things in my four years at Harvard. The first is that an equally intelligent, rational, and valid argument can be made on all sides of a question from any and all premises. The second is that those arguments have no relationship to anything but themselves. We are trapped in a philosophical system of cause and effect. Rationality binds the mind and restricts the soul. It might even destroy the brain cells. We need to be liberated, we should be constrained no longer by possible rational consequences. With all the words and images we have around us, it may be that action is the only way to open fresh areas of consciousness. In any case it will take a complete destruction of the material foundation of the wrongs we are fighting before we are rid of them. And only then will we be able to plant trees and flowers over all our woes and begin again.

People my age have to be terrorized by the idea of throwing over reason and the whole of the past in the hope that we'll be able to plant flowers over our woes. To think that someone's been at Harvard for four years and has been so unaffected by a liberal education as to write this just makes you want to cry about how far we are from where we should be!

It seems to me that for teachers and for liberal arts educators the time has come to yield to the young people's demand for institutional change, to get them out of the cages that we have built in the educational system. I am not saying that the young possess any special wisdom, but the fact that they're so energetically pushing against the cages we've built should suggest to us that we ought to open up and let them try their wings. We must accept them, even if it means taking away the conveniences of our own curriculum, the conveniences of our own administration. Sure, it means running a much seemingly looser ship, perhaps even a much looser ship intellectually. But I think we've got to be open enough as adults and college administrators to allow new things to happen, to temper them only when in our judgment they are at the very brink.

I would hope that if a liberal arts education could be a reality for the students I see, then they will devote their education to questions rather than to answers; they will not accept the easy idea that if we could either elegantly engineer our way out of our problems or just destroy the whole superstructure, then suddenly paradise would grow again. If they have the right questions they'll accept neither of these two polar positions but will be willing to pick up the kind of crazy and frightened world that they will inherit, that before them we've fixed up a little bit here and torn down a little bit there.

I see a need, and in a curious way I see it in looking back over all my management experiences—a need to restore a belief in several important dimensions of human consciousness. I do believe that it's very important to restore respect and faith in form and order (not "law and order"), for somehow a man's language and his experience and his remembrance are a treasure and that treasure has a form that has got to be kept alive. Form is a continuous and continuing attribute of knowledge, whether it be language, art, philosophy, politics, or history. Without form men will slip back to barbarianism. We can't burn the books, we can't throw away Shakespeare and Greek drama. Language and poetry weave together all of our experience. They make us able to endure the hurt that so much of our lives has to be. I think what Mr. Arrowsmith was saying last night about imagination and what Mr. DeMott said today about sympathy for the other, or the ability to "imagine the other," is vitally important in a world such as ours where we are—merely by living in this technological world—divorced from any direct engagement with the world. We are shielded by layers of plastic unreality. Sometimes I pause at the end of a day and try to remember what natural phenomena other than my own body I have touched during the day. There are days when I have moved through nothing but machines and plastic and a synthetic reality. If we don't develop a vital imagination we're destroying our ability to reach beyond this plastic world and become human. And I believe we must follow the lead of many of the young and begin to believe that there are many more ways of knowing than those language alone provides: the beauty of just being able to move properly, to dance, is a joy of knowing.

As a society, I think we should be able to afford to put aside the idea that the only reason to know is to make money, that the only reason to know is to have power or to further the practical uses of knowing. Knowledge is the basis for insight as well as use, for defining one's self as well as one's course. I applaud, and I hope to learn from, some of our black students and their beautiful demand to go back, to seek the roots and to know life in some other way. I watch what they are doing and want to share in it.

We finally must come, and as a society we can afford it, to realize that beauty is now about to become a supporting economic commodity. I think beauty has now reached level of consciousness and taste where it can influence our market economy; it can be something that is "profitable." It seems to me to make a great deal of sense in the early years of elementary education to teach the kids, not only how to letter and reckon, but to understand what beauty can be; to throw out much of the historical facts, the spelling facts, and the number facts. Let us rather teach what it is to demand beauty so that as consumers in a market economy they can set standards—so that the world can be made profitably beautiful.

This conference has impressed upon me that the liberal arts provide a key with which to open up the world of love. It is interesting that at least half of the speakers I've heard here really talked about the urgent need for man to love man. We don't, in this society, speak very easily about loving other people. We just don't know how to talk about emotions.

But there's another side of this coin of the liberal arts and loving. It seems to me that it's also necessary to restore, if not the approval of, at least the ability to endure, suffering. I don't want to get into any discussion of the Judaeo-Christian ethic, but it seems to me that we take something out of life, that we diminish man, in our endless quest to trade suffering for security, happiness, or drugs. I'm not saying that we should all go around chopping ourselves up in order to know pain, but, as Mr. Arrowsmith said last night, the liberal arts should make people recognize the necessity of understanding suffering. If one understands this, if one feels for people, then it is a bit more difficult to fire someone (firing ought to be a little tough) or to inflict unnecessary embarrassment.

Finally, it seems to me that the liberal arts should restore something else: all of us, I think, sense that we've lost something beautiful and simple. I think of the cosmetic culture we have, a culture wherein everybody wants to be ageless, where the people my age are in a contest with twenty-year-olds to see who can look the most attractive. It seems to me that we've lost a sense and knowledge of the fact that we're going to die; that when we die there's a rebirth; that life is a cycle; that there are seasons; that we're a part of a process. Without the fruits of the liberal arts to make me aware of this age-old tradition I think I would go mad. I don't see how men could endure without this sustaining force. The sense of time, the realization of the ocean of blood we are, that we have only a short time to be is the price of consciousness. In a poet's words:

> We recede from our fathers,
> We drift from our rooted shores
> And we fear the sea of oneness;
> Oh, where is my land,
> And where are my fathers:
> How shall I be.

Not what shall I be, but how shall I be—this is the quintessential thread. How can we go about our business as teachers and educators without wanting people to feel that same sense of—I can only call it being one with the cosmos, that kind of poetry, those kinds of thoughts?

And that brings me down to Don Bigelow's invitation and full circle. He asked me to come because I'm practical. I tell you, as a practical man, that it is urgent that we keep this society from destroying itself, to keep it from being insanely sane. This is what the liberal arts can do. Without them we are terribly lost. Because of this need, the conflict that Don mentioned earlier between teacher education and liberal arts comes into focus. Frankly, I'm not much interested in it as a problem. I know little about teacher education and curriculum development in the liberal arts. But it seems to me that our needs are urgent, and that we need what I believe a liberal arts education can provide. This need is too urgent to allow the kind of cabalistic rigamarole that pervades the entire credit system. Perhaps all notions of credits and units should be thrown out. We should give everyone a bachelor's degree along with his birth certificate—except that if they're particularly heavy at birth, they should receive a masters. And if they're prodigies of size, they should get a Ph.D.

We've got to realize the urgency of having people such as yourself dedicate your lives to helping men like myself, people who are still in the business world and in the government, to come to very human and very humane conclusions about their work. They have all the answers and very few of them know how to ask significant questions. I would hope that for whatever it's worth you'll take my words, the words of a practical man, that yours is a vital spot, and not only that you can add a great deal to our society, but also that you can add ultimately that which will set our course and keep us straight.

B. OTHANEL SMITH

The Liberal Arts and Teacher Education

These addresses impress us with the discriminations, special privileges, provincialism, and power controls of the social system, and the apparent dehumanization of social relations by technology. They claim that we have been brought to the brink of disaster, as witnessed by alienation, escapism, cults, frustrations, violence, and loss of communication. Furthermore, they tell us that institutions of higher learning are permeated by scientific, technological, and professional mentalities that have all but rendered them incapable of dealing constructively with the problems of individuals and society. And they tell us that university faculties are preoccupied with problems of the disciplines and with the knowledge and skills peculiar to the professions and technologies. In consequence, the liberal arts have become subservient to scientific and professional studies and have lost their sense of direction, their concern with man as man and his problems. For the same reasons, teacher education has been reduced to the acquisition of skills on the job and to preparation in a subject matter that provides little human understanding, sense of history, feeling for one's fellow man, or capacity for creative thinking.

This bill of indictment is fraught with a sense of urgency and impending disaster. It is exciting and disturbing because it depicts the surface of social reality while pointing first to one eruption and then another, to this crevice and that sinkhole. It fails to look beneath the surface to the underlying influences and to recognize the great cohesive forces that keep intact the social fabric.

It is important not to distort the social and educational picture of our times. One distortion holds that our difficulties are not serious, that we can go on with business as usual. This view measures present conditions by those of the past and inflates the gains. Another distortion overemphasizes the seriousness of the times—revolution is just around the corner. It measures things as they are against high ideals and sees the achievements of the past as trivial and the present as intolerable. If we are to preserve some semblance of sanity, we must remember that idealistic outlooks must be tempered with historical perspectives, and that cries of impending disaster are perennial.

Our task is to explore the role of the liberal arts in teacher education and we must ask some hard questions. We need to know what the liberal arts can contribute to teacher education—what they can and cannot do. We need to know their strengths and weaknesses as disciplines. And we need to know also what changes should be made in the purposes for which they are used and the ways they are taught.

There are hints in the addresses that not all is well with the liberal arts. They have been taught in isolation from social realities, and the feelings they are to engender and the lessons they are to teach are too often lost in the intricacies of interpretation. Very little is said about the liberal arts themselves, their nature, needed reforms, and applicability to the problems of man in mass society. This omission is unfortunate, because we can no more tolerate "the liberal arts as usual" than "business as usual."

Historically the liberal arts were those which were deemed fitting knowledge for freemen. They consisted mostly of literature, philosophy, and languages (especially classical Greek and Latin). In sharp contrast were the servile arts, which were assigned to the slave, or to those in bondage. In modern times the liberal arts have been equated to the humanities, which are concerned primarily with the nature of man, human relationships, man's hopes and fears, his appreciations and enjoyments, and his purpose and destiny. They are thus said to be different from technical and scientific studies, which treat the physical and biological worlds, and from professional studies, which provide preparation for the rendering of services. Liberal education is then defined as learning in the liberal arts without reference to preparation for any specific occupation.

THE ECLIPSE OF THE LIBERAL ARTS

The eclipse of the liberal arts increases the difficulty of utilizing them in teacher education. During the last fifty years they have sustained considerable loss of status. Evidence of this is found in the fact that the study of classical Greek and Latin has almost disappeared from American academies. Even graduate departments are reducing requirements in foreign languages and in some cases eliminating them altogether. Furthermore, no classical Greek is taught in the public schools, as it was at the beginning of this century, and Latin does not enjoy the status that it held only a few decades ago. Although work in philosophy still flourishes, it does not have the same prestige among students and faculty that it had at the beginning of the present century and the proportion of students who actually take enough philosophy to learn what it is all about is small. Literature and other art forms, together with history, enjoy somewhat greater attention, but their prestige as academic studies have been on the wane.

A number of influences can be suggested as probable causes of this depression of the humanities, but only two will be mentioned. For one thing, scientific knowledge has grown at such a rapid pace that the accumulation is little short of being fantastic and almost overwhelming. But it is not merely the growth in scientific knowledge that has challenged the liberal arts. Rather the challenge is that the sciences have pushed the quest for knowledge into domains that were once the exclusive territory of philosophy, literature, and history. Science deals not alone with questions whose answers feed technology, but also with questions which from the beginning of man have puzzled the race: When and where did it all begin? Who is man? What is his purpose and destiny? The domain of metaphysics has been invaded by physics, and man's psychic and physical natures have become the territory of psychology and biology, respectively.

For another thing, the liberal arts, as pointed out above, have for centuries been associated with the genteel class. As society becomes democratized, accompanied by increasing emphasis upon the education of the masses, the liberal arts have been depreciated because of their long association with the wealthy and the well bred. Those who defend the liberal arts have not been successful in convincing any considerable number of the academic community, certainly not of the masses of the people, that the liberal arts have a content that is as relevant to one social class or occupational group as to another. The supporters of the humanities, and especially those who teach them, have done little, if anything, to neutralize the onus that comes from this long association with the genteel class.

The Revival of the Liberal Arts

If the liberal arts are to play a significant role in the education of teachers, and they should, they must be given a breath of life. How they are to be revived is a question to which scholars of the liberal arts should address themselves. The question is certainly one that an outsider discusses at the risk of intellectual embarrassment. But be that as it may, we shall here record some imports of these addresses for that question and add some reflections of our own.

We can hardly disagree with DeMott when he supports, at least by implication, "studies that move out from classroom and library situations to the field, confronting the social and political (as well as natural) intricacies of immediate experience," or when he calls attention to the apparent emergence of community-oriented teaching styles and "the taste both of younger teachers and students alike for ... ways of thinking that ventilate problems and situations with general air, that acknowledge the interdisciplinary character of events in daily life, that drive hard for the human meanings in any natural, historical, or cultural event." By moving in these directions the liberal arts may come to grips with life as men in mass society experience it, and thereby neutralize the age-old conception of liberal arts as the exclusive privilege of the well born and the well-to-do.

These are familiar aims and hopes. The cries raised for them in the years of the Great Depression still ring in our ears. It is not for lack of goals and hopes but the want of a program by which these may be realized that schooling in the liberal arts suffers. To design such a program, to say nothing of its development, requires down-to-earth thinking. For when community-oriented teaching begins to involve the social and political experience of youth or their elders, we must ask the hard question, What can the liberal arts say in answer to their quandaries? Can they say that here is a fresh, constructive view—a breath of fresh air? Or can they say only that here are some interpretations—some old ways of looking at your experience—based on the ideas and insights of this or that classical, medieval, or renaissance figure? These queries are raised not in an attempt to discount the perspectives of great thinkers as we grapple with current realities. Rather the purpose is to remind us of the magnitude of the task, and to save us from the tendency to romanticize approaches to educational problems.

Industrial society is in a transitional period, not a decadent one as is sometimes claimed. This need hardly be said were it not for the fact that we have yet to recognize the potential good in an electronic age. We see the events about us and react negatively, because in themselves they are often evil and frightening. We imagine an electronic society and fear that our lives will become even more dehumanized, because we know neither the shape of the new society nor the range and extent of the freedoms to be enjoyed in it. But if these images and events are seen in the context of a transitional period, they can take on a different significance. They arise from the miseries and spasms of distress that attend the uprooting of man from the psychological and social ground that has given him stability for centuries. The social picture that frightens us now is transitory, it is a phase in the movement toward an age in which for the first time in history the humblest person can have a noble life.

We can imagine that a resurgent liberal arts program can awaken man to the good that inheres in the emerging age and thus help to assure that it will not go awry. Man must have a fresh interpretation of his problems, his purpose, and his social destiny in this transitional period and in the new society that will be partly shaped by man's creative energies. This need of man for positive approaches and interpretations of his experience partly sets the task of the liberal arts. The magnitude of this task is great. We talk of educating for leisure, but this language is already obsolete. For ages the source of man's personal discipline has been work. In the electronic age the demand for labor may almost disappear. Soon it will be necessary to find a moral equivalent of work—to discover ways of using surplus human energy constructively. Indeed, we are already at the edge of this necessity. Even now the absence of this moral equivalent is one of the conditions of the anomie and aggression of college youth. To conceive of the function of liberal arts in the context of this unparalleled demand for the constructive use of human energy gives only a glimpse of the significance the liberal arts can have in the emerging age.

If the liberal arts are to be viable in a mass democracy, they must also develop an intellectual discipline appropriate to the nature of their normative content. If efforts to revive the liberal arts consist solely in the reinstatement of the literary humanist's modes of thinking, they are doomed to failure. According to this brand of humanism, humanistic studies carry convictions; they convince us because they describe man's condition in terms which we recognize as true to our own inner experience. This is good so long as the liberal arts are concerned with the enrichment of experiences, with man's deeper and more fundamental enjoyments and appreciations.

But when they leave the campus and go to the people who are confused in their political and social activities because of a multiplicity of perspectives, the liberal arts must offer more than a mere reinterpretation of these outlooks. For in mass democracy men must act in groups, and group action requires uncoerced consensus, or at least enough agreement to sustain the action. If rationality is to be achieved and maintained in an extreme social heterogeneity, it is necessary that personal convictions be tested by a criterion that is broader than inner experience.

A hard fact about modern man is that he must act in concert to an unprecedented extent. It is impossible for one person to cope with pressing social problems because of the multiplicity of perspectives and values. Social, not individual, action has become the only effective alternative. Yet our inner experiences are so different that what is convincing to one man turns the other off. At this point, too, the conference papers are deficient. They present no mode of intellectual discipline, no basis of rationality, and for this reason the conception of teacher education they reflect must be taken with serious reservations.

The various kinds of discipline to be obtained from the pursuit of the liberal arts have seldom been described. Yet the discipline to be acquired from the study of science is sensed, if not understood, by the masses. They carry in their heads some sort of picture of the scientist as a man in possession of methods of finding knowledge that turns the world to man's advantage. When one asks about the conception of method in the liberal arts, he finds no corresponding picture of how the questions that arise in the philosophical, literary, or historical study of man's nature, his relationship to other men, his thought, and his ultimate destiny are answered. Indeed, some leaders in the liberal arts assert that there cannot and should not be any objective criteria by which knowledge in these arts is tested for its worth or its truth.

It is not the purpose here to present a concept of intellectual discipline appropriate to the liberal arts or to the age that lies before us. Perhaps there are many sorts of such disciplines, depending upon the art and the requirements of the age. The norm by which Isadora Duncan judged perfection in the dance was probably different from the norm of a Cezanne or a Beethoven. But these are not the arts that the liberal studies encounter when we attempt to adapt them to "imaginative gaps existing within communities." Here we encounter the art of personal interaction, intrapersonal and intragroup persuasion. This art calls for, among other things, sensitivity to perspectives, to ascription of one's feelings to others, and for the ability to see the world through the eyes of others and to seek new outlooks inclusive enough to incorporate the broadest range of interests. It has its own norms of adequacy, adherence to which constitutes an intellectual discipline.

One of the reasons why the pictures of society that men carry around in their heads are "blurred and incongruous," as Louis Wirth put it, is that there is practically no common normative context of thought. Western society, like Western science, has proceeded on the basis of a common set of normative concepts. These have become eroded by the acids of specialization, class differentiations, minority perspectives, and conflicting cultures and ideologies. Liberal arts education should be concerned with, among other things, the task of helping man to reestablish a set of normative concepts to use in settling issues that confront him from day to day. A society can progress only if there is a basic set of norms which for the most part can be taken for granted as a basis for settling practical issues. Such a set of normative concepts would constitute the criteria by which personal convictions are evaluated, and they would serve the same persuasive role in social action as the concepts and attitudes of science play in solving problems and resolving disputes. They would constitute the basis of rationality and social objectivity. In doing so, they would no more rule out the interests and preferences of man in the social realm than the concepts and norms of science rule out the interests and preferences of scientists.

Perhaps the main point of the preceding discussion can be put in another way. Value judgments always incorporate the character of the one who judges. There is a sense in which one's value judgments tell as much about the judge as it does about the object of judgment. This is true in the domain of natural science no less than in the domain of social thought and action. When a scientist renders a judgment, he reflects his character as a scientist as well as his knowledge of the world. It is therefore an error to contrast the scientific man with the liberally educated man without taking into account the fact that their judgments reflect their respective characters.

What is necessary for rationality in this period of extreme social unrest and confusion are men who have comparable value characters, just as in science they have comparable descriptive characters. The normative content with which to develop value character is found in the intellectual tradition. To be sure, this tradition is not all of a piece; it harbors inconsistencies and many of its concepts are either vague or ambiguous. If this were not the case, the task of educating people liberally would be much easier. But since it is the case, a program of liberal arts education must come to grips with the task of clarifying and reconstructing the normative concepts that constitute the tradition.

It may be claimed that this emphasis upon a common set of values rules out individuality, creativity, and dissent. Of course it does not. In the sciences, where insistence upon a community of concepts, values, and techniques is emphasized, no one raises the question of whether or not such a community snuffs out individuality, creativity, and disagreement. As a matter of fact, it is a necessary condition for the growth of scientific knowledge. There is no good reason for assuming that the contrary would be the case in the domain of social thought and action. The irrationality that threatens to thwart the realization of the potential good of an electronic age and to push us into a new form of tyranny is partly attributable to the failure to develop a common normative ground from the study of intellectual history.

The Liberal Arts in Teacher Education

The teacher's preparation consists of a number of constituents. Among these is a pedagogical and an academic, or nonpedagogical, component. The latter consists of the fields from which is drawn the subject matter the teacher uses while teaching. The liberal arts make up part of this component of the teacher's preparation.

The content of the field of liberal arts which is taught to prospective teachers is partly determined by the subjects offered in the public schools. Traditionally these subjects have been, and continue to be, literature, history, languages, and fine arts. Literature and history now dominate the liberal arts program of the public school. The history taught in the schools is a mixture of political, social, and military history. The history of ideas is almost completely neglected except for a few courses in literature where intellectual history is given a brief and spotty treatment. In most schools the fine arts are given even less attention.

Today there is a groundswell of excitement over and interest in the development of a program of instruction in the humanities at the public school level. As with many educational innovations, efforts will be weakened by attempts to develop a program in the humanities in too many directions. Some programs appear to stress work in aesthetics in which all the various art forms including the mass media are given a place. Others attempt to build a program that incorporates history and literature with only minor attention to the other art forms. Then a few programs attempt to combine the literature representative of the various significant epochs from the ancient world with that of the present. Others stress the cultural history of the world. It would appear that these diverse approaches indicate the need for a program of humanistic education that will include a systematic integration of the various subjects that make up the field of the liberal arts. Such a development would require the cooperative efforts of the teachers of the humanities in the public schools and scholars in both the liberal arts and the field of education.

Unless there is a program of teacher preparation in the liberal arts appropriate to the work in humanities in the schools, it will be difficult, if not impossible, to find appropriate personnel to man the public school program. This will require, among other things, that in the universities and colleges we abandon the policy of "liberal arts as usual." Instead it will be necessary to develop a program for the preparation of teachers in the liberal arts through the cooperation of the same mix of personnel as recommended for the development of the public school program. In any event, a program in liberal arts must come to grips with man's problems and experiences, his purpose and his hopes, his conditions and his destiny, in and through a content representative of the intellectual tradition and also of the various media of communication. It must also provide for an intellectual discipline that is not purely literary and subjective.

It should be pointed out that the liberal arts already play a significant role in the preparation of teachers with respect to the component of pedagogy. A considerable proportion of the intellectual history of man has been concerned with educational problems, as seen in the work of a long line of renowned philosophers from Plato to Locke and from Locke to John Dewey. Furthermore, many of the great pieces of literature—plays, poems, novels, and short stories—tell in unforgettable language the experiences of teachers and students from which the prospective teacher can gain many insights into the processes of education and schooling. These materials in the liberal arts which are relevant to the preparation of the teacher have been a concern of scholars in the field of educational philosophy and history for almost a century. And almost every program of teacher education requires that the prospective teacher show some proficiency in these subjects.

It is well to bear in mind that the liberal arts are neither a place, a college department, nor even a college. They are a depository of a certain kind of knowledge, and any program of education that has need of such knowledge can and should appropriate it. This does not mean that liberal arts education should be the business of everyone. If it is to be well done, it must be carried on by a group of devoted scholars. But neither does it mean that such a body has a monopoly on the territory of the liberal arts.

JOSÉ MARIA BURRUEL

The Simplicity of the Liberal Arts Colleges and Mexican-American Community Needs

I have some simple questions I want to ask of the following groups:

THE UNITED STATES OFFICE OF EDUCATION AND COMMUNITY POWER:
The first question that I want to ask you is a question about TTT: Who educates the U.S. Office of Education? How do you know what is going on, you who are in the U.S. Office of Education? Do you really know who controls the power groups in the Mexican community? I was born down here; I got isolated from these groups when I went back to California; when I came back, I had to get the oils and the ointments poured on me all over again. I now know who makes up the power structure in the Mexican-American community. Do you really know who makes up the power structure in the black community? Or the Puerto Rican community? And how can you say that each teacher needs a knowledge of the community, that he needs encounters with the community, if you yourselves don't have direct interpersonal contact with the community? I ask this because some of you here today are both close enough to the problems and close enough to the power—if not close enough to those that have the franchise—so that you could affect these changes that we so direly need. You could help the Chicanos.

UNIVERSITY ADMINISTRATORS, FACULTY MEMBERS, AND EDUCATORS:
Those of you who are in the universities, you who are graduate professors, superintendents of schools, deans, you who set policy for

the liberal arts and education, from you I want to know what you've done in the language departments, in the psychology departments, and in the area of linguistics. Where are you going to produce graduate professors, deans, or superintendents of schools who know a thing about bilingual education? We know from the Chicano community of discoveries and recommendations that could alter the teaching of English as a second language. We also know that many of you in the audience, many of you who are linguists, will go back to your departments unable to affect any changes because your department is under the direction of your college of liberal arts. The college will be reticent to change to meet social needs: e.g., Bob Shafer and Jim Ney at the Arizona State University want to establish a center for the teaching of English to non-English speakers and to those who do not speak standard English. The plan is a beautiful thing, but it may take a very long time before that center is established because of what is happening in the college of liberal arts.

COMMUNITY POWER AND ECONOMICS:

How many of you people in the liberal arts know about "barrio economics"? When you teach Chicano people, you teach us the (great economic principles): marginal utility; the law of diminishing returns, and so forth, but such principles taught as they are presently taught do not help my people to buy a chuck steak. They do not help my people to cope with situations where they buy pure grease when they are supposed to be buying hamburger.

THE COMMUNITY AND ITS DROPOUTS:

I was deeply impressed by Tim Healy's statistics concerning Puerto Ricans and blacks in New York; on the way home last night— I don't live very far from here, about a mile—I thought about those New York kids. It really was disturbing that 88 percent of the kids in New York don't make it. But, only 20 percent of the Mexican-American kids in this town of Phoenix and in this state of Arizona *get into the high schools.* Of that 20 percent, only 2 percent make it over to the university. Seventeen percent of the population of Arizona is Mexican-American; Arizona State University, which has 353 Mexican-American students (of these approximately 40 are Latin Americans), this year will graduate only approximately 40 Mexican-Americans. Of the 2 percent who came to the university,

55 percent will drop out at the end of the freshman year; more will drop out after the sophomore year; and these first two years at our university are under the auspices of the college of liberal arts.

The college of liberal arts is teaching our people the wrong subjects in the wrong way. The university is not getting our students, and is losing those it gets.

DR. BERNARD C. WATSON

Questions Without Answers: A Response to Dr. Charles DeCarlo

Dr. DeCarlo noted that he would be satisfied and happy if a liberal education prompted students to raise questions or to pose the right questions. I agree with him up to a point, but it is ironic that some antiliberal attitudes and behavior are displayed in the products of our so-called liberal education. Perhaps we should consider what happens to an individual when he raises the right questions and gets no answers: what happens when he asks questions about racism, poverty, repression, and intolerance, and the answers are inadequate? How then should the liberal arts graduate respond? He may very well react with despair or with irrational behavior. I think evidence of this was given in the essay by the Harvard University student whom Dr. DeCarlo quoted in his speech. Questions *are* being raised, but actions and behavior are not being changed rapidly enough or in appropriate ways. This is precisely what generates the kind of despair and irrationality displayed in the statement of that young Harvard undergraduate.

What I am suggesting is that not only must the proper questions be asked, but appropriate action must also be taken. Certainly we should, in Dr. DeCarlo's words, "loosen up" our education and our liberal arts colleges. But we must also loosen up the options for students within all educational institutions, and provide a wider access to these institutions, and a wider access to the other institutions which comprise our society. Until the options within universities and colleges, whether liberal arts colleges or schools of education, are buttressed by similar options in the larger society, we will be headed on a collision course, particularly in relation to the poor, the black, and the Spanish-speaking.

Dr. DeCarlo talked a good deal about beauty, and who can disagree with that? But beauty has its antithesis—ugliness—and students must know the one to know the other. They must be given the opportunity to view, to deal with, and to confront the ugliness in our society, so that they will have an opportunity to value the beauty. Commitment must be based on knowledge as well as on feeling, and there must be a firm basis for choice. Otherwise, commitment is at best rhetoric and at worst hypocrisy.

Words are not enough; behavior is what we must begin to deal with. Only from behavior can we infer attitudes, values, and commitment. The test of a man's humanity is humane behavior. I would agree with Dr. DeCarlo that we need men who love—but love is not enough. What we need are feeling, caring, loving, *acting* men—men who act out of their love: men who demonstrate their love through their behavior. To confront the problems faced by this society at this time, we need men who not only have had liberal educations, but men whose very lives are an exemplification of their basic humanity. The education and development of such men, I would suggest, is the most compelling and significant challenge to all of us in this day, in this time, in this country.

IV
PANEL DISCUSSION: *THE EDUCATION OF TEACHERS AND THE UNIVERSITY OF THE PUBLIC INTEREST*

DAVID BRUMBLE

The Panel Discussion: The Education of Teachers and the University of the Public Interest

The panel discussion was in many ways a reflection of the conference as a whole. According to the conference plan, on the stage, under the lights, were to be William Arrowsmith, Charles DeCarlo, Benjamin DeMott, Timothy Healy, Paul Olson, and Robert Cross—all men deeply concerned with the need for change in American universities, all consciously aware of the indignities minority people suffer at the hands of American education, all distinguished academically, in the liberal arts, by achievements that could be pointed to with certain pride. It perhaps goes without saying that all were white. In addition, and singled out here not merely because of his obvious status as a minority representative, there was Father Henry J. Casso. The light that Father Casso threw on the conference by the way in which, without irony, he served both as a translator of the Chicano young and an interpreter for the white audience, is an additional index of the scope of perception of the panel.

Father Casso was one source but far from the only source of the morning's climactic minority report, which included a proposal for a follow-up conference which would recognize and draw upon the talents of blacks, Chicanos, and Indians. Resolutions were put forward by the minority representatives and passed by the conference without a dissenting vote. They are part of the record of the conference.

What is reflected in the remarks of all the panelists is a profound sense of the necessity for change. The general problem they confronted was, How to effect change? To be more precise, they addressed themselves to three basic questions: (1) What direction change? (2) What methods should be employed in bringing about change? and, closely related, (3) Where lies the power necessary to achieve change?

There seemed to be unanimity among the panelists as to the necessity for getting the schools out into the streets, for getting the liberal arts to recognize Whitehead's "sacred" present. Yet the focus was remarkably various. William Arrowsmith referred to an "institution of the public interest" and cited Senator Gaylord Nelson's suggestion that a university might well become a drug testing center; Father Healy described not merely the beauty but also the worth of "the grammar of inner-city speech"; Paul Olson urged the liberal arts to acquaint elementary children with the vocational world of their parents and something of its realities.

Conclusions about how change could come about ranged from Benjamin DeMott's reliance on the development of the natural course of our "democratic society" as it changes into "something closer to a truly democratic society than it has ever been in the past" to the proposals of Charles DeCarlo and Father Healy, which involved various elaborations of Boulding's notion of a competitive educational system wherein federal education money would go directly to the students, a system which would change things drastically by changing the power base of educational institutions. If money were given to students rather than to colleges or to public schools, there is a strong likelihood that both colleges and schools would have to change in order to attract the students (read: "dollars") they would need in order to remain operational.

And how is the power to change things gained? For one thing, there is self-motivation (the black, Chicano, and Indian movements are models), a self-motivation which would come were the colleges of education and the liberal arts colleges to be visited by a sufficient sense of pride. There is the power of the students, of the community, of the professional societies, of imagination and appreciation of the other man's rattrap. But in general this final question was worried over by both panel and audience and left unresolved. The question is a crucial one for community, public schools, schools of education, and the liberal arts.

The following does not purport to be a complete transcription of the proceedings; the mechanics of the discussion are largely deleted, as is some of the banter and some warmup. The remarks of Edward Powell have been deleted, since he was asked to expand upon those remarks in writing; the result appears under the title "Haraka," in the section of black and brown responses to the conference, below. One of the responses of Father Casso is similarly transplanted, as are the minority resolutions. The format of this session encouraged conference participants to write out *questions, which were then read from the platform by Donald Bigelow, who was careful to be partisan to no one side, feeling his function as an officer of BEPD to be one of urging participants on to their own determinations. The questions were discussed by the panelists and are presented in what follows.*

DONALD BIGELOW: Let me say one word by way of beginning this morning's panel. Some of you have said to me, "I still don't know what to do about the liberal arts back home." You must remember, if we had known that, we wouldn't have held this meeting; we would have tried to fund a proposal to do it. We are asking you to explore the matter. That is your charge. Remember that most of you belong to one of the forty-one groups that are getting between ten and twelve million dollars of federal money next year to come up with solutions. Now, first question?

QUESTION: The concept of a liberal arts education has been in existence long enough so that we are now living with the results of such education. Why does everyone here seem to think, with those results before us, that we'll now suddenly do something if it has not already been done up to this point? Shouldn't we first determine why the liberal arts have not been the salvation of the people? Is it the content of such programs or is it the way they've been taught?

BENJAMIN DEMOTT: I think the answer to that question goes like this: In the past, the liberal arts tended to be a means by which certain already well placed human beings placed themselves more firmly at the top of the heap by mastering particular kinds of vocabulary—to be precise, the vocabularies of taste, so there would be something called educated taste, differentiating it from the appetite of the mob. . . .

Why will the liberal arts change? They will change because the social structure that supported the liberal arts as an elite organization of learning has undergone an enormous transformation. One of the best evidences of the inevitability of change is that even such an abstract entity as the federal government appears now to be engaged in the task of encouraging people to think about the transformation of the liberal arts so that as an organization of learning it can have something to do with the facts of society, the newer facts of society as they are beginning to dawn upon us. This transformation of society is central to what I was talking about the other day. So

I'd base my hope for a transformation of the liberal arts on a simple historical transformation of a democratic society into something closer to a truly democratic society than has existed in the past.

QUESTION: How can those in the liberal arts as well as those in professional education assume greater accountability for what the teachers educated under their direction know or can do as practitioners in classrooms?

TIMOTHY HEALY: From where I sit it looks like accountability in college teaching is coming, and coming fairly fast. It's perfectly clear now that the student movement has its eye on tenure. There is still a lot of middle ground left. Perhaps a lot of that middle ground will be chopped out by institutions like my own where the entire faculty is unionized. In institutions where this is not so, there is still plenty of maneuvering ground, but the notion of teacher accountability is growing very fast.

Just look at the fact that there is probably not a campus represented in this room where there doesn't exist some form of teacher evaluation, formal or informal. If there isn't any, you can be sure the kids are talking about it. In practically every major eastern school I know of, teacher evaluations are published. Now it's all very well for people to say, "Well, this is just the kids talking," but more and more this kind of evaluation, particularly when it exists on a stable and fairly mechanical basis, is getting into the evaluations made by departmental chairmen, by deans, and by other administrative officers. So one form of accountability in college teaching at any rate is already on us. And to be perfectly honest, I think that for both teachers and administrators this is a very good thing.

QUESTION: What do you mean by saying that the liberal arts and teacher education can or should be the same? How? In what ways? With what kinds of curricular provisions? Involving what kinds of new roles for liberal arts and education professors? And how would you relate such efforts to further community and social problems?

WILLIAM ARROWSMITH: Perhaps I can answer best by indirection. I tried to say that I think the heart of our problem is that we are suffering a crisis in the professions. It's not just your profession, it's all professions, and these professions are of course deeply involved with the traditional liberal arts. I think the important thing is to develop wholly new institutions which will put the liberal arts into a very different kind of relationship with society, by accepting the crisis of professionalism and going, as it were, with it, not fighting against it. This may mean that everything that we do in the name of courses and structure and curriculum will vanish. You can't reform the university without making the changes that will allow you to cut through the armor of departmental interest. Right now university reform is in a desperate way all over America simply because there has been no way of cutting through the fact of departmental or faculty power. Despite ten years of outraged talk about the impasse in the liberal arts, we really haven't succeeded in making any major reforms or reforming any major institution in an important way.

All right, so much is obvious. What I'd like to suggest is that we start thinking about how to create an institution with a different mission. I've tried to suggest elsewhere a university in the public interest. That seems an important way of putting it, a university that would function as a spiritual institution in our society. We don't have spiritual institutions so we've forgotten what these things mean. We don't have any other spiritual institutions except the churches, and they've not done very well. Invest these universities with the care of the public. This might mean that you transform laws utterly. I think the university should hit the streets. We do need new institutions for a mass society.

This will mean that you've got to go beyond the classroom. Create a national newspaper, for instance! If the First Church of Christ Scientist can create a national newspaper, why in the name of God can't six major universities? Think how that could transform learning. It would put the focus on the present—and the present is, as Whitehead said, holy ground. This present is where we live. All our past, all our access to other ages, should be focused right here, on improving the quality of the now. That's what we need, above all, an active quality of mind directed right at our society. Ecology, for example, belongs in the university. We mustn't allow ecology to become merely another mirror in which the schizophrenia of our culture will be reflected. What we want is moral intelligence— intelligence made moral, morality made intelligent.

As a classicist, I'm sick of a system that tells me the only purpose of knowing about Hippolytus or Theseus is to read Racine. That's the only use that's suggested. That's why we've become so damned decorative. Our institutions suggest no use for our talents, but, in fact, the use for such energy is everywhere visible. People want reform. There is real danger here because if there isn't a real attempt at reform on a national level—soon—we're going to sink into an ever deeper well of rancor, rancidness, fatigue, bitterness. We go to meetings like this and somebody says we must go home with a new commitment; we must start with ourselves. All well and good, but at the same time those commitments have got to be concertive if we're going to effect change. TTT is an important thing; institutional reform by enterprising and intelligent administrating is damned important. Mr. DeCarlo is a beautiful example of a college president; he is all the things that are involved in liberal education. But such able administrators alone? TTT alone? They don't stand a chance. There's got to be concerted effort, some umbrella program under which all these energies can be collected and channeled.

I suggest that the time has come to create institutions of public interest. There are ways of doing this. Senator Gaylord Nelson asked, "Why can't we create in the universities of this country an independent drug testing center?" A great idea. You could found a university on that program. You could also suggest to a few scientists the mandate of sympathy that Paul Olson was talking about yesterday. That would put them in a kind of relationship with society.

QUESTION: This question is concerned with parity within the TTT. The liberal arts have more prestige and power than the other three elements in TTT (community, schools of education, public school systems) put together. How can this imbalance be changed?

PAUL OLSON: I'm not at all sure that, in the education of teachers, the liberal arts have more power than the other three put together. One of the hideous things—and one of the potentially good things about the education of teachers in our overly centralized society—is that the power is distributed everywhere. It is given to the state departments of education, in their credentialing agencies; it is given to their allies, the schools of education, which do the recruiting, evaluating, and recommending of teachers-to-be.

Given the power of state departments of education and the schools of education, I would deny that the liberal arts have more prestige and power than other elements in teacher education, but I do think that one of our problems is that we don't know where the power is. There are an infinite number of points where people can be stopped and very few places where the stopping of people has much to do with their competence as teachers. We seldom ask any questions as to whether the sanctions applied to people in the credentialing process have anything to do with their teaching competence.

Within the university the liberal arts do have one important power. They may provide good or bad models for teaching. The impetus to provide bad models may, ironically, be very largely a creation, over the last two or three decades, of the federal establishment. There has been a tendency at this conference to hesitate to name villains, but I think that we ought to name *some* bad guys. I would suggest that the federal government is a very dark villain in this piece. We ought to insist that the Office of Education develop a plan whereby NSF, the National Endowment for the Humanities, and the Office of Education's own Bureau of Research would not fund projects by university teaching staffs unless they could show how those projects have implications for the betterment of teaching as well as research. That would produce a great deal of change in higher education.

The liberal arts colleges have the power to do a better job of educating teachers—if they are encouraged to invest in teaching. The public schools can help to support the development of new ways of teaching in arts colleges through their control of the public school classrooms where teachers are trained, their future control of the clinical schools to which teachers-to-be will have to be admitted if they are to practice their art. Presently most schools of which I have knowledge do not allow teachers-to-be or even master teachers to do much but replicate their college professors' models; hence, the schools primarily reinforce bad liberal arts practice—the lecture method, dependence on textbooks, etc.

Finally, as to the future and the balance of power: I think we shortly will meet a situation where the communities will have the greatest power. They will be able soon to remove us from their midst. Organizations like the Woodlawn Organization in Chicago can now remove teachers in training from those sections of town over which they have authority; the black community in general will very shortly in my opinion be able to remove people if it doesn't like them.

How can this mishmash be changed? Federal funding patterns can be changed. Evaluation, like that Tim Healy has talked about, is already coming into the picture. The changes will be so great that I am not exactly sure what the college of education will be like in the future. Perhaps we all will go to the college of education to learn something about teaching and learning theory: we need such learning —on a broad scale and in depth. But most of the colleges of education of which I have knowledge are pretty illiberal institutions; we may not have a hell of a lot to learn from them about either teaching or learning unless they reform. To change American teacher education in a serious way, we may need to change patterns of federal funding to liberal arts colleges and graduate colleges, to free the schools, and to recognize the power of community. But we may also need to get the colleges of education to a position where they have some sense of pride, dignity, and enterprise. Their present lack of pride is something that the liberal arts colleges have fostered.

QUESTION: Can we identify those sections of our society which are economically and culturally disadvantaged? How can the arts and the sciences prepare teachers to serve the needs of these neglected groups?

T. HEALY: This goes right to the essence of what we've been doing here. Let me look at the question from two angles. I can give you one clear and hard fact at the moment. To all of our teachers at City University who have been engaged in the SEEK Program—which is probably our largest single remedial enterprise (4,500 kids)—it is perfectly clear that there is a pattern of speech in the ghetto in New York City which is different from what we call standard English. This pattern of speech has existed for years; yet English teachers in the high schools have been sitting there correcting kids, correcting conjugations, saying, "That's wrong, that's wrong, that's wrong, that's wrong," and putting a D on the paper. Someone happened to mention this phenomenon to a bunch of linguists, who said, "You know, that's interesting." So we are now churning out a grammar of inner-city speech. The churning out of such a grammar would seem to me to be one of the essential services that the liberal arts can render to teachers, particularly in the primary schools, but also in the high schools.

The ghetto kids of whom I speak talk a different kind of language; their problem is not that they don't know standard English. It's that they are bilingual; they have to be taught how to make a bridge between a perfectly satisfactory street language and standard English. Their street language is a language in which declension and conjugation are performed by additives and not by morphological change; it is a damned sophisticated language. But these youngsters have to be taught how to bridge the gap between such language and standard English. This is a clear case of a research potential lying in a liberal arts establishment put to the service of teachers to meet a clear and pressing social problem.

Now there is no question that the beauty of ghetto speech is very real. You realize this every time you ask these kids to try their hand at verse—but they do have still to learn standard English; they have to be able to function in standard English too. Well, let me tell you a story.

Some years ago, in the course of an Upward Bound program, I tutored a kid one night a week. What I tried to do was come in under his high school English course. This kid had had four teachers during his fourth-year high school English course—four different teachers. We abandoned *Macbeth* at about act three; we abandoned *A Tale of Two Cities* at about chapter twenty. So it went. Finally, we came to *The Brothers Karamazov*. This kid honestly had about as much need for *The Brothers Karamazov*, as much ability to cope with it, as I have to cope with a pamphlet by Ludwig Wittgenstein at breakfast.

At any rate, the last teacher was something of a genius. She said to him—she said to the whole class—"I want you to read a play, a classic play. The definition of a classic play is anything not by an American." That's all right. It's a good operational definition. You need that kind of thing. So I said to this kid, "Why not read a really classic play, a Greek play?" He's sixteen, so you get that weary look, "What garden path are you taking me up now?" So I said, "Greek plays have one advantage. They are all short." This was a contract. I wouldn't screw him because it was short, and he'd go along with my kooky notions. So I thought, "O.K., what is the shortest Greek play I know—without too much religion?" So I said, "Let's do the *Medea*."

I got more out of this exchange than the kid did. I said to him, "Now, look, before you get started you've got to realize the context. *Medea* is the story of a stranger. It's the story of a woman who depicts emotion and warmth and really a kind of odd personalism, in the face of a society which is ruled by law, which is structured and cold, a society that is not understanding. When the moment of crisis comes, when she finally decides that she has a chance to destroy that society, the only thing she destroys is the only thing she really loves."

Then it suddenly occurred to me that this piece out of my grab bag was this kid's life story. He is a black from Harlem in the middle of New York City. All of a sudden I realized that if I could ever get this youngster tooled up to deal with my text in the same way that I could deal with it, if he had the skills and the training and the understanding, he could read that text with an immediacy and an understanding that

I could never have acquired if I had lived to be five hundred. I have never lived as an Asian woman in a Greek society. This black kid from the center of New York City has lived as an Asian woman in our Greek society.

I know I risk being somewhat smug in saying that's what I think the liberal arts can do for the training of teachers—particularly as concerns the economically and culturally disadvantaged.

QUESTION: How can the reward systems in the colleges be changed?

ROBERT CROSS: I think that the only forces capable of bringing about such change are those outside the faculty and administration. It is only as faculty and administration come into collision with students, or, perhaps, with the government that change will come. There are other outside forces which perhaps will move or be motivated to move. There has to be a lot more forceful pressure from parents and alumni for a change in the reward system in college than what we now feel. I guess that, like every other college professional, I'm simply appalled by the disposition of the alumni. The people who are made in the colleges are the kind of people they can love, and they hope the college will preserve it that way. They hope the college won't have very many troublemakers. They hope the college will be able to resist changes. Now, this isn't universally true. The great flood of alumni since the Second World War is, I think, less worried by change. If, however, they don't come through very strong for a change in the reward system, then the chances for such change are small. Of course, I speak only from my experience in a private college.

QUESTION: Dr. DeCarlo, would you comment on Dr. Foster's observation that change within the present structure is almost impossible, that we need to develop something new?

CHARLES DECARLO: In general, I would agree that no institution changes from within, and I'd like to see the establishment of competitive models. First of all, the small colleges, small private colleges such as the one where I'm located, could be encouraged to rip off the curricular moss and to open the college up to be absolutely a place where adults and young adults meet—a place where, hopefully, both could be transformed. A man comes with some special skill as a teacher; he teaches what he wants to teach, without worrying about sequentiality or packaging. It would not be unreasonable to have a collection of teachers grouped around one common interest, or around their own friendship, as a qualifying body which would assert at a certain point in time that this or that young person is now eligible for the first ladder of collegial association.

Further, I think something must be done about the appalling size of universities and colleges. They should be broken down. I happen to believe this about business, too, in spite of the fact that I was with IBM for eighteen years. I always believed that IBM should have been broken up. Everybody would have been better off, including the stockholders. I think we need to find ways to break large institutions down to a human scale. When you get that small scale, you then begin to be responsive to the interest that the students have in running their own lives. Then you can help them organize their own community.

If small colleges would quit trying to act like little universities and admit that their role is simply to transform young people, the cost of education might be relatively modest. And we could set up one competitive model by stocking maybe fifty small liberal arts colleges with good teachers and then letting them go.

A second competitive model could spring from changing the whole method of funding educational institutions. The ghetto youngsters of a given locale might be selected. They would be given money and freedom as long as they could demonstrate some minimum of progression so that they could shop for their education. Thus, you would let the market economy work. That would be a long-term operation, but it fits the American mind—let people shop. In the end the colleges would then be forced to compete for such students, and so, presumably, change would be effected.

T. HEALY: I want to come in very strongly behind Dr. DeCarlo on this question of leaving kids free to move, free to shift from college to college. The only way we're going to do that is by getting rid of the whole tuition and payment structure. We at CUNY are the only absolutely free public system in the United States. There is no tuition charge. There is a fee charge, and we're having riots now because Lindsay's come round to us and told us we have to raise fifteen million dollars more on fees—so we're raising fees from forty dollars to eighty dollars and the kids are screaming. What they are really screaming about is not the lousy forty bucks—what they're fighting is the erosion of free tuition. Now it seems to me absolute nonsense that Dr. DeCarlo at Sarah Lawrence has to charge twenty-three or twenty-six hundred dollars' tuition, just as it's absolute nonsense that those up-state Republicans should come down and tell us to charge four hundred dollars so that we'll be like the state system.

We talk about ecology, but I'm from a big city and I think that ecology is essentially a cop-out. This whole fuss is a cop-out because these are solvable problems; they are technically solvable and we can solve them. But let's take another natural resource that we're kicking around—the young. We are the only major industrial society that charges tuition. We pat ourselves on the back about how forward we are in our public education: look at Europe, where nobody has to pay to go to college if he can get in. There is France and Germany and England and Scotland and Wales—and even Spain provides free tuition for the minimal percentage of kids it lets in. OK, we let more in, and therefore we want to charge tuition. But we need these people! We need every intelligent human being we can turn out, and the more intelligent he is, and the better trained, the better use he is to society. It is absolutely criminal to waste generation after generation of kids from the inner cities, and it is equally criminal to charge tuition for a natural resource that the nation needs.

I'm perfectly willing to see the state of New York pay Sarah Lawrence whatever it is they need to run and keep free tuition in the public institutions. This is one of the essential focuses of liberty. If all the kids at Hunter College decide that Sarah Lawrence is doing much better, they'll all go up to Sarah Lawrence. Then we might get around to changing something at Hunter College.

This question of free public higher education is under a hell of a lot of fire, particularly in California. I really bleed when I watch happen in California what ultimately is going to happen to us. Every nickel we charge kids to get into our school keeps somebody out, and this nation simply cannot afford to keep kids out of college.

B. DeMott: I want to come back to the matter of the reward system. The question is, How can the reward system be modified so that liberal arts professors would be more willing to cooperate and participate in teacher education? Now I think that in order to effect any change here, you're going to have to change your point of view. You must enter the point of view of a liberal arts professor. You have to know the field from inside before you can begin to speak to it. Now it is true that when people like myself speak to this problem they tend to turn the liberal arts professor—and I'm one—into a satanic, demonic figure. "Let's kill the bastard," etc.

I think it's very important in TTT, where we've got community and education people working in a relationship with the university faculty, that we take into account certain facts. One fact is that the university professor who is oblivious to the needs of the community, and oblivious to everything except the pursuit of his own private scholarship, may nevertheless feel behind him an extremely honorable tradition that has been a leader for years in American society. He feels, whether rightly or wrongly, that he has, over the years, stood up in protest against the cash basis of American civilization. He remembers the thirties, and indeed the forties and fifties, when his situation as a university professor was not a comfortable situation; he was often beat upon the head by public leaders. He has always been beaten upon the head by his older brother who became a banker, or something else, and made it in the American way. Within the faculty clubs of America—those bastions of privilege—there is a sense of extreme commitment to personal integrity. Whether we like it or not, the people in question do not see themselves as villains, and you cannot begin to deal with them if you assume that shame is their natural response to the life they lead.

They feel that they have stood up for the right. They also feel that the very protest that is moving through American society now would not be there if the university had not kept alive certain values in American society over the past thirty years. It kept those values alive. Nowhere else—certainly not in the press and nowhere in the pulpit—was anything like a social vision being expressed. It was only in the universities. I know there are many people in the room who don't want to hear about that sense of personal probity and integrity, and I don't blame you a bit. But if you're going to change the reward system, you have to understand that you must begin by addressing yourself to that sense of honor. Appeal to that sense of honor in telling the liberal arts professors that they have distanced themselves from the needs of society, and that this distance constitutes a denial of the tradition they have stood for.

W. ARROWSMITH: With some aspects of what you say, I am in passionate agreement—with other aspects, I am in passionate disagreement. I agree that a feeling of honor, of personal probity, is there. I agree that it has to be addressed in terms other than cries of shame. Nonetheless, to put it another way, our elite institutions, though they may have created individuals with a strong sense of individual honor, do not really deserve to be called elite institutions.

They've not succeeded in creating an elite. They have not succeeded in creating men who could put this personal probity to any social use. They were built essentially on the code of the gentlemen, and this is precisely the point where the liberal arts are going to suffer a necessary transformation. The liberal arts curriculum, once adequate for the gentlemen, must be given to a nation. The role of these elite institutions must change. I'm not arguing that all institutions should be the same. I am pluralistic. We need institutions for contemplative people and for active people. We simply can't do without that kind of pluralism; we're going to educate different kinds of men.

But we've got to get our elite institutions into the job of creating culture. One of the reasons they're blowing to pieces is that, as Michael Novak has said, they're becoming babysitters for the youth culture. There's no need for courses, for curriculum. What we want to do is deacademicize the culture; get it out of the academy and back into the civilization. This you do by evidencing it. And you can only evidence it by, as it were, taking the war into the streets.

One thing this means is taking the task of diffusion with a kind of seriousness that the university has never granted that task. This means a different kind of theory of knowledge. The academic people act as though the job of diffusion, of popularization, were a vulgar one instead of a high calling; hence, they will not perform it or undertake it.

A final point. Put the motive back and all this debate about form and matter, form and communication, form and style, form and material begins to vanish. I really can't take very seriously the claims of the teachers' colleges simply because I believe that what's absent in both liberal arts and teachers' colleges is the motive that makes a man clever and cunning and inventive. You don't need to be taught how to communicate if you really want to do something for a certain reason. A man in love is damned cunning. He uses his full intelligence—and more than he knows he possesses—in getting where he's going, because he knows where he's going.

I don't argue with Ben DeMott, but I do want to make one point clear. We must make the crisis of our country's native moral and educational situation known. It must be known not only by the people in this room. It must be generally known. Now how do you make the full weight of the difficulty come across? For me it is a matter of our being obliged, each of us, to see as far as he can into his own obliviousness to the social needs, the social urgencies, the intellectual urgencies of this country. In order to do this, we must change the system within our institutions. And one of the most important barriers here is that extreme sense of personal integrity which is built into the people who are now the university teachers of liberal arts. They do not see themselves as criminal, and they cannot be moved by men who don't understand that they don't see themselves as criminals. They can only be moved by men who say to them, "It is time to reclaim your personal probity, to reclaim the integrity that you have been a witness to in the American past." I see this very well. You cannot change a man's motives by calling him shameful any more than you can convert him by banging him on the head with a stick.

I do believe, however, that we must suggest some new goals for our institutions themselves, goals which will give a man something besides the professional mindlessness which he will, for all his personal integrity, lapse into so long as there is no other suggestion of any larger purpose in his life.

T. HEALY: I want very seriously to enter into this talk about pluralism. The Roman church has had a pluralistic experience for a long, long time. There is a clear division of the great religious orders into the Jesuits, who went traipsing all over northern Europe fighting Lutherans, and the Trappists, who sat in their monasteries and said their prayers. Now I know that it's a matter of clear historical fact that there have been a lot of nutty Jesuits. It's also a matter of clear historical fact that a lot of the monks who took to the contemplative life were lazy bums who went into the monastery for three square meals a day. I think in any one of our larger institutions, and by "larger" I mean even our liberal arts colleges, there is a place for the Trappist as well as the Jesuit. There is a place for the contemplative. There is a place for the man who is not involved—whether he doesn't want to be or because he can't be or because he recognizes that sometimes the quiet things are the best things. Somebody has to do our dreaming. Those of us like Dr. Arrowsmith and myself who are out talking to legislatures and screaming and yelling and trying to pull together programs and harassing very patient teacher education folk, such people fall back on these contemplatives. The breath of the university is contemplation, and frankly, it is only when the kids themselves get a whiff of this priesthood that they begin to understand what a fascinating enterprise the university is. If we liquidate all these good men who have admittedly been weak in social conscience, I think we're really going to liquidate what we know as the university. Now maybe Dr. Arrowsmith would feel that that would be a hell of a good idea. I don't. I just want to get a word in for the Trappists. They weren't all lazy. The slow-breathing rhythm of their contemplation accomplished an awful lot of good.

P. OLSON: I want to speak on the issue of responsibility which has been raised by Ben DeMott and Bill Arrowsmith. It seems to me that behind Bill Arrowsmith's response to Ben DeMott is the assumption—I may be misreading—that if you hold a man guilty, if you hold him responsible, then in a sense you don't take the stance which Ben DeMott has suggested; it is almost as if we were saying, "If you regard a man as responsible and as having done wrong, then you cannot respect his sense of personal probity." But my sense is that only if you hold a man responsible can you assume the stance of respect for probity. Our difficulty is that we regard people as guilty, hold them responsible, and then treat them as incapable of learning. With the concepts of responsibility and probity go also such con-concepts as "capable of learning." I learned this first from O. K. Bouwsma, who wrote a maxim once—I think in the context of a confrontation. He said, "Hold a man responsible so that he'll hold himself responsible." The most profound, insightful thing I've ever read in this area are the last chapters of Erik Erikson's *Gandhi's Truth*, which display, in ways which I can't exactly, the psychological processes involved in saying, "You're a devil, and you're redeemable." It seems to me that what we've lost is the redemptive insight.

B. DEMOTT: I think I usually do try to hold onto the redemptive insight Paul's talking about. I'm speaking as seriously as I can. I can only show you what I mean by telling some anecdotes, some experiences. When I just talk about this business of entering another point of view, I think, "My God, how could anybody believe that, anyway?" The whole life of the notion depends upon stories, it depends upon interactions between people in particular situations. So I'll give you an example.

I was in a teaching project two or three years ago in Washington. We ran a seminar for ghetto schoolteachers in which we tried to show what it was we thought the teachers might do in the classroom, or what they weren't doing, and so on. Now, most of the teachers in the group were black teachers and I was a white, Harvard, Ph.D., flown in from "the North" for two days every two weeks. The only reason I was flown in, the only reason the project was floated at all, was that the director of the Central Education Laboratory down there would not let such a project go on unless he had the cachet of an ivy Ph.D. behind it. I was very ineffective in the seminar, and I knew I was ineffective. I was not getting to these people at all, and they put me off.

Finally someone in that laboratory suggested that if I could find some black people who would work with me, and teach with me, that maybe this thing might get off the ground. So we hunted, and at length we found two black poets, Sam Corners and Lucille Clifton. They're damned good poets; they're excellent teachers; and somehow they managed to tolerate me. So we started the seminar up again. The three of us would sit together at the end of the table; Sam and Lucille played the game with me and made me feel that I could get to these people. We established better relationships, and the school visits went better.

At the end of every day of school visits we'd always wind up at a kind of black and white saloon called "Mr. Henry's." It was a nice, comfortable place, a good place to end the day. We'd talk about the teachers; we'd talk about the kids; we'd have a literary conversation—finally I'd go to catch a cab to the airport and they'd get a cab back to Union Station. There was one small problem. They seemed to have trouble getting a cab. So we worked out an arrangement whereby I would go out and flag a cab for them. When I opened the door they would come from across the street and get in. (Usually Lucille would make some kind of light-hearted remark like, "Sam, you got your knife?")

Then I'd get a cab for myself. You know, I'd sit back in the seat of that cab and I'd carry on a little self-congratulatory monologue: "Well, boy, you really are doing something for public service, aren't you. You know, you wouldn't think that somebody like you could really work comfortably with—and be taken as an OK guy by—people like Sam and Lucille. But they really do dig you, you know they really do. And, oh, at the end of their day when you get that cab for them, their bosoms must just swell with what a wonderful guy you are."

Do you see? Well, I know you're proof against any overindulgence in your sense of personal probity—but I'm saying that I wasn't. And the only reason that I eventually saw through my self-containment, my capsulation, and my own virtue, was that one day a cab driver picked me up who'd seen me get the cab for Sam and Lucille. He turned around to me and asked, "What were you doing there with those two blacks?" I told him that I was getting them a cab, because they had a little trouble sometimes. He drove on a bit longer, then he turned around and said, "I'll bet it makes you feel like Jesus, uhn?"

Well, all at once, it dawned on me—what you would say any perceptive human being should have known all along, what any man who spends his life with imaginative literature should have known all along. You might say, "Surely he couldn't have lived in so circumscribed a world that he couldn't imagine what it would be like to be Sam or Lucille, to be any way dependent at the end of a day on this big bloke, with his ivyness and his whiteness and his Ph.D., just to get home at night." Nevertheless, that is what I call closure, do you see?

Now that closure easily merges into a sense of integrity, a full sense of integrity. That closed-inness, you see, is what you have to try to break through, not by saying, in effect, "You are Satan," but, like the cab driver, saying it in a bit nicer tone. You have to say, "Well I know you think you're Jesus, but you're not quite." You have to say, "Look, for the following reasons you're not Jesus." You have to say, "Let's go and reason together on this general theme of why you're not Jesus, and why it would be a good thing for you to try to become something a little closer to just being a decent human being." That's what I'm talking about, and I think that's what Paul is talking about.

W. ARROWSMITH: I find it difficult to argue with this. I feel that I'm arguing against the metaphysics of fair-mindedness. And again, I agree that crying Satan is wholly wrong. You might better try the other adjectives; you might better charge him with being God in the hope of shaming him into some sense of his limitations. But I'm simply worried—perhaps practically, perhaps platonically—that this is merely the same sort of high-mindedness which has so often been used by the academy as an excuse to do nothing.

This isn't what DeMott means. I'm absolutely clear on that. But what DeMott intends will immediately be translated into the ethic of disinterestedness, of noble detachment, of no-care, of going on with what we have always done in the name of some kind of spiritual fulfillment. It will be used in selfish ways. I don't really think Ben and I are too far apart; but let me turn to a passage from Whitehead which supports what I'm trying to say. Whitehead was addressing a group of engineers at a technical institute:

> The insistence, in the Platonic culture, on disinterested intellectual appreciation is a psychological error. Such education strives to divorce the intellectual or aesthetic life from the life of action. Herein lurk the seeds of the decadence of civilization. Essentially culture should be for action, and its effect should be to divest labor of any association with aimless toil. Art exists that we might know that the deliverance of our senses is good; it heightens the world of sense perception. Disinterested scientific curiosity is a passion for an ordered intellectual vision of a connection of events. But the goal of such curiosity is the marriage of action to thought. This essential intervention of action, even in abstract science, is often overlooked. No man of science wants merely to know. He acquires knowledge to appease his passion for discovery. He does not discover in order to know; he knows in order to discover. The antithesis between a technical and a liberal education is fallacious. There can be no technical education which is not liberal and no liberal education which is not technical; that is, no education which does not impart both techniques and intellectual vision. Education should turn out the pupil with something he knows well and something he can do well. This intimate union of action and theory aids both. Firsthand knowledge is the ultimate basis of life. To a large extent book learning conveys secondhand information and as such it can never rise to the importance of immediate action. Our goal is to see the immediate events of our lives as instances of our general ideas. What the learned world offers is one secondhand scrap of information illustrating ideas derived from another secondhand scrap of information. The secondhandedness of the learned world is the secret of its mediocrity. It is tame because it has never been scared by facts.

I refer in closing to the thought of the Benedictines, who saved for mankind the vanishing civilization of the ancient world by linking together knowledge, labor, and moral energy.

> Our danger is to conceive practical affairs as the kingdom of evil in which success is only possible by the extrusion of ideal aims. I believe that such a conception is a fallacy directly negated by practical experience. In education this error takes the form of a mean view of technical training. Our forefathers in the dark ages saved themselves by embodying high ideals in

great organizations. It is our task, without servile imitation, boldly to exercise our creative energies, remembering amid discouragement that the coldest hour immediately precedes the dawn. The future of the country lies with you. The crown of your success is the promise of future work, often unrecognized and done under discouragement, but done steadily and often cheerfully. It is on you the country depends for the maintenance and the growth of those ideas without which a race withers.

I want to stress those lines especially in opposition to Professor Smith, who, it seems to me, does not believe sufficiently, profoundly, in the possible impact of education. Do not be discouraged by difficulties which seem insurmountable. The conditions of life which mold us all are modified only by our will, our energy, and the purity of our intentions.

[At this point, Mr. Moses Davis introduced the minority report; cf. section V for the report and its follow-up.]

QUESTION: All of us are self-oriented. We have put up with the hassle of our parents and our training and what church we went to and the chemicals popping around in our brain. But it seems to me that one of the things we're trying to do is to figure out where that "other place" in reality is, where that other connecting place is. So we've asked ourselves, Where do we turn? Who are our best supporters as far as change is concerned? The liberal arts? No. They're aloof and professionally oriented. We've heard about that. The colleges of education? No, they're usually smugly businesslike and product-oriented. The community? Sometimes, but not in my community. My nine-year-old daughter is still getting grades and report cards on patriotism and work habits. I don't want the consensus of my community to decide my daughter's education. Science and research is always after the fact. Linguistics can analyze inner-city speech and tell the elementary teacher or the high school teacher the nature of inner-city speech, but the teacher must first be got to recognize that fact that inner-city speech is more than a grammatical aberration. This just won't come through research. And I'm afraid it won't come through the university, or through curricular change.

Where, then, will the force come from which *can* bring change? Obviously from the students. Thus it is that every advance for students as regards self-direction and student selection of curriculum —every student-taught, student-organized, and student-controlled class in the university—is an advance toward reality. The students are the ones who are going to change the nature of the liberal arts. I am tempted to run through a number of my reasons for this view, but I would like to ask the panel to respond to this: How can the liberal arts and teacher education use the only thing in education that really changes from year to year? Whether they are black, white, Mexican-American—how can we help these students bring about change?

JACK GORDON: I would like to object to one of the suggestions of the minority report. I think that it is a serious error to request the opportunity to have a black scholar contribute a paper to the proceedings of this conference; that would be permitting the Office of Education, the TTT Program—and I speak as a member of the LTI—to cop-out and say, "OK, here is a little response after we've managed to conduct a conference in which the racism implicit in our society has been very well reflected." I would think that, since the Office of Education has money to conduct other conferences, a much better demand to make would be to ask those twenty-four minority people to sit down and plan the next conference for this same group. The theme of the conference should be "How do we get at the problems of racism that are implicit in the liberal arts and teacher education and the public schools?" In fact, there ought to be a committee formed for just such a scrutiny. That is the basic problem. We can't afford to capitulate to the tokenism implicit in saying, "OK, contribute a chapter to some book that nobody is going to read anyway."

MOSES DAVIS: I can't really answer for the twenty-four minority people who made the minority report. I can only give my opinion. We didn't ask for "tokenism." We didn't say, "Get a representative of a minority group to put just anything into the publication." We said, "Find someone to make a *significant contribution*." This does not mean representation; it means adding to this report a dimension that it needs. I think that your other suggestion is excellent.

QUESTION: Mr. DeMott described the liberal arts professors snuggling up to their sense of probity. Now, I really can't take very seriously my responsibilities toward the gentleman who solves current problems by remembering how he kept the American Legion from firing John King Fairbank. Such people live in systems. One of the things a liberal education might do for one would be to free one from the sense that one is a creature created by some sort of deterministic necessity, free one from the determinism putatively imposed by the system in which one works. You cannot tell me that there aren't a good many changes which can be made in the reward system of higher education. These are things one already knows. One simply cannot refuse to identify the villains; one must say that the promotion committee which parcels out the money in any given department is making its decisions about teacher education wrongly if it refuses to support those who teach well and who educate teachers to teach well. It is generally in the power of such committees to make their decisions correctly.

What we need is not respect for the honorable professors who make such decisions. What we need is more of what Mr. Olson has called "low cunning" and less of what Mr. Arrowsmith has called "high-mindedness."

QUESTION: I came to this conference persuaded that I might learn something about the problems of the arts and sciences in relation to the preparation of teachers. I'm from Cleveland State University, and I'm sure Cleveland has problems as serious—racism and all the rest—as regards teacher preparation, as any community in the country. I have listened very carefully, and this has been a disappointing conference. Supposedly, we have now learned that the reward system, the way in which we pay and promote our professors, is a serious stumbling block. We're been aware of that for some time. We're making efforts at our university to improve in this aspect.

I have also heard the complaint that professors in liberal arts dissuade their best and brightest young students from becoming school teachers. I admire them for this if it is an expression of their best and candid judgment about the future lives of those people. The irony, to my ear, is that it has been said that the reason they dissuade them is that the reward system in the public schools is corrupt. This is treated as a cruel or foolish reason for dissuading young people from teaching. But the public school is a very frustrating place for a bright, creative, energetic, ambitious person to go, especially if he expects confidently to starve to death if he makes the decision. We ought to expect all reward systems to be reformed.

I had hoped there would be more constructive comments about the liberal arts. One of the things that puzzles me is why they need to be involved at all; I don't recall that *the liberal arts* ever made any demands that public school teachers should be prepared in the liberal arts. The demands were made by others for reasons that I suspect are still valid.

I'm really issuing a challenge here! What do *you*—the schools, the community, the colleges of education, the Office of Education—want the liberal arts to do to put *your* house in order?

FATHER CASSO: I'm amazed to hear that statement. I'd like to make a suggestion, especially now that we've heard from this distinguished gentleman. You see, it's very difficult for men like me, or like Moses Davis, to convey to you what's going on among our people. Hence, while I don't particularly like conferences, I want to make a recommendation, in the form of a request to Don Bigelow and the Office of Education: in view of the fact TTT is committed to educational development, to educational change; in view of the fact that TTT is committed to a concept of parity, to the inclusion of community, and, most importantly, to the inclusion of students; in view of all this, would it not be possible to come up with a follow-through conference which would include students from the black, brown, and Indian communities, as well as community people? Then key speakers, such as you have here, key individuals from some of your recognized institutions of higher learning, would have the task of letting you realize from their own lips and their own hearts what they see and what they wish to do about what they see, their ideas and recommendations. Let this be put out into the form of a document.

Our youth would then be able to take these documents, quoting men like yourselves, and show these documents to their parents, to their principals, and to their teachers, their counselors, and so forth. Many people out there are beyond the reach of your institutions; they do not believe the youngsters, and when the youngsters raise these kinds of questions, naturally the teachers feel threatened. No teacher in his right mind is going to admit that he has been doing something wrong for twenty-five years. Somehow or another you have got to provide the youngsters with the data, the facts, the notions that you can come up with. You know, if the young could have this document—why it would be bullets to the young people in the community.

The changes needed in education are not going to come in this room, that's for sure; it was especially obvious to me that change cannot come from this room when I listened to the gentleman just before me. The change is going to come from the community, from the young, or from the masses of people. We can give direction to this change by our notions and our ideas. I think that's what we ought to be doing here.

Now to take a position—to recognize the importance of the right document—is not easy. We just had a running battle with the U.S. Commission on Civil Rights. They have a major document, the result of a million-dollar study of 540 school districts, with statements by principals and superintendents. I wish that I had time to take ten minutes to tell you of the battle we have had to get that document out; a million dollars' worth of data, admissions by principals and superintendents—and we have to fight to get it out!

What is such a document going to do? It is going to give credibility to those kids out there who are walking out of the schools. They don't know precisely what is happening to them, but they know that what is happening is not good. And they would like to tell you; they would like to share it with you. They have good ideas. In Crystal City, a rural, predominantly Mexican-American community, the Mexican-Americans had been held down by a strong white school board. The kids decided to get to work. They did the negotiating themselves. When they went into the negotiating room they brought their pillows with them. They were asked why they brought pillows. They said, "If need be, we're going to stay here all night long." Those kids came up with some very buyable ideas—*any* idea generated by such youngsters would be commendable.

P. OLSON: I want to speak to Father Casso's notion. I think that what we're talking about is something that can't be done in one conference, although I, too, would appreciate having the conference he describes. What may be more significant is that we, in the liberal arts, are, most of us, very ignorant people.

We are not very cosmopolitan; we have, most of us, never been part of another culture significantly different from our own. We need to have long-term experiences in the educational institutions that are emerging which represent cultures other than our WASP culture. I'm thinking of the Navajo Community College; I'm sure that one could find, in San Antonio, Chicano intellectual resources which could train us. The black colleges are another resource. If most of the education that is to be done in this country is going to be done in institutions which are large, within these large institutions will have to be created colleges or enclaves which represent a variety of cultures in exactly the way that the medieval university represented a variety of cultures through its Italian nation, its English nation, and so forth. We will never peacefully create the tolerance to include multinational enclaves in the university unless we give the perception and sensitivity to people like me and the other people on the platform. That perception can only be gained if we are trained at the institutions and in contexts which really embody another cultural style (as the Navajo Community College does).

W. ARROWSMITH: I'd like to respond to some of the sense of dissatisfaction being voiced, some of the bitterness. I've been to a large number of conferences; that I have been is perhaps an indication of the low state of the liberal arts. I'm sorry that you're so disappointed,[1] but in fact I've not heard better talk about the liberal arts in my memory. I'd really like to make some kind of appeal from both sides and arising from Paul's remarks, an appeal to the effect that what we face after all, in our situation, is so incredibly awful that it ought to instill a little humility in all groups. What is appalling to me is that, after three days of talking about the liberal arts, the same hubris I complained about is so bloody visible still everywhere. It seems that not a word is being heard.

It was not, I believe, mere rhetoric, beautiful words that were being talked, about the liberal arts. I really don't want to make this a speech of defensiveness, but we all are in our own rattraps. Anybody who has experienced what it is to be in a university—and I feel our experience is limited, it is not cosmopolitan, as Paul has pointed out—but anybody who's been there and tried to reform it knows the sheer hell of reforming it. We are in a hell of a jam; all of our problems are rolled into a knot, and while I feel enormous sympathy with those who want, because their urgencies are so enormous, to talk about problems of the community, I still want to return to the point made by Mr. DeCarlo that the reforming requires a complexity and subtlety of mind which simply can't tolerate simplism.

The universities are going to be reformed if at all by the energies available in such complex communities as the Navajo community represents, or the communities present here, or those communities of professionals eager to reform their professions. The communities to which I have referred are very different from one another, and there has got to be some respect for the integrity of those intending reform or otherwise the whole bloody society is doomed.

[1] One takes Mr. Arrowsmith to be referring to the sentiments of the speaker from Cleveland State University.

We've got to stop talking to other human beings as though they were simply free and unable to appreciate *our* rattraps. It is in the nature of our conditions that we're all in a hell of a rattrap; to look for complex solutions requires the intermeshing of precisely the areas that were supposed to be discussed here: what learning is, what the past is, what the "other" is. There are other "others" than the cultural communities represented here; there are those that have not yet been born. Who speaks for them? The Pope speaks for fetuses. Who speaks for the unborn? Women speak for babies. Who speaks for the dead? They have some stake in the present; else, why did they live? This is what we need, it seems to me, a large complexity of mind to embody into all our institutions. The community is a crucial factor; it is our immediate experience of the "other," and it will be invaluable to the reforming of the university. But even the community must not indulge itself in what is really its own form of hubris. Hubris after all is a human trait; nobody has a monopoly on it. I suppose that was what DeMott was saying. The very fact that we believe the "men of stone" are stone men maybe, that they are not human but subhuman, is a defect in our own humanity.

RUBY RINEY: Today we were supposed to be concerned with "Where do we go from here?" It was mentioned by one of the reactors that the professions and technology are closing the job markets. What do you panelists see as the role of the arts and sciences in the preparation of the future teachers who will equip non-college-bound students for a life which is fulfilled?

C. DECARLO: If I had one recommendation to make to this conference, and to all people in our society who are concerned about making this country a decent place to live, I would ask that we address ourselves to what I think is the deepest problem all of us face. That problem is neither racism nor war. I'm convinced that our gravest problem is the disappearance of meaningful work. I spent a major part of my life designing work for machines. It is my belief that when a job or pattern of human behavior can be designed to be done by a machine, then at that point that particular human behavior which the machine can perform becomes meaningless. Anything that can be done by a machine should be done by a machine. I make no apologies for a lifetime spent in trying to automate people out of business.

Your question is, What's left? I think that it's high time to make a study of what's going on in the work world, not in terms of vocational preparation, but in order to find out what men and women really do. I feel certain that what such a study would find is that the work, not of the DeMott or the Arrowsmith but of the white-collar worker or the professional, is being fragmented so that most tasks are interchangeable and can be best taught within the process itself—that is, outside the liberal arts.

I grant that for the next decade, perhaps, we will need to train people who are going on to college to perform jobs that we're probably going to make up, but in the long run—make no mistake about it—meaningful work is not going to be available and that changes the whole ball game. This is the reason I'm interested in the liberal arts—as a key to sanity. Through their contemplative life, the Trappist monks may preserve some keys to a sanity we're all going to need.

But I'd like to come closer to the school situation. I think that in the great urban centers, the logical conclusion of open admissions is open enrollment. A university should be a group of people, young *and* old doing their own thing, saying to the rest of the world, "If you would like to come in and join us for a space of time, you're welcome—you're welcome at eighteen or nineteen; and you're welcome at twenty-four; you're welcome at fifty, at sixty."

A great university ought to be a place of total welcome. We're finding out, for instance, that one enormous source of talented and motivated students is that great pool of Vietnam veterans. If these people are superb students, why hang some derogative title like "adult education" about their necks? So what if they're over twenty-one? Then there are the women who have had a few years of school and then went off and raised their kids. Precisely because they haven't been professionalized, as Whitehead points out, they are among the most sophisticated, knowledgeable adults in our society—precisely because they've lived with reality. They have been scared by facts.

Let's have them back into the universities at forty and at forty-five. Like Bill Arrowsmith, I'm not a youth cultist. Possibly the only thing worse than the sort of hierarchy of incompetence that we've built into the university would be an oligarchy of adolescence.

P. OLSON: Ruby's question concerns something important to me; implicit in the question is the question of how one makes this society display a decent respect for the energies of the species and for intelligent ("healthy") methods of moving people from childhood to adulthood. The whole business of the present separation of youth from age in our society is related to what Van Den Berg talks about when he says that children in our society can't envisage what their fathers are doing. My kids have no idea as to what I do. I take them down to the office, but they can't figure out what I'm up to all day. They sit beside me, and they still can't figure out what I do. I think we have to make the world of adult vocation a world which is open to kids. This means doing at the secondary level the kind of thing which the Philadelphia Parkway School is doing: kids are going out into the streets, seeing what the adult world is like, evaluating and studying it on the basis of their experience. Such an interaction between the vocations and study should perhaps be central to the operation of the school in which the adolescent child is placed.

To turn to the elementary school: liberal study there need not necessarily direct one toward a vocation, but a liberal education should provide one with a sense of what the adult vocations are and what knowledge is embodied in their comings and goings. We ought to have lots of vocational training in the classroom in the elementary schools, but vocational training should be there because of the liberal intellectual principles embodied. Vocational training should not be part of any curriculum to get people into a vocation. It should be part of the curriculum because it educates.

I taught in a ghetto school a bit; I taught kids who had been turned off. I taught them about electricity, about mathematics, and about physics because they were interested in motors. I wasn't trying to get them to spend a lifetime working with motors.

It seems to me we've lost a sense of the great potential of vocational education to make people understand what it's like to be alive intellectually in a relationship with objects. The fact turned up by one study that, in some areas of the country, 75 percent of the people who don't learn how to read in America's schools do learn how to read within five years after they drop out, after they get into a vocation, is the most savage indictment of American education I know.

One other thing in response to Charles DeCarlo: I don't think we have any right to render work meaningless. We have to ask, as we go about the business of automating, just how many people's lives we're rendering meaningless, what the aesthetic is of what we're doing, and what other implications for social disorganization there might be. We allowed cotton fields all over the South to be mechanized, we allowed thousands of people to be thrown out of jobs without considering the social consequences; we've done this to black people and to Mexican-American people; and we might have reduced our problems had we contemplated what we were doing as we did it.

W. Arrowsmith: I'll try to be brief. To go back on my point again and perhaps elaborate a little: earlier I mentioned that we have a responsibility to create what I would call Socratic institutions in a mass society; I suggested a new "university of the public interest." I'm trying to answer the question raised: How do you get the liberal arts out in the street? How do you educate a society that maybe can't get into the "university of the public interest." That's the problem also raised by Tim Healy.

Institutions seem to me no longer the ideal way to change the intellectual tenor of the country. You go to war with the culture. I mentioned the possibility of a newspaper; I mentioned it in deadly seriousness. A real commitment to the diffusion of high-level intellectual work has never been undertaken in any serious way by, say, a national press in this country. This is a job universities can do; they have the talent for it, they can redeploy their talent, and the redeployment of their talent may also renew the dying professions and relieve the malaise of which we've all complained when we've looked at what has happened to the liberal arts tradition.

It goes in further and deeper. We've got to create a culture. Right now blacks are trying to work out an interesting relationship to Africa. But they're working out an interesting relationship to Africa just as the Africa to which they're working out their relationship is being everywhere eroded by the appearance of the same technological mass society which is ours. Nobody yet has ever devised a satisfactory alternative to what is happening now all over the world. We haven't yet managed to save the traditional cultures of others who know a relationship to the land and to others not known to technological man, a relationship which makes it possible to be human. Such saving of the older culture in the midst of technological change is a work requiring, I think, the intellect; it has to be brought to bear. We can't just work our way back into sentiments we no longer feel; we are, in fact most of us, deeply cut off from the earth. Only a university using its powers to the maximum and making the maximum effort to diffuse its powers, only a university making the kind of effort which was once put into universal education, can ever succeed at the tasks which I have described. You do not educate a whole society by sending it through institutions, making people sit in dreary classrooms, taking dreary courses under mostly dreary professors who are busy with nothing except their professional routine.

V
REPORT FROM THE
BLACK AND BROWN COMMUNITIES

Minority Report: Observations of Minorities in Attendance

During the morning panel discussion session, Mr. Moses C. Davis arose to read the following position paper, which had been drawn up by twenty-four members of minority groups present at the conference, representatives, in the main, of the black community, though some Chicano people were also included in the writing of the report. The report went as follows:

As participants (or, more truthfully, pseudoparticipants) in this conference, we feel it is our sincere obligation to help you to see this weekend session through black eyes, as only an exercise in verbal gymnastics—an exercise which continues to disregard the potential in the black, Chicano, and Indian brother for making contributions in a more vital way to any effort to examine the present frightening condition of this nation. This setting, though quite comfortable, is irrelevant in the context of the real concerns and implications of the TTT thrust. Despite the fact that these activities were long ago scheduled to take place in Phoenix, the Phoenix real-life community was not in any way involved in preparations to host or conduct this conference. A local "maxi-problem," of housing in the black community of this city is experiencing an innovative—to profane the word "innovation"—"mini-solution" in a plan called MINI-HOUSING. The conference analogy to this is that education's "maxi-problem," of America's historical failure (and the word "failure" here is an utter euphemism) to come vigorously to grip with the real issue of the impact of racism upon present plight of education in America has here met with the "mini-solution" of beautiful (?) rhetoric in a traditional conference setting.

Thus, this minority position paper declares that this conference has violently raped the entire TTT plans which have been in operation during this past year. "The Year of the Liberal Arts" should respect the TTT guidelines. These specifically call for (1) parity of school, university, and community in their involvement in the programs, and (2) impact upon the "economically and culturally disadvantaged" student.

(Personally, I don't like the term "disadvantaged." There are large segments of our society who have been placed at a disadvantage because of a deliberate design of social *robbery!* This nation's customs, practices, and even laws have, in too many instances, been designed to rob some members of this society of any real avenues through which they can develop to their greatest or highest or best potential. So the term should be *robbed*—not disadvantaged!)

Initial plans were made without true consideration of the community of black and other minority educators. Some received "invitations" to participate scant hours before they appeared on this stage. Although this and other conferences are supposedly designed ultimately to deal with the educational-social-psychological problems of the minority and poverty groups in this affluent nation, rarely are such groups honestly and creatively involved as part of the total planning. This now appears to be a consistent practice of verbal mouthing of meaningful involvement while skillfully avoiding *real* meaningful involvement. Certainly, this is true of this conference.

"The Year of the Liberal Arts" conference should be designed to reclaim and discover the intellectual energies of the traditionally overlooked and socially robbed person. Although you who are white are victims in a way that you may not see, we—the minorities and the poor—are victims of your problem in a more devastating and dehumanizing way; therefore, we *must* have input into sincere efforts to find solutions.

Although in more than one instance there was expressed real concern about preserving the study of Chaucer, Shakespeare, and the heritage of the Greeks, there was no concern evidenced to introduce for serious study the works of W. E. B. DuBois, Langston Hughes, Leroi Jones, Malcolm X, and other minority writers. One notable exception to this absence of concern was Paul Olson's moving response in which he read significantly from Ralph Ellison. You refused to involve as a major speaker on the liberal arts a person from the black or other significant minority community. Is the argument that one cannot be found?—or that we no longer want or believe in parity? Whatever the argument, we strongly recommend that the Office of Education *immediately* contact a black or other minority person to contribute an article of note to be included in publication of the report of this conference.

The liberal arts are charged with the production of scholars in the various disciplines who must provide liberality and the liberating of individual potentialities for future growth. When such unshackling is consistently denied to an exploding and vocal minority, the liberal arts themselves must carry the responsibility for any subsequent decline of these arts.

Two points in conclusion:

1. In presenting this minority report, although I most assuredly know who I am, I most assuredly know my name, such individuality is at this time subordinated to our role as a black observer viewing (studying) this conference through a filter of the Black Experience. Therefore, any of the comments in the report are subject to additions and expansion by any one of the other of the twenty-four persons who were involved in preparing this paper.
2. We leave you with the challenge that the greatest need in liberal arts and teacher education (if the two can indeed be separated) is vigorous and immediate action necessary to recruit and utilize the vast untapped reservoir of minority and black intellectual power.

> Moses C. Davis, for the twenty-four minority people who prepared the report

This report was heard during the panel session; it set the tone for many of the later remarks, most specifically those of Mr. Jack Gordon, above. At the end of the panel discussion Mr. Davis rose again to make a motion:

MOSES DAVIS: I have a motion to make. The motion is that (1) this conference direct that the Office of Education contact a minority person to contribute a significant paper, treating the topic of "The Year of the Liberal Arts," in order to enhance the eventual report of this conference, and (2) that this conference direct that the LTI of the TTT be urged to evolve plans for the follow-up conference suggested earlier by Mr. Jack Gordon.

Mr. Davis was followed by Mr. Theodore Johnson:

TED JOHNSON: I want to second that motion, and as a representative of the heretofore silent minority, I would add that in planning such a conference we will not neglect the problem of racism; we will take into full account the components of education for the poor and bilingualism. Let us take the opportunity of planning your increased liberalism—we will hungrily accept it.

Mr. Bigelow was somewhat hesitant to turn the discussion into a legislative session, but then decided to do so:

DON BIGELOW: I think that while that is a good motion, it's out of order. It seems to me that a vote is unnecessary. You are a collection of senators from the forty-one TTT projects. Each of those projects has a vote—a vote as to the direction of American education.

I beg your pardon? The vote? I had assumed that no one would deny it. All right. The motion that I heard was (1) that there be included in the report of this conference a paper by a minority person of note, and (2) that the LTI organize another conference, which would seek to represent the interests of those minority people not here adequately represented. Could we vote on that motion?

Those in favor?

Those opposed?

The ayes have it. Thank you.

The conference closed at this point. Later Mr. Anthony Gibbs wrote to Mr. Harry Rivlin of the TTT LTI concerning the resolutions. Mr. Gibbs noted that the resolutions:

1. *Directed the conference organizer to make arrangements for a representative of the minority community to prepare a paper (to be included in any printed document of the conference) to enhance the material growing out of the conference.*
2. *That LTI be responsible for putting the machinery together necessary for holding another conference, at which the minority groups in this country would present papers for the purpose of bringing another dimension of "The Year of the Liberal Arts" to the project directors and representatives from prospective liberal arts departments involved in the forty-odd TTT projects.*

Later Paul Olson was asked to get in touch with Mr. Gibbs and Mr. Johnson, leading community spokesmen. They determined in consultation with the community people they could reach that Mr. Preston Wilcox should be asked to write the paper "to enhance the material growing out of the conference." Mr. Wilcox's paper follows below.

Mr. Wilcox suggests in his paper that Chicano and Indian leaders comparable to him prepare papers analogous to his. These could not be prepared in time for the publication of this book. However, Mr. Wilcox's wish will be followed up in the later conference provided for in the resolutions of the Phoenix conference. Independent of Mr. Wilcox's suggestion, Mr. Edward Powell, a faculty member at a black college (Jarvis Christian College) expanded his remarks during the panel discussion session and made them into an article for publication in this book. Whereas Mr. Wilcox speaks primarily of the black presence on white campuses, Mr. Powell speaks primarily of the functions of the predominantly black college, but these remarks also suggest how a less ethnocentric liberal arts program could come into existence on all campuses.

Father Casso's speech to the panel discussion group representing Chicano community needs is a beginning toward making a meaningful representation of what meaningful liberal arts responses to Chicano needs might be.

Finally, Les Whipp, one of the "white establishment" participants at the conference, independent of Mr. Wilcox's suggestions and those of Mr. Powell and Father Casso, wrote a set of comments stating his sense of the need for something like the conference proposed by the minority resolution and his sense of the potential uses of the skills which he, as a rather typical liberary scholar has. Mr. Whipp's response was written up to be included in section VI but is included here because of its special relevance to this section.

PRESTON WILCOX

Liberal Arts and Teacher Training: A Pan-African Perspective

This paper was requested to ensure the inclusion of a minority group presentation in the final document from a TTT conference entitled "The Year of the Liberal Arts" held between April 30 and May 2, 1970, in Phoenix, Arizona. Despite the good intentions of the minority group caucus, whose actions precipitated the request for this report, and the actions of the conference leaders, who responded to the demand of the caucus, this statement will lack the legitimate pluralism the caucus sought to engender. One white presenter wrote, "I think we need the session run for minorities or we'll lose them for good." He seems to be expressing the feeling of the participants. One group (the minority caucus) was concerned that they were being left out; the other group wanted to deal with that feeling—and little else. My hurried review of several speeches and a tape recording from the conference lent powerful support to the notion that good intentions were not the means to an end at this conference; they were the end!

This author seems to have been placed in a quandary. The conference leaders appear to have conducted a white nationalist conference and are now attempting to cover their tracks by including a minority group statement. By doing so, they have placed me, a Black man, in the position of overlooking the legitimate concerns of my Third World brothers—Chicanos, Indians, Puerto Ricans, and Orientals.

At a recent Techni-culture conference held in Chicago in February, 1970, the participating ethnic groups developed a final document which included the total statements of all of the groups present—Blacks, Chicanos, Puerto Ricans, Indians, and Orientals. Each group discussed and did its own thing. Neither group had a need to evaluate, approve, or produce a statement for any other group. Each group guarded the right of the other to participate. All were performers and spectators, consumers and participants. They refused to treat each other in the fashion in which each had been treated by white America—left out, divided and conquered, and oppressed.[1]

The lesson for me is that I have no need to speak for my Third World brothers and sisters. I neither feel capable of meeting such a challenge, nor do I have a need to do so. I also do not have a need to bypass their interests. Rather, I am concerned that they be included. In the spirit of authentic pluralism, the submission of this statement is being made with the proviso that a representative selected by the respective Third World groups be chosen—as I was by the minority group caucus—to ensure the inclusion of a statement comparable to mine by each one of the minority groups. I am unwilling to replicate the behavior of the conference leaders. I am not content to pave the road to hell with their good intentions.

Further, if their good intentions are more than a warmed-over exploitation of minorities, the conference will move to install TTT programs in places where minorities will have to count on themselves and not the benevolence of white good will. Black college campuses, inner-city community-control-oriented public schools and independent minority group educational institutions await the actualization of these good intentions. It is suggested that the minority report which led to the commissioning of this paper and which is referred to elsewhere in this publication should be reviewed before one reads further (see pp. 159–63).

Introduction

This paper is an effort to state the issues as one Pan-African perceives them as they relate to the subject of the uses of the liberal arts in the education of teachers. The terms "Pan-African" and "Black" are deliberately used interchangeably in describing the

[1] "Resolutions, Demands and Recommendations: Techni-culture Conference," New York, National Federation of Settlements, February 11–13, 1970 (mimeo).

subject ethnic group. In either instance reference is being made to an African origin, a concomitant cultural heritage, and a common experience: victimization by colonialism, imperialism, and racism, all of which are intellectual rationalizations for gradual or abrupt genocide. These latter phenomena are seen in their educational form in the systematic fashion in which the contributions of over twenty million people have been overlooked on college campuses. In addressing my subject, I discuss first the issue of the Black presence on white campuses and then the concept of intelligence from the Black perspective. The succeeding section, one dealing with the myth of oppression, raises the question of who is really being oppressed. The implications of these three analyses for teacher training are then drawn and a new model proposed. The summary concludes with an effort to restate the real problem.

The Black Presence on White Campuses

The Black presence on white campuses has unleashed several forces which were obviously lying dormant on campuses heretofore; college faculties are being confronted with their tendencies to separate academic counseling from social counseling or to avoid the latter altogether. They are being called upon to remain *relevant*: to enable students to acquire the skills to participate in and hold accountable the society of which they are a part—and not the one that made it possible for present faculties to secure tenure.[2] Similarly, the credibility gap is being narrowed. Faculties are being asked to teach about history as it occurred and not as they "apoliticized" it. Another strand is the demand that thought not be separated from action and feeling, that apprehension not be separated from comprehension and theory from practice. For far too many years students have studied Thoreau, Emerson, Camus, Sartre, Rousseau, and the like without being summoned to *act* upon their learning.

Black students, despite the depth of their Americanization, have their origins in Africa. Their ancestors were brought here against their will, enslaved, dehumanized, freed to make it on their own with minimal enforcement of the laws presumably designed to protect their rights. Their group suffering within a pronounced egalitarian society is unparalleled; they remain psychological refugees,

[2] Lawrence E. Metcalfe and Maurice P. Hunt, "Relevance and the Curriculum," *Phi Delta Kappan*, March, 1970, pp. 358–61.

not because they have not been acculturated, but because they have never been permitted the right to assimilate on their own terms. This sustained state of psychological uprootedness has made Blacks perennial newcomers despite the fact that the presumed "old residents" followed them to this land. Importantly, the white-hyphenated groups—the authentic refugees—came to these foreign shores voluntarily in order to escape domestic deprivation in their home lands. The authentic refugees have turned Blacks into permanent refugees even though the Blacks were torn away from their homeland against their wills.

It is of unequaled credit to Black people that they are striving to refurbish a cultural heritage of which white America deliberately sought to rob them. It is of unestimable credit to Black people that they have survived a master plan that was designed to destroy them or turn them into cripples. It may be that white America is uptight because white racism failed to do the job; that the souls of Black people survived the seventh-son designation, discussed by DuBois.[3] Maybe Blacks have now achieved a true self-consciousness: an ability to see themselves through their own eyes. If this is the case, this view by Blacks of themselves has altered their views of the white society which surrounds them. Black people simply want to be themselves!

Unlike any other men who have resided on American soil, Black men know the devastation of being prevented the opportunities out of which one matures to manhood. When Black men perceived themselves through the eyes of others, they found themselves emulating men whose manhood was essentially based on the freedom to oppress other men. When Black men began to see themselves through their own eyes, they recognized two startling facts: that manhood cannot be denied one who believes in himself and that their right to be men was nonnegotiable. Education must incorporate this concern. The Center for Black Education in Washington, D.C., states it this way: "We have maintained that the essential problem within the African community is its dependency upon whites. And that Black Education is valid in so far that it seeks to break that dependency. Black Education must be committed to the self-reliance of Black People."[4]

[3] W. E. B. DuBois, *Souls of Black Folk* (New York: New American Library, 1969), p. 45.
[4] *The Fight for Black Education* (Washington, D.C.: Center for Black Education, 1969), p. 3.

It is no accident that Black students began to act under the guidance of those great teachers; Martin Luther King, Jr., Malcolm X, and Frantz Fanon.[5] W. E. B. DuBois, long accredited as a scholar-theoretician and whose works are read and understood, now turns out after death to have been a creative pragmatist.[6] Garvey's writings are now being dusted off and reactivated along with those of the founders of the Pan-African Congress, George Padmore and C. L. R. James.[7] Even Booker T. Washington now seems to have been saying "power to the people" in his historic Atlanta address.[8] White students who have been conditioned to read history have now become activated by Black students who have compelling need to rediscover their own history and to actualize it.

If one can examine the above analysis without placing colonialistic value judgments on it, he will understand why Black students within an acknowledged white racist society will be compelled to learn how to reshape the context of this society. Their survival as humans demands it. The differential treatment which they have received and will receive for far too many years to come requires that they acquire a set of thought-action skills that frees them to perceive and respond to the society as it really is. To the degree that their own self-confrontations can engineer similar confrontations by white students, this differential will be minimized. Another alternative is to involve Black and white students with faculty in redefining the context and form of liberal arts curricula. As these Black and white students look at curricula on their campuses, they will find both African studies programs and Black studies programs, being developed frequently to prevent self-confrontation and to preserve the existing system.

A recent report issued by the African Research Group suggests that the white denial of the accreditation of manhood to Blacks is based largely on the refusal of Black men to turn against the best interests of their home land—Africa. The ARG reports that African studies programs on many white campuses were heavily involved in

[5] Preston Wilcox, "The Black University: A Movement or an Institution," in *Negro Digest*, XIX (December 1969), 2.

[6] Meyer Weinberg, ed., *W. E. B. DuBois: A Reader* (New York: Harper & Row, 1970).

[7] C. L. R. James, *A History of Pan-African Revolt* (Washington, D.C.: Drum & Spear Press, 1970). The Action Library, Afram Associates, Inc., 103 East 125th Street, Harlem, N.Y. 10035, is now developing a bibliography on Pan-Africanism.

[8] Booker T. Washington, *Uptown Slavery* (New York: Dell, 1965).

CIA and AID activities—a kind of scientific colonialism designed to keep the African nations psychologically and politically colonized. It is interesting that Howard and Lincoln universities have not been used for these purposes. They have been utilized as training centers for African diplomats and bureaucrats.[9] This report probably also explains the resistance of white institutions to the Pan-Africanization of their curricula and the ease with which they set up separate Black studies programs; African studies programs on white campuses have usually trained missionaries and State Department officials, both of whom are colonizing agents. Had Black students gotten on the inside, they would have probably "blown the whistle," as has Curt Flood done in baseball, as Muhammed Ali did on the Vietnam war, and as have the Black Panther party on the court system in this country.[10]

As white students and faculty confront themselves on white liberal arts campuses, they will ask themselves, "Who is to blame?" and create a variety of accounts. It is appropriate to comment on what I refer to as the "theory of white blame." Whites have systematically denied Blacks opportunities and blamed them for being poor. They blame them for smelling; yet whites buy up most of the deodorants.[11] In the main, whites have projected their superior technological advancement as a measure of white supremacy while concealing their efforts to systematically deny such opportunities to Blacks. One Pan-African writes: "During the period of colonization, the European did not show his African captive how to produce and employ muskets, cannons and sailing ships because the only way that the European was able to maintain his position of superiority was to maintain a technological edge."[12]

The Concept of Intelligence: The Black Perspective

Curricula are one part of the liberal arts; college standards and rules are another. The Black man in America has been bedeviled by steadily being held accountable by standards, criteria, rules, and

[9] *African Studies in America: The Extended Family, a Tribal Analysis of U.S. Africanists, Who Are They, Why to Fight Them* (Cambridge: Africa Research Group, October 1969), pp. 29, 31.
[10] See Haywood Burns, "Can a Black Man Get a Fair Trial in This Country," *New York Times Magazine*, July 12, 1970, pp. 5, 38, 44, 45, 46.
[11] Dick Gregory, *The Light Side: The Dark Side* (New York: Poppy Industries, Inc., 1969) (a record).
[12] "The Importance of Technology to Black People" (Washington, D.C.: Center for Black Education, 1970), p. 1 (mimeo).

procedures which were essentially stacked against his own humanity. Neither the original Declaration of Independence (July 4, 1776) nor the Black Declaration of Independence (July 3, 1970) spoke to his legitimate needs. The former counted him as being only three-fifths of a white man; the latter appealed to the descendants of the authors of the first one to treat Black men as being equal to white men.[13]

The pattern of looking at the Black man as "three-fifths of a white man" or "equal to a white man" is consistent with the concept of intelligence defined by mainstream scholars. Intelligence is viewed by mainstream scholars as being the act of thinking. The authors of the Black Declaration of Independence fell into the same trick-bag. What Black people in this country require is a Declaration to Act Independently: to guard their collective right to be autonomous. Intelligence, when perceived from that perspective, compels one to think, feel, and act in one single effort. The evidence for the assertion that we have separated thinking from acting is that we have used technology in this country essentially as a tool to destroy, a tool to control, or as a tool of economic exploitation. Far more technological skill is employed for these purposes than is utilized to develop a human technology. Recall that we reside in a society where it is still illegal to be Black and illegal to be human.

The concept that we have failed by separating thinking from acting has relevance for the educational controversies that currently bedevil us. As suggested above, institutions of higher education operate to separate academic counseling from social counseling, gown from town, theory from practice, and that which is essential from that which is existential. It is literally illegal to feel strongly about anything, or to suggest that one can learn experientially as well as experimentally on many college campuses. Importantly, the separation of class from field learning is itself an instrument to control, since few faculty members are emotionally equipped to participate in, or evaluate, a real-life experience. Witness how long they rationalized failing their students into service in Vietnam.

This concept that intelligence cannot separate thinking from acting, and its operational dimension, is of key importance to Black students. Many concepts cannot be learned in a classroom—and many cannot be taught devoid of experience. The increasing desire of Black students to remain "relevant to the Black experience" has meant that they have had to endure a white nationalist experience as

[13] "Black Declaration of Independence," *New York Times*, July, 1970, p. 7.

a means to achieve the credentials to provide educational leadership within a Black nationalist community. The absence of any real concern for learning how to become human on such campuses further cripples them. They frequently return to the Black community with a white nationalist indoctrination and present themselves as white liberals rather than as authentic members of the Black community. They end up far too frequently as mainstream advocates and not as advocates of the Black experience.

The inclusion of Black content does not measurably alter this factor. Exposure to Black content without building in a systematic learning experience as a member of the Black community merely produces Black scholars who perceive themselves as being "equal to whites." They seldom become "equal to the occasion," since they are ill equipped to function as participant-theoreticians within the Black community.

It may be unthinkable to request that white institutions of higher education educate Black students to recover the revolutionary zeal which is embedded deeply within the gut of all Black men in white America. It would be equally unthinkable to assert that this revolutionary zeal can be totally erased by any pattern of indoctrination. White institutions, then, have two alternatives: to postpone the revolution or to remove the need for it. The people who have the most to gain by removing the need for it are Black people.

Nathan Hare's definition of the Black scholar may be instructive:

> He is a man of both thought and action, a whole man who thinks for his people and acts with them, a man who honors the whole community of Black experience, a man who sees the Ph.D., the janitor, the business man, the maid, the clerk, the militant, as all sharing the experience of blackness, with all of its complexities and rewards.[14]

The presentation of educational materials for use by Black students on white universities suits the interests of Black scholars and the Black community as little as do white intelligence tests. Much of what has been written by white scholars flows from a scientifically colonialistic frame of reference.[15] It presumes white people to be superior to Black people. It converts the myth of white supremacy

---

[14] Nathan Hare, ed., *Black Scholar*, I (November 1969), 1 (inside front cover).
[15] Johann Galtung, "The Lessons of Project Camelot: Scientific Colonialism," *Transition*, XXX (1967), 11–15.

into a legend—and proceeds to support that point of view. White students who are exposed to it come to believe that they are legitimately superior. They are taught that the privilege of the white skin is a basic human right for whites. Black students, in turn, are taught that they are inferior and that that is the way things are supposed to be.[16]

But it is not only what has been written that does not suit the interests of Black students. The very organization of the material is such that its utility for Black students is not readily apparent. Few libraries have a category labeled "white institutional racism."[17] (If they did, they would probably have to put that category up as a sign in front of the whole library building.) Few have books organized into such categories as "Black Economic Development," "Pan-Africanism," "Black humanism," "Black political thought," "police community control," "school community control," "women and race," "Black history," "Black periodicals and publications," and the like. Libraries organize their files in such a way as to encourage Black students to depend on white salvation rather than urging them to acquire the skills to manage their own. The inhumanity of it all is apparent. White people are not even free enough to respect Black people *in writing*, let alone on a face-to-face basis!

THE MYTH OF OPPRESSION

The events of the past few years have raised some fundamental questions about the processes of victimization; victimization derives both from the illusions of success and the illusions of failure. Despite the strength of white institutional racism, its most vaunted political impact is the message it has conveyed to Black men about their essential resiliency and the indestructibility of their culture. On the other hand, the benefits which have accrued to white men deriving from their comfortable exercise of the privilege of the white skin are increasingly becoming a source of their own self-crucifixion. Witness the ingrained fear of Black men by white men. White men are becoming the victims of their own "successes"; Black men are learning to "succeed" despite their victimization. When one

[16] Preston Wilcox, "Social Policy and White Racism," *Social Policy*, May–June, 1970, pp. 37–46.
[17] Catherine Havrilesky and Preston Wilcox, A *Selected Bibliography on White Institutional Racism* (New York: Afram Associates, Inc., May 25, 1969). See introduction.

considers that the objective criteria for accrediting the humanity of this society reside within the purview of authentic Black men, then one can honestly raise the question about who the oppressors really oppressed: themselves or the targets of their disdain.

White men—the authentic Uncle Toms—are finding a declining number of Black men who want to emulate them; Black Uncle Toms are learning that they cannot achieve authenticity by adopting white nationalism as a survival philosophy. "Uncle Tomism" can never be any more than a temporary tactic, for it is the Black men who have been fully involved within the white world who are most adept at reading the white racist agenda. The kinship between the poor Blacks and the African Bushmen is, interestingly enough, stronger than the bond between those of African origin on African and American soil who perceive themselves as being middle-class. They, poor Blacks and the African Bushmen, hold in common a rare ability to value themselves and their latent cultural beliefs above the rewards of destructive Americanization. They not only can read the white man's agenda: they want to begin to deal with it. My point: Black Uncle Toms are African warriors in Brooks Brothers suits; they are not white men with a warrior's coloration.

The purpose of this interpretation is to direct attention to some fundamental educational issues. What is the function of education within a society that suppresses dissent, celebrates thinking in isolation, and commits its members to enact and reenact the status quo? What is the function of education that denies minorities equal access to a white racist curriculum and proceeds to evaluate them as failures because they reject its essential inhumanity? Who is qualified to call himself an educator when the basic social problems are addressed on the streets and not in the classrooms? Prison cells served as study halls for Malcolm X, Martin Luther King, Sr., Eldridge Knight, Eldridge Cleaver, Huey Newton, and Bobby Seale! Parole boards served as their doctoral committees; their dissertations did not sit on shelves. Their writings served to begin to redefine the context of this society. All of these men engineered their own psychological liberation while being denied personal freedom because they attempted to enforce the white man's laws. Who are the authentic educators, I ask?

The so-called ivory-towered centers of learning are now engaged in using the issue of academic freedom to infringe upon students' rights; they are continuing to evaluate Pan-African students according to white nationalist standards; they are continuing to attempt to imprison the minds of students in the name of free intellectual inquiry. Doctoral committees ordain rather than accredit authentic performance. The priesthood of academia has become its own prison in isolation. It offers students two opportunities: to participate in their own intellectual imprisonment or to exercise their right to authentic intellectual liberation. The first alternative sanctions the exercise of nonphysical violence against students by their teachers; the second has sanctioned the exercise of physical violence by the national guard under the supervision of institutions of higher education. Who's really in prison and who are the perpetrators of violence, I ask?

The masterful skill of projection which white racists develop as a technique to justify the denial of the white racism from which they benefit is increasingly being understood. One function of white racism is to convince Black men that they are inferior to white men in order to remove from white men the need to justify their own presumed superiority. The name of the game was to substitute the myth for the truth—as a means to blur the truth. Hence, the search for truth—even on college campuses—is illegal. The only men, Black or white, who foster their own oppression and that of others are those who believe that white people are superior to Black people. The only oppressed men are those who want to oppress others or subscribe to those values which require the oppression of others. The projection of the white sense of oppression by whites and on other people is part of the projectors' game to conceal their own oppression.

In this context, one may look at the conference reported in this book. The omission of a minority statement was a deliberate game to convince the minority caucus of the reality of their oppression when, in fact, it was and is a myth. Oppressed peoples do not take the kinds of actions taken in the minority caucus, and people who have no need to oppress do not force the kinds of actions that the minority caucus took. They include them from the beginning.

I would like to suggest that the issues confronted by the conference under discussion arose because the conference leaders perceived minorities rather than themselves as having been oppressed.

Implications for Teacher Training and Parity

The Black presence on white campuses has heightened the awareness about the reality of white institutional racism and its consequences for Black and white men alike. It has white institutions uptight because they want to continue to conceal their colonialistic tendencies rather than confront them. The liberal arts curriculum, which was used to get white students to line up and to orient them to avoid responsibilities, is being rejected by Black students.

The standard measures of intelligence applied by white institutions condition their students to separate thought from feeling and to become adept in applying rationality to nonrational problems. They literally become ill prepared to act in the real world.

Institutions of higher education have attracted Pan-Africans as students and not as members of the Pan-African community. Their goal is to turn them into mainstream advocates and not advocates for their own people. A problem exists: the traditional oppressors are losing their ability to oppress and are ill equipped to deal with their own oppression. Gouldner describes their oppression as follows:

> For tenured faculty, the university is the realm of congenial and leisured servitude. It is a realm in which the academician is both esteemed for his learning and castrated as a political being. Indeed, it is this trade-off in which the academician may be a tiger in the classroom but must be a pussycat in the Dean's office, ...[18]

The implications of these analyses for teacher training are clear, particularly for the TTT Program, whose guidelines call for (1) parity of school, university, and community involvement, and (2) impact upon the "economically and culturally disadvantaged" student.[19] The guidelines as defined are replete with the language of racism: they conceal the elements of power and politics and the illegal deprivation of the students they seek to serve. They imply that parity, like power, can be given, not taken. They suggest that minority group students are ill equipped to survive in the real world when in fact they are consummate masters at it. The basic premise of the TTT Program conceals the racism it proclaims to confront.

If TTT programs are to have any future viability, white liberal arts courses must be replaced with humanistic curricula that cause the students to confront themselves first.

[18] Alvin W. Gouldner, "Toward the Radical Reconstruction of Sociology," *Social Policy*, May–June, 1970, p. 24.
[19] "Minority Report: Observations of Minorities in Attendance," The Year of the Liberal Arts Conference, Phoenix, Arizona, May 2, 1970, p. 1.

Faculty, in such programs, should be required to enroll in courses on southern Black college campuses in order to learn what it means to perceive Blacks as human, the experience of being a minority within a Black community and earning the wrath of the white establishment. The experience of John Morris at Miles College in Birmingham is a case in point:

> In my previous incarnation, when I was a dues-paying member of the white community, I had a hard time taking seriously that I and my well-meaning liberal-minded church-going friends were bigoted racists. And a couple of years back when I heard young black people accusing us good white folks of "genocide," I considered the accusation dangerous, and also rather paranoid and absurd. But I see things somewhat differently now. I find it a particularly rich experience to live and work in a black community, mainly because in the black community you develop a clarity of vision about the realities of American life.[20]

(Before any proposals are written for such a retreading of white academicians on Black college campuses, permit me to suggest that a reparations fee, not straight tuition, be charged. Such a fee would include tuition costs and a special fee for the real-life learning opportunities that are provided. No course credit should be given and such faculty should be required to engage in community work under the leadership of Blacks.)

Students in these humanistic programs should be heavily engaged in learning how to redefine the condition of their own groups on human terms. Some of the important consequences of their learning experience should be: (1) a love of learning, not teaching; (2) an understanding of the racist nature of the society; (3) an ability to perform the tasks for which they are being educated based on the judgments of their communities of origin in ethnic terms; (4) an ability and desire to be held accountable to and by their own people. Their education of these students should take place on the site where they hope to perform beyond graduation. They should become students of their communities and not university students. Seminars should be held on the site in which community members are involved as full members—without cost but for appropriate credit. An

---

[20] John U. Munro, "Escape from Dark Cave," *Nation*, October 24, 1969.

important part of their student role should be that of enabling the local community to define educational policy on its own terms.[21]

An important part of the community's learning should be that of reasserting one's ties to his own cultural heritage. Such students should live with and pay rent to poor families. They should not study such families. Rather, they should learn from them. The bond of the poor with their African heritage has been retained despite years of victimization. Hopefully, the student in such a community will learn what white institutions have failed to teach: that Black people are human and educable. The president of Mississippi's Tougaloo College recognized this. He was quoted as follows: "We don't place the stigma of disadvantaged or inferior symbols on our students. They are college people, and we expect them to perform college level work. We don't indoctrinate them in their alleged inferiority or disadvantages."[22]

The university's facilities should only be used for library study in order to deepen the student's understanding of the field learning. A part of this process should involve the reorganization of the cataloguing process and the inclusion of publications by Pan-Africans. Such a process would make the library relevant to the real world and increase its utility as a public service—and not just its utility as a place of privilege for university scholars.

Heading Home

The essence of my position is that the liberal arts must become life arts—and that such a transformation cannot occur on a college campus. The authentic educators are not located there: students seeking authentic intellectual freedom would not be caught dead on a college campus. Pan-Africans with a desire to participate in transmitting knowledge to the brothers on the street must demonstrate, as a sine qua non, an ability to be taught by their brothers. In the last analysis what is required is a Black university for white scholars.

[21] See *Position Paper: The Future of the Arthur A. Schomburg I.S. 201 Complex Demonstration Project* (New York: I.S. 201 Complex, April 1970).

[22] Thomas A. Johnson, "Poverty Is a Boast at Tougaloo College: A Black School in South Sees Students Succeed Despite Lowly Origins," *New York Times*, July 25, 1970, p. 15. George A. Owens is the person referred to. See also *How SEDFRE Staff Works with Students* (New York: Scholarship, Education and Defense Fund for Racial Equality, March 10, 1970).

The problem has been that white racist scholars have been forced to pretend that they were teaching Blacks as a means to learn about them. And that's the problem.

NO MORE BULLSHIT

BIBLIOGRAPHY

ARTICLES

Abrams, Morris. "The Eleven Days at Brandeis—As Seen from the President's Chair," *New York Times Magazine*, February 16, 1969, pp. 28, 29, 113, 114, 115, 116.

Anderson, S. E. "Toward Racial Relevancy: Militancy and the Black Student," *Negro Digest*, September, 1967, pp. 10–12.

Boggs, Grace Lee. "Towards A New System of Education," *Foresight*, October, 1968.

Bray, Thomas, and Lehner, Urban C. "Black Collegians: Enrollment of Negroes Will Jump in the Fall at Many Institutions," *Wall Street Journal*, July 28, 1969, pp. 1, 8.

Caldwell, Earl. "College Chiefs Urge Ethnic Centers," *New York Times*, June 28, 1969, p. 15.

Cass, James. "Can the University Survive the Black Challenge?" *Saturday Review of Literature*, June 21, 1969, pp. 68, 69, 70, 71, 83, 84.

"Campus Reform: The Faculty Role," *Life*, May 23, 1969, p. 42.

Crystal, Josie. "Changes in an Ofay Curriculum," *Center Forum*, Vol. III, No. 5 (March 1, 1969), p. 24.

Darnton, John. "New Black Studies at Yale Covers Slavery Era and Up," *New York Times*, May 15, 1969.

Dixon, Norman R., and Barnes, Edward J. *Liberal Education for the Black Student* (Pittsburgh: University of Pittsburgh, 1970). 2 pp.

Dunbar, Ernest. "The Black Studies Thing," *New York Times Magazine*, April 6, 1969, pp. 25–27, 60, 65, 68, 70, 75, 76, 78.

DuPree, David. "Angry Young Man: Tough Black Militants Browbeat Opposition at San Francisco State," in *Wall Street Journal*, May 18, 1969, pp. 1–18.

Farber, M. A. "Learning + Experience = Knowledge Survey Shows," *New York Times*, July 8, 1970, pp. 1, 12.

——. "Eleven College Presidents Caution Money Crisis Imperils Future," *New York Times*, July 13, 1970, pp. 1, 24.

Genovese, Eugene. "Black Studies: Trouble Ahead," *Atlantic Monthly*, Vol. CCIII, No. 6 (June 1969), pp. 37–40.

Gregory, Dick. "Studies in Black and White," *Renewal*, IX (May 1969), pp. 9–10.
Hamilton, Charles V. "Black Students Need Relevancy," *Essence*, I (May 1970).
Harding, Vincent. "New Creations or Familiar Death?" *Negro Digest*, March, 1969.
"How Black Studies Happened," *Yale Alumnae Magazine*, May, 1969, pp. 22–27.
Lasker, Lawrence. "A Whiter Shade of Black," *Esquire*, July, 1968, pp. 61–65.
Lewis, Arthur. "The Road to the Top Is through Higher Education—Not Black Studies," *New York Times*, May 11, 1969, pp. 34, 35, 39, 40, 42, 44, 46, 50, 52, 54.
———. "Black Studies: A Black Professor's View," *Wall Street Journal*, May 15, 1969.
"A Look at What Americans Know and Can Do," *New York Times*, July 12, 1970, p. E9.
Mahome, Otello." Incident at Cornell," *Liberator*, IX (June 1969), pp. 4–7.
Maidenberg, Michael. "Black Studies Programs: Are They Successful?" *Washington Free Press*, undated.
Nolan, David. "White Control of Black Education," *New South Student*, Vol. VI, No. 1 (January 1969), pp. 22–30.
"On Being Black at Yale," *Yale Alumnae Magazine*, May, 1969, pp. 28–33.
Poussaint, Alvin, and McLean, Linda. "Black Roadblock to Black Unity," *Negro Digest*, November, 1968.
Raskin, Barbara. "Federal City College: Militancy in Microcosm," *Washington Monthly*, Vol. I, No. 3 (April 1969), pp. 52–61.
Rich, Evelyn Jones. "Black Is Beautiful . . . But Not Enough," *Bryn Mawr Alumnae Magazine*, Spring, 1969, pp. 2, 3.
Roberts, Steven V. "Black Studies Aim to Change Things," *New York Times*, May 15, 1969.
Robertson, Nan. "Racial Approach Urged in College," *New York Times*, May 31, 1969.
Walton, Sidney F., Jr. "Proposals for Black Directed Change," *College Board Review*, No. 71 (Spring 1969), pp. 18–20.
Wentworth, Eric. "Giving the U.S. an Exam," *New York Post*, July 8, 1970, p. 37.
Wilcox, Preston. "It's Not a Replica of the White Agenda," *College Board Review*, No. 71 (Spring 1969), pp. 6–10.
Woodward, C. Vann. "American History (White Man's Version) Needs an Infusion of Soul," *New York Times Magazine*, April 20, 1969, pp. 32, 33, 108–14.

BIBLIOGRAPHIES

Havrilesky, Catherine, and Wilcox, Preston. *A Selected Bibliography on White Institutional Racism.* New York: Afram Associates, Inc., July 1, 1969. 7 pp.

Ramsay, Annette M. *Understanding White Racist Thought: A Bibliography.* New York: Afram Associates, Inc., Action Library, August, 1970. 5 pp.

Wilcox, Preston. *The Black Condition: A Bibliography.* New York: Afram Associates, Inc., October 15, 1969. 10 pp.

―――. *Black Economic Development: A Bibliography.* New York: Afram Associates, Inc., June, 1970. 4 pp.

―――. *The Revolt by Black Students on College Campuses: A Bibliography.* New York: Afram Associates, Inc., January 30, 1968. 6 pp.

―――. *Black Position Papers: A Bibliography.* New York: Afram Associates, Inc., December 7, 1969. 6 pp.

―――. *Pan Africanism: A Bibliography.* New York: Afram Associates, Inc., August, 1970. 5 pp.

BOOKS

African Studies in America: The Extended Family, A Tribal Analysis of U.S. Africanists, Who They Are, Why To Fight Them. Cambridge: Africa Research Group, October, 1969. 52 pp.

Augusta, Georgia and Jackson State University: Southern Episodes in A National Tragedy. Atlanta: Southern Regional Council, Inc.'s Special Report, June, 1970. 76 pp.

Black Students in American Colleges. Washington, D.C.: American Council On Education, 1969.

Black Studies in the University: A Symposium. Edited by Armstead L. Robinson, Craig C. Foster, and Donald Ogilvie. New Haven: Yale University Press, 1969.

Egerton, John. *State Universities and Black Americans: An Inquiry into Desegregation and Equity for Negroes in One Hundred Public Universities.* Southern Education Foundation, May, 1969. 93 pp.

Undergraduate Enrollment by Ethnic Group in Federally Funded Institutions of Higher Education: Fall 1968. Washington, D.C.: Office of Civil Rights. U.S. Dept. of Health, Education and Welfare, 1969.

Woodson, Carter G. *The Mis-Education of the Negro.* Washington, D.C.: Associated Publishers, 1933.

PAPERS

Boggs, James. "Curriculum Suggestions for Black Studies Institutes." New York: National Association for African American Education, February 12, 1969. 3 pp.

"The Fight for Black Education." Washington, D.C.: Center for Black Education, n.d. 4 pp.
Gaines, Lonnetta, and Skaggs, Victoria. "Working Paper for the Learning House: A Community Pre-School." Atlanta, 1970. 63 pp. + Appendix.
Hare, Nathan; Lynch, Acklyn; and Wilcox, Preston. "Black Power and Black Education." New York: National Association for African American Education, 1970. 13 pp.
"The Importance of Technology to Black People." Washington, D.C.: Center for Black Education, n.d. 3 pp.
Kent, David B., Jr. "Proceedings of the First NAAAE Conference." New York: National Association for African American Education, August, 1968. 77 pp.
Mamis, Nancy. "Guess Who Is Still Speaking with A Forked-Up Tongue?" New York: Afram Associates, Inc., 1970. 1 p.
"Minority Report: Year of the Liberal Arts." Chicago: Woodlawn Organization, 1970. 2 pp.
"New Perspectives: Findings of a Five-Day Black University." New York: National Association for African American Education, April 15, 1970. 125 pp. + Introduction.
Wilcox, Preston. "Blackenizing the Curriculum." New York: Afram Associates, Inc., n.d. 2 pp.
———. "A Reader on Black Power and Public Education." New York: Afram Associates, Inc., 1968.
———. "A Think-Piece: The Multiple Forms of Black Studies Programs." New York: National Association for African American Education, February 20, 1970. 6 pp. + footnotes.
———. "Black Communities on White Campuses: Patterns of Fragmentation." New York: Afram Associates, Inc., March 25, 1970. 4 pp.
Williams, Russell Spry. "An Open Letter to the Students and Faculty at Spelman College." New York: Afram Associates, Inc., May 18, 1970. 3 pp.

POSITION PAPERS

"Atlanta University Position Paper On Racism and Violence in the United States." Atlanta University Center, May 25, 1970. 3 pp.
"Black Declaration of Independence," *New York Times*, July 3, 1970, p. 7.
"Declaration of Independence." Dayton: Model Cities Joint Community School Council, September 13, 1969. 1 p.
"Excerpts from Speech by NAACP Head Calling Administration Anti-Negro," *New York Times*, June 30, 1970, p. 25.

"Resolution by the Committee of Twenty College Presidents." New York: Afram Associates, Inc., July 17, 1969. (The statement was developed at a meeting in Mobile, Alabama.)

"Text of White House Telegram Replying to NAACP Head's Criticism of Administration as Anti-Negro," *New York Times*, July 1, 1970, p. 34.

EDWARD C. POWELL

Haraka

The discussions of this conference were long overdue. Every paper presented has led me to a deeper insight into the complexities of the problems and the creative opportunities we face. The word *Haraka* means "hurry" in Swahili. *Haraka* is an appropriate title at this time. Our institutions and large segments of our society have moved beyond value conflict to more rigid postures and even overt conflict. We must hurry if we are to rescue the American dream. Those of us who are knowledgeable in the wisdom of the past, unprovincial in our appraisal of the present, and steadfast in our quest of the free and enhancing society must be able to reason and build together.

In the recent past the schools or colleges of education and the liberal arts disciplines have not come to grips with the fundamental problems of our society. Liberal arts and education, each viewing the society from a different perspective, have spent too much time in sarcastic exchange and in competition for limited resources. The effectiveness of institutions of higher education, and therefore of society, is adversely affected by this lack of understanding and acceptance of a legitimate role for each area in the development of a free and responsive society. The small, developing institution, black or white, red or brown, public or private, has a vital interest in the resolution of these conflicts. Many of these institutions are acutely aware of the need to review, reconstitute, and refocus their efforts toward the learning environment, efforts which will add creative power to those now deprived and inject new vitality into the accelerated development of the free society.

Our society is in need of major changes. The very fact that so much conflict exists at the verbal level and elsewhere is proof in itself that changes must be made, and made effectively and rapidly. We have made staggering changes in the area of technology. Concurrent with these changes in technology there have developed other cultural, socioeconomic, and demographic pressures which are inevitable consequences of the nature of social systems. American society, viewed as a system of interacting variables, comes under increased stress when the rate of change in any subset of variables does not keep pace with the other variables. Functions leisurely performed will no longer suffice, under present conditions. Many of our young people think that institutions of higher education are in league with the establishment in either a witting or unwitting process of depersonalization, that we lack authenticity—proclaiming noble ideas but actively pursuing the ignoble.[1]

This is not the occasion to trace the development of a concept of liberal learning in Western thought. I will be content, therefore, with giving my perception of the present situation. Typically the liberal arts tradition has been too narrow in its perspective. Not all beauty, wisdom, and noble ideals have been echoed in the temple at Delphi. Men have struggled with the great questions relative to man's relationship to man and to the unknown in all cultures, on all continents, for thousands of years. I wish that I had time to read more Greek plays, African stories, and Eastern philosophy. Those which I have read have given me a sense of kinship with other men which I dearly cherish.[2] Everyone needs a sense of identity and a sense of continuity with the past even if he chooses to break clearly away from that past. There are many red Americans, brown Americans, black Americans that seek to renew their inner spirit through the study of the sources of their identity. To many such persons this has been denied. Our limited experience, our own blindness, has led us to think and act as if the only source of wisdom, beauty, and creativity is Greece.

[1] Jack F. Padgett, "The New Breed in Search of a New Morality," *Liberal Education: Bulletin of The Association of American Colleges*, LIV (October 1968), 435–42.

[2] See Jahnheinz Jahn, *Neo-African Literature: A History of Black Writing*, trans. by Oliver Coburn and Ursula Lehrbuger (New York: Grove Press, 1968); S. Dasgupta, *A History of Indian Philosophy* (London: Cambridge University Press, 1955).

There is an old African saying: "Not to know is bad, not to want to know is worse."[3] Many of us have not wanted to know ourselves or to permit others to learn. For example, at a time when many foreign-language teachers wish more students would learn a foreign language—one which they teach—the young people who wish to learn and speak Spanish and Swahili are discouraged.

Our curricula have been limited in their perspectives; they have dealt with problems, however legitimate and eternal, packaged in archaic form and expression. One must recognize that the socioeconomic, demographic, and technological situations have changed faster than either our programs in higher education or our programs in the liberal arts. I hope that we still have time to redirect the liberal arts from what seems to be an almost total preoccupation with drawing eternal truths from Western classics to a wider search for authenticity, beauty, and justice in man under varied life situations —black, red, Eastern, Western, rural, urban.

This is not to say that classics have nothing to say to the New Breed. They speak to us as well. *Oedipus the King* is obviously a classic; a man is caught in a web of circumstances; he has a sexual relationship with a woman who is later discovered to be his own mother. In our time and in his time that was and is judged the worst of fates. Although there are many ideas in this story which deserve consideration in the education of people for politics and leadership, I am concerned here with Oedipus' reaction to the truth of his condition. What does he do? He is sorry about the situation and feels that he has to take some appropriate action. I will not argue with *Oedipus* at this point about responsibility, whether it was chance, society, culture, or Oedipus himself. In any case, Oedipus judges himself or, more pointedly, parts of himself, guilty. His sentence upon himself is to pluck out his own eyes. Using Oedipus' own frame of reference, I question his choice of his eyes. To me one of the most instructive aspects of Oedipus' story is his decision to blind himself. He does not wish to see. He does not wish to face reality. Many other illustrations could be drawn from this story, many illustrations concerning the appropriateness of Oedipus' actions as head of an institution; but I believe that there are non-Western stories, some black American stories, and some modern urban stories about the struggles of the individual with change, society, culture, and power which might also be considered relevant to the perception which

[3] Richard F. Burton, *Wit and Wisdom from West Africa* (New York, 1969), p. 6.

I have gathered from Oedipus.[4] Learn, for instance, about Bigger Thomas, a native son presented to us by Richard Wright.

As a final word about the liberal arts, I know that I have distorted the position taken by many progressive persons and institutions, but I believe that they are atypical and that they must do more to make their voices heard today. In all my enjoyment of the Greek classics I cannot help remembering that the democracy of Greece was an "equality" for only a few—existing on a base of institutionalized slavery.[5] Except in a very few instances Plato would have very little difficulty in adjusting to the present institutions of higher education. The American college is somewhat different in its purpose from the Academy, but fundamentally we teach and manage as though the technological revolution had not happened, as if the behavioral sciences did not exist. There are a few institutions that have taken bold steps to reconstitute themselves in order to refocus their attention on building a free society. There are too few such institutions.

The federal government, through the Department of Health, Education and Welfare, the National Endowment for the Humanities, the National Science Foundation, along with a relatively few foundations, has tried to help us. However, most of us organize our materials and our teaching experiences in such ways that it is difficult for a young person seeking to be free to find his place. With so much remaining to be done, I am discouraged by the destruction of the integration concept, by its misuse in the struggle for power, by the addition of long hair to skin color, sex, and socioeconomic circumstances as superficial rationalization for hate and repression. Those of us in education should beware. It is not racism alone. What is at large is even more sick and disfunctional to the American dream of the free and enhancing society. The undercurrents of repression which flow from distrust of long hair, skin color, sex, etc., can destroy all of us. The "little" repression which we condone to support our favorite prejudice can give those who lack faith in the American creed an opportunity our future does not deserve.

[4] Earle H. West, "Editorial Comment: The Concept of Relevance," *Journal of Negro Education*, XXXVIII (Winter 1969), 1–3.
[5] Gerrit P. Judd, *A History of Civilization* (New York: Macmillan, 1966), pp. 43, 45; also see Alfred North Whitehead, *Adventures of Ideas* (New York: Macmillan, 1933).

It is a tragic commentary on the level of our democratic achievement that red, brown, and black men have had to walk around the ivy-covered "walls of Jericho" in order to get the opportunity to unfold their natural creative talents for the benefit of the whole society. Our colleges are as prepared for open admissions as they are for restricted admissions. The Carnegie Commission on Higher Education said that "inequality of opportunity must not continue to sap the strength of our nation."[6] They propose that "all economic barriers to educational opportunity be eliminated," that "the curriculum and the environment of the college campus not remain a source of educational disadvantage or inequity."[7] We are all brothers in sweat, tears, blood, and hope in seeking to build the free society; yet many of us are strangers distrusted not only in the house of intellect, but also in the society generally. I firmly believe that greater cooperation, greater effort toward mutual understanding of the respective circumstances and aspirations of education and the liberal arts, is essential. Attacking the problems which we face requires the coordination of our respective energies and capabilities in a massive effort seen only directed toward the attainment of technological objectives. I think we can achieve this closer relationship, this mutual respect, this marriage to give a new birth of creative freedom. If for some unforgivable reason this is not possible, there is still a great deal that can be done within education and within the liberal arts which could help us achieve the kind of society that is congruent with our dreams.

I am encouraged by such projects as the TTT projects which seek to involve the full spectrum of our society in developing an effective educational environment. I am also encouraged by the new models program which the U.S. Office of Education initiated in October, 1967. Ten models have now been developed which seek to bring a greater degree of cooperation in the development and implementation of more effective teacher education programs than has existed in the past.[8] It is such programs, involving as they do the individualization of instruction, the community, behavioral objectives, and decent

---

[6] John A. Crowl, "Carnegie Panel Sets '76 Goal: Equal Access," *Chronicle*, Vol. IV, no. 21 (March 2, 1970), p. 1.

[7] Ibid.

[8] Joel L. Burdin and Kaliopee Lanzillotti, *A Reader's Guide to the Comprehensive Models for Preparing Elementary Teachers* (Washington, D.C.: ERIC and AACTE, December 1969).

planning, which will allow the freedom necessary to cultivate the development of feeling, justice-loving individuals.

I hope that those people with power over the allocation of resources will not overlook the creative potential of the small, developing institution in this task ahead. We so commonly think in terms of bigness that it is unthinkable that a small college such as Jarvis Christian College, in East Texas, could possibly have anything to say or do about a task so awesome. Yet I believe that it is with the help of such institutions when they are properly supported that significant advances in education will take place. They know that they will have to change. They do not have a great deal of vested interest in the status quo. If there are institutions where education and liberal arts are in a hurry to change in order to be more creative, these institutions are among the best candidates.

REV. HENRY J. CASSO

My People Are Crying

If I were going to give a title to what I am about to say, it would probably be "My People Are Crying." I accepted a position on the LTI, TTT advisory because I believed it to be necessary both that one make people aware of the difficult issues of the street and community and also that one work for change. You who come from the various schools represented in this program come from the institutions of higher learning that will probably have the greatest impact on the formation of teachers.

Are you, then, aware that 80 percent of my people drop out before they graduate from high school? They drop out in the first grade, in the second, in the third, all the way to the twelfth. Just last night I had to explain to the leaders of the Mexican-American UMAS's Committee why it is that, after they have raised money sufficient to bring young Mexican-Americans from all around the state, money sufficient to house them and provide them a fine conference, one principal can refuse categorically to allow his children to participate. By the way, that particular principal loses 50 percent of the Mexican-American students that go into his high school. How do I explain to that committee that a counselor refused to get the information out? Our Mexican-American Legal Defense Fund is now meeting with parents in San Diego, trying to initiate a lawsuit demanding $400,000 because of the misplacement of brown and black children in mentally retarded classes. This is what I call the great rape of the mind. You know, each one of these parents, right down the line, both brown and black, says, "We were never told that our children were going to be placed in mentally retarded classes." One parent said that she asked her child's teacher why her child was in that special room; she was told: "Your child is going to be in that room for six years, she's going to be in that same room, and she's going to have the same teacher."

Do you know that when students down at the southern tip of Texas demanded quality education, the kids involved were suspended? We went to the federal court and had the decision of the administrators changed, but do you know what happened to those young men, the leaders of that movement? A senior leader, if he wanted to stay in school, had to get under the desk of the teacher and remain there for the remainder of the class. Another leader who was at home during all of this was arrested because he was supposedly loitering on the school grounds.

Four thousand young men walked out of the schools in Los Angeles. Two years later absolutely nothing had been done, so then they burned the records at one of the schools, and now, a week later, they are burning down the school building. How can I explain all of this to my people? Teachers so glibly say, "This is the land of the free; you're able to get quality education; educational opportunity is for everybody." And yet we see these gruesome things taking place. And so I come to you to make a plea, a plea that each of you who is in a position of responsibility go back to your institution of higher learning, remembering that our people are crying out here.

If one were to judge by the agenda of the Phoenix conference, he would never know that Mexican-Americans constitute the largest minority in this part of the country. If he were to judge by its agenda, he would never know that there are 500,000 Mexican-Americans in Chicago and the Midwest. From its agenda, one would never know that bilingualism is the issue that is molding a coalition of Mexican-Americans and Puerto Ricans—all Spanish-speaking people. Bilingualism is very important to us; yet many teachers who have come from your areas have fought us tooth and nail on the issue of bilingualism. Yet someday, in the not too distant future, this country is going to have to begin to deal with the twenty-six countries to the south and the 260 million people from those twenty-six countries. You know what they're crying? Do you know what the first Mexican-American law student conference resolved? "We will no longer recognize the political division, the territorial division, that divides the United States from Mexico."

These are the words from the lips of our young. How about us? There is a tremendous opportunity in this Phoenix conference; the opportunity is yours. One four-letter word which we have heard frequently at this conference is the word "love," and it is an attribute which we hope can be instilled in the teachers whom you form in the arenas of your institutions of higher learning. More practically, you can contribute to the national concept of bilingualism and biculturalism.

If you do not help, if the present thrust continues, some of the most valuable characteristics we know are going to be destroyed: warmth, trust, respect, devotion, and loyalty.

I sat in on a student world affairs conference at the University of Colorado. I saw there students from your campuses talking about the complete destruction of the system. I had to come to the defense of our people and say, "It is an amazing fact that you're talking about the destruction of the institutions of higher learning, while some of us are dedicated to getting our people into them." The present revolution faces us with a damnable dilemma, and I would suggest that none of our voices are going to be heard for long if we do not put our ear to the ground and hear the thunder of those marching, those running, feet.

My challenge to all of you? Get our students on your campuses; take our educators and bring them to your campuses. Give them the opportunity—as the original design of this conference did not—to expose their minds so that you can know what they're like, so that they can help you be that bridge between Spanish-speaking Americans and the rest of this country. I urge you to do your utmost to make the concept of equal educational opportunity a reality for our young.

LES WHIPP

Rescuing the Perishing

One feature of the conference which remains significant for me is a negative feature, and I want to focus in my remarks exclusively on that feature. In doing so, I am acutely aware that the very nature of the criticism which I must make inherently attests to the significance, and hence success, of the conference. That its failure was *clear* is its significance and its success.

The failure was superficially represented in the very program of the conference: no important black or Chicano from Arizona was originally scheduled, I gather, to be on the program, and no attempt was made to lead the conference participants to get into the minority cultures present in Phoenix. Gross as that lapse came to appear, one misses the point, I think, if one sees this solely as an inadequacy. How many conferences for academicians in liberal arts have paid any attention to the minority cultures near the conference site? And how many have made it obvious that this was an oversight, a gross neglect of fundamental responsibilities? The success of this conference was in discovering and recognizing the fact of the oversight.

One also misses the point, however, if one sees the oversight only in terms of the surface arrangement of the program. It also includes the focus of the subject matter. Implicitly, the focus of the speakers was repeatedly on the relationship of the traditional content of the liberal arts to the needs of the excluded minorities in our culture. For example, one speaker at one point expressed considerable concern about enabling a young black man from the New York ghetto to appreciate Greek drama; his stance was not an unusual stance. It is one which I have taken repeatedly and one which was repeatedly taken at the conference. Let me overstate, and perhaps misrepresent, what was going on here in order to make my point quickly: the liberal arts representative is thinking of himself as possessed of instances of imaginative experience, of the boy as deprived of them; of himself as needing to convey to the boy, of the boy as needing to absorb. We tend to think of the academicians as people who have, and of the minority people we seek to serve as have-nots.

Now with respect to our—the liberal artists'—area of competence (imaginative experience), that position strikes me as boxed in. My professional preparation, my professional experience as a professor of English, must—at least implicitly—have taught me that the imaginative life is indigenous to every culture and subculture, and inescapable in the life of any individual human being. What the young black lacked (it seems likely to me) was not an immensely rich and varied repertory of imaginative experience; he had that. What he lacked was far more simply a body of imaginative experience peculiar to the formally educated subculture, a body of experience which I and most of the humanists who spoke have worked very hard to acquire and one which is to us extremely valuable indeed. That body of experience is scarcely coterminous with the range of all valuable imaginative experience.

What we should have in cases like the one elicited which is relevant to the situation of the young black man may be precisely a series of insights into the nature of imaginative experience which tell us how to come to know and be enriched by the dreams of the young black person's culture; what we should also have is a methodology for dealing with such experience. Possessing these, we could perhaps come to discern, for example, the myth systems by which the subculture of the young black had been formed and educated, we could really help the young black both to discern and to know how to discern the operation of these myth systems. People like me have to get our eyes off those particular instances of the imaginative life which we have spent so much time and effort cultivating. We ought to be able to apply the expertise we have developed for dealing with those instances to instances we have ignored, the instances indigenous to the subcultures we have excluded.

That is to say, at the conference we tended to overlook one of the most significant applications of the professional competence of liberal arts academicians to the problem of social injustice in our culture. We tended to perpetuate the problem by assuming, sometimes rather subtly and sometimes very openly, that ours was the only valuable imaginative life. Concomitantly, we tended to overlook the application of the methodologies of the liberal arts to the culture of the excluded peoples in our country.

I am, for instance, a specialist in Donne; I know very well that in Donne's "A Litanie" and in Vaughan's "Regeneration" one finds a *simultaneous* representation of the history of the growth of the Church and the history of the recreation of an individual soul. What this should suggest to me is something beyond itself: namely, that the imaginative language of subcultures alien to our own is accessible to us only when we have come to see the *system* (or *systems*) of analogies upon which that language is based. As literary critics and scholars, our task, insofar as the theme of the conference is concerned, should be less the teaching of Donne's poems or Vaughan's poems or Greek drama, and more the perception of, and teaching about, the analogizing process which composes our imaginative life, specifically, the analogizing process which informs the imaginative life distinctive to the subcultures of the minorities with which we were concerned at the conference. To conceive of our task as the task of giving *them our* riches is, at best, gross; our job, if we have one, may be to gain insight into their riches, giving them the means, perhaps, of gaining insight into their own riches, as well as the means of gaining insight into ours should they so desire. We have to be prepared to recognize that the great imaginative formulations which we have come to cherish may be of no value to other people. (The "them"-"ours" language is odious to me, too, but surely it is an apt language with which to reflect on the proceedings of the conference.)

This criticism, that in substantive focus as well as in programmatic form the conference successfully bared the deeply felt, deeply internalized ethnocentrism of those of us who are liberal arts academicians, this criticism, it seems to me, implies certain ways of proceeding further. It certainly implies the need for further conferences. It certainly implies that the role of the members in any conference who have grown up as a part of the culture of excluded minorities, having a handle on that culture should be greatly emphasized. It certainly implies that the role of the academician needs to be changed from the role of the preacher to the role of the student.

Further conferences should not feature the luminaries of the liberal arts establishment. They should feature the luminaries of the subcultures which that establishment has excluded. The competencies of these luminaries should include, among other competencies, these three:

First, the competence persuasively to represent the substance of the imaginative life of the peoples in the excluded minorities.

Second, the competence persuasively to represent the shortcomings of the dominant values of the canon of the liberal arts.

Third, the competence persuasively to represent possible applications of liberal arts methodologies to the substance of the imaginative life of the peoples in the excluded minorities.

VI
REFLECTIONS AND RECOMMENDATIONS: *THE JESUIT AND THE TRAPPIST*

Reflections and Recommendations: The Jesuit and the Trappist

The following is a series of excerpts from the eight group discussions and from the letters invited and sent in after the conference. These remarks are divided into four parts: (1) Responsibility and Accountability of the Liberal Arts College in Educating Teachers; (2) The Liberal Arts College's Involvement in the Community and Teacher Education ("Getting Out of the Plastic Tower"); (3) The Possibilities for Changing the University and the Methods Needed to Change It; and (4) Changes in Our National Life and University Change. In accord with the conference's charge to the discussants that they seek suggestions for actions by the liberal arts regarding teacher production, the third section on change is the longest and contains the most detailed statements. For the most part, these suggestions are neither startlingly new nor profound. But lest this be seen as an entirely reprehensible piece of dullness, it should be remarked that the homogeneity of many of the excerpts implies something very like a common direction for discussants as diverse as Anthony Gibbs of the Woodlawn Organization and Henry J. Hermanowicz, Dean of the College of Education, University of Illinois. The reality implied by Don Bigelow's question, Is your campus still intact? is obviously in the background. Perhaps a word was in the whirlwind after all. The quotes are arranged in mosaic to form a picture, or an "argument by design."

I. *Responsibility and Accountability of the Liberal Arts College in Educating Teachers:*

A. *Accountability and Ethnicity*—Robert Cross, President, Swarthmore College. (Letter written after the conference.)

Before we become completely engulfed in the twin streams of college agitation over the extended war and the onset of graduation, let me send you a few words about the TTT conference which I attended in Phoenix. First, let me say that I think the conference was a very considerable success, that I found the wide variety of perspectives offered helpful, even though I am not now immediately involved in a TTT project. I think it was an excellent idea to devote the session to the question of the liberal arts. I think the liberal arts are central to the education of cultivated people, and I think that on the whole they have been badly taught. I think they play a central role in the education of teachers, and indeed of all educated men. Certainly to call something liberal or liberalizing is not necessarily to make it so. And I think that the conference highlighted that problem very adequately indeed. It is perhaps a bit of a luxury to engage in cataloguing the sins of pedantry and professionalization, but I suspect that in our society such meetings are good for the souls of all of us.

I was glad to find the conference coming to a clarification, at least among most of its members, of the distinction between the liberal arts as a liberalizing force and as merely the acquisition of certain techniques that may fall within the purview of liberal arts—for example, higher algebra—which *may* also have specific liberal value. I was also interested that no one at the conference apparently chose to confuse the liberal arts with religion, though they indeed are closely connected. Apparently, that intellectual battle is no longer high on the agenda for most people today.

My sense of the rationale of the conference is this: that almost all teachers will become more teacherly in the best sense if they, at the same time, acquire a deeper sense of the liberal arts. I found Bunnie Smith's talk on craft and technique, while no doubt defensible in itself, unfortunate in emphasis. While I would not turn over all responsibility for training of teachers to liberal arts courses, I would insist all liberal arts courses be taught in the context of the transmission, whether from teacher to student, or from parent to child, or from neighbor to neighbor, of what the liberal tradition consists of. In that sense, the heart of teacher training must be training in the liberal arts.

I did not sympathize with the disposition of some speakers to suggest that the traditional liberal arts amounted to or should be replaced by an emphasis upon love. I am sure that good teaching always does involve extremely close relationships between teacher and taught, but I think that subject matter of importance should be the major term of discourse between the two parties. I had a feeling that some of the people in the conference seemed to think that the opposite of hateful teaching was the teaching of love; this seems to me a false conclusion.

Finally, I would want to say that I abhor the introduction of racial and ethnic power plays into the discussion, though I suppose I recognize them as inevitable in our society. Judging by what I have heard, I have no particular reason to believe that I will learn more about the role of liberal arts in education or teacher training from a conference run exclusively by black Americans or Mexican-Americans than I would from a conference run, as this one was, from the perspective that all people have something to say on these matters. Let me be clear on this last point—that I am not complaining about certain emphases in the conference, only squaring it with my conscience that, although I did not say anything to the contrary while I was there, I would not wish my silence to be construed as intellectual or moral consent to an inverse form of racialism.

B. *On Visiting the Schools and Accountability: The University's Interest* —Group 4.

Early in Chicago's Urban Fellowship Program, fifteen major corporations could not get people from the public schools who were qualified even as beginners. So they felt they wanted to know how their tax dollars were being spent. They sent some executives out to visit the public schools and find out why. Yet *professional educators* don't even feel the *need* to look.

C. *Accountability and Ethnicity*—Milton J. Gold, Dean of Programs in Education, Hunter College TTT.

The second problem that we face is finding ways of working with militant groups in the inner city so that they have a sense of real participation in the design of programs and yet recognize the need for professional expertise. Both the education and liberal arts faculties have little experience in this kind of approach, and we are developing new sensitivity to the attitudes of the minority community. We are doing so, however, with a considerable amount of difficulty and conflict partly because of our inexperience.

D. *On-the-Site Training and Accountability*—Group 8.

Both the academicians and the educationists working in collegiate education programs should have direct responsibility for the training experiences of teacher candidates in on-the-site teacher education centers within communities having culturally diverse pupil populations. Academicians must become responsible for the pedagogical application of knowledge from their disciplines as it is applied in working with children from a variety of ethnic backgrounds.

E. *Accountability and Change: Being on the Spot*—David Willis, Portland State University TTT. (Letter written after the conference.)

Many in the audience, including several of my own people, were turned off a good bit of the time because they were having to struggle too hard in trying to think how one speaker's points were related to the preceding speakers' and how all were related to the processes of educating teachers and children as *the individual knows them*. Therein lies much of our problem in trying to improve communication and cooperation between the liberal arts and educationists, as well as the schools and community.

It is this very thing, if you will permit me, which our project at Portland State is getting at and which appears to be achieving more than a small degree of success. Just yesterday, for instance, the chairman of the mathematics department and two of his henchmen who are to be with him on our TTT team next year, all of a sudden, whoosh, expressed great anxiety that the sanctity of mathematics and of the instructional relationship between student and subject matter might be cut to ribbons in the context we are proposing for them. His apprehensions were deep and honestly expressed. You would have thrilled at the way two English professors, a geographer, a physical scientist, and two education professors turned to him to explain how they too had had such anxieties but had come around to realizing that content could be taught and probably learned better in other settings and by other means of communication than the college classroom. At the close of what had become a very heated discussion, he was willing to consider the possibility that perhaps the orderly sequence normally held so dear by mathematicians might not be inviolable. Anyway, he didn't back out after all, although it was touch and go for a few moments.

My suggestion is that the next step for TTT as a whole, in following up on the Phoenix conference, would be to look hard at instances of cooperative activity and productive communication between liberal arts and education. Portland State, I am suggesting, is worth looking at as just such an example. It might be revealing to study why and how English and education professors are willing to observe and analyze together video-tapes of each other's instruction in regular college classes, to sit down together with a few students to do a similar analysis of instruction by a junior in English education in a ghetto high school or by a junior who has taught a reading lesson in an elementary school. Equally challenging might be the kind of interdisciplinary conversations we have in our seminars when we tear into problems of why disadvantaged kids aren't learning better at both levels.

My point is that the kind of theorizing that went on at Phoenix may be fine as long as your objective is merely to inform and to upset. If you want to change behavior, you'll have to go deeper to a study of particular cases; without that kind of more intensive study, there is little likelihood that there will be any transfer.

F. *Accountability and the Selection of Candidates for Teaching—* Groups 4 and 8.

What about prospective teachers who don't care about kids—who may even hate kids? Who sees that they don't get into classrooms as teachers? The liberal arts don't have knowledge to screen out those students who don't love kids.

Professional educators don't do their job either—they should be out in the field with their teacher candidates, know what those candidates need and be able to give it to them. They ought to be held accountable for that teacher product.

How can both academicians and educationists be made accountable for the knowledge and performance competencies of the prospective teachers they are educating?

We represent hundreds of years of what society wanted and wants us to be: the mantle, the published articles, the Ph.D., etc.—and when we get these, then we know where we are, and we're not going to move.

G. *Responsible Teaching*—Wallace Douglas, Northwestern University.
(Letter written after the conference.)

I thought that the Phoenix conference was generally a satisfactory experience. The main speakers were all very interesting; and I enjoyed listening to them. I did think that they spoke rather too much about the ethos or spirit of the liberal arts and rather too little about teaching techniques. To put it more bluntly, by and large, college professors have a variety of reasons—self-interest, size of enrollment, devotion to discipline—for sticking pretty closely to a lecture system. What they call discussion is always pretty much teacher-directed; that is, the discussion goes on through the teacher: Student A says something, teacher responds, student B comments to the teacher on student A's remarks, and so forth. And this is characteristic of teaching not only in liberal arts but also in education. The result is that students preparing to be teachers carry away a most inadequate model for any kind of teaching except that which involves either transmission of information or inculcation of the values of routine and discipline. The amount of talking to that was done us at Phoenix is symptomatic of the college situation.

I had the feeling at Phoenix that most of the representatives of the disciplines were far more interested in the disciplines than they were in children engaged in the act of learning. This was so at the Grove Park conference, too. Their notion of improving subject matter work in the schools consisted only, so far as I could see, of Bruner's old suggestion of finding the basic principles of the subject, or of finding more adequate logical organizations. Such organizations and principles are always adult in origin, and the problem, even for high school, is to find natural learning situations which will express the child's natural way of living and learning.

H. *Accountability and Liberal Arts Teaching*—D. T. Oviatt, San Fernando Valley State College TTT Director.

We felt, for example, that the academic majors might be classified into some grouping such as Exact Sciences (math, biology, chemistry, physics, etc.), Social Studies (history, political science, geography, anthropology, etc.), Communicative Arts (English, foreign language, speech, etc.), and Esthetics (art, music, drama, etc.). The teaching styles and practice (of liberal arts professors) might then be identified by certain leading characteristics such as lesson presentation, use of illustrative materials, attention to individual learning, patterns of evaluation, cooperative efforts such as team teaching. There are probably a dozen other characteristics that could be identified for some kind of quantitative measurement or rating. An evaluative study might then be devised, working either with student teachers or perhaps, better, with first-year teachers, to find whether there is any commonality in the chief characteristics of teaching that relates in turn to the basic nature of prior academic training.

I. *Responsibility and Accountability: Irresponsible Attacks on the Liberal Arts*—George Harrington, Associate Dean, College of Liberal Arts, Temple University. (Letter written after the conference.)

Different people interpreted TTT in different fashions. One version seemed to be the direct training of teachers as opposed to the teachers of teachers; another seemed to emphasize the training of inner-city teachers. A third version saw TTT as a vehicle to reform liberal arts programs. In connection with the latter it seemed that some of the remarks of the principal speakers were ill-placed, if the intent of the conference was to involve liberal arts departments actively and enthusiastically in this program. I commented after one of the talks, that the title of the conference should be altered to read "The Year of the (Attack on) Liberal Arts." *I know* that within our own college, our departments are very much concerned about teacher preparation and are anxious to participate and cooperate in such programs. We need concrete help and advice, however. Inflammatory rhetoric and ill-founded charges are hardly very constructive. I found, in general, that the remarks of principal speakers were in some cases very entertaining and interesting but not very useful. Small group discussions concentrating on specific problems, and their solutions, and perhaps the exchange of experience between different schools and programs would be extremely useful to all concerned.

Perhaps such a conference does serve a purpose, however, in that we have permitted the rhetoric to be said and we can now feel free to get down to the real job at hand. In terms of follow-up, I would suggest small meetings involving participating individuals from similar types of schools, with, hopefully, the liberal arts people from the various schools having an opportunity to interact and learn from each other's experiences in the program.

J. *Accountability, the Training of Elementary Teachers and How Teaching is Taught*—Jack Soules, Dean, College of Arts and Sciences, Cleveland State University. (Letter written after the conference.)

I note that a liberal arts degree, or even an education degree, is irrelevant for a first grade teacher. *Motherhood* is a far more effective preparation, along with academic preparation in psychology, explicitly in such areas as growth, normal and abnormal behavior, and learning. The entire relevant content of the necessary curriculum takes about two years and is definitely not a liberal education. In fact, since existing baccalaureate degree programs deliberately filter out students on sociocultural criteria, the holder of such a degree is, statistically speaking, likely to be especially unsuited to elementary school teaching.

Secondary school teaching requires the teacher to demonstrate a life-style as well as teaching craft. I believe, therefore, that a B.A. degree has some value for the secondary teacher. It is my strong prejudice, however, based on a wide range of examples drawn from psychological research, industrial experience, and military training programs as well as foreign educational systems, that teaching is a science, a craft, and a skill. Although a liberal education is valuable for its own sake, it is largely irrelevant to the specific responsibilities of the teacher.

I would like to see colleges of education as functionally effective and behaviorally oriented as colleges of business and colleges of engineering. The arts college contributes economics and statistics to the business program, mathematics, physics, and chemistry to the engineering program. The balance of the liberal arts program would be general cultural offerings valuable to all citizens.

II. *Involvement in the Community: Getting Out of the Plastic Tower and Finding a Humane Community.*

A. *The Truth and the History of Communities*—Group 4.

We need to teach the truth about what really has happened and is happening.

B. *The Liberal Arts and the Black Community*—Group 4.

"Outsiders" (such as blacks) find education hollow. When they are crying out for black studies, they are really crying out for sensitivity, honesty, and relevance. In looking at these kinds of needs, the *community* should be heavily involved. Especially they should be involved in a *community college.*

C. *The institutional "Community"*—Group 2.

A comprehensive work-study program in institutional studies could be developed which would bring liberal arts and education students into hospitals, schools, factories, etc. Such a program would teach education students about the nature of institutions and would expose uncommitted students to career possibilities in education and other fields.

D. *Liberal Arts and Community Schools*—Group 8.

What kinds of working relationships can be established between the collegiate academicians and educationists and the community schools which serve as the consumers of the teachers?

E. *Involvement*—Group 4.

There is a great need for real community involvement, not tokenism but real interaction and contribution.

F. *The Liberal Arts, American Communities, and Traditional Documents* —Group 1.

The real purpose of the liberal arts today is to help to interpret the events of the contemporary world, e.g., the Fourteenth Amendment, due process, etc.

G. *Ideology and Multiplicity of Perspectives*—Group 4.

Is there a national ideology of what we'd like to create as a human being? Is there a national theme?

H. *Moving the Community to the Campus*—Group 2.

Since teachers are prepared largely by the liberal arts faculty, faculties in both the liberal arts and teacher education should include people drawn from the community who can provide the university with some notion as to what kind of education the community desires for its children.

I. *The Community as Laboratory*—Group 2.

The community can be used as a general education laboratory for experiences which draw upon liberal arts skills.

J. *Community-Based TTT Projects*—Warren Rasmussen, College Teacher Education Program, San Francisco State College. (Letter written after the conference.)

It would, as a matter of fact, be my impression that liberal arts faculties in our colleges and universities are not going to make any significant changes in what they do and how they do it. Small changes may come about as individual schools pay more attention to hiring dedicated teachers who may also be noted scholars, rather than the reverse. Beyond this, if educators see the need for change in liberal arts instruction, they need to be much more specific in their suggestions than I think they have been so far.

I would recommend consideration of the following:

1. That we establish as our first priority the training of teachers for sensitive communities whose needs are particularly ill-served by the standard product of current teacher education programs—I am thinking of the ghetto, the disadvantaged, the ethnic-bound, the bilingual, etc.
2. That this priority training program be administered jointly by colleges, local school districts, and community boards.
3. That no later than the third year of college, applicants be accepted into the program, and that from that point on their essential educational home base be the community rather than the college.
4. That beginning at least with this third year, the government, the college, and the local community jointly subsidize the student's education and living expenses, where need is demonstrated.
5. That some sort of contractual arrangement be explored which would guarantee the community the educational services of its graduates for at least some minimal period of time—perhaps two years.

Such a proposal as this, "off the top," may not be the right answer, but it does, I think, address itself to the most important problem we presently face.

K. *The Community and the Liberal Arts*—George J. McMahon, Dean, Fordham University. (Letter written after the conference.)

I would like to make a few suggestions:

1. If there is another national meeting held, or if there are regional meetings, it would be advisable for the principal speakers to have met themselves for, say, one day about a month prior to the meeting. With the assistance of your office they could determine what direction each would take in his paper, etc.
2. It would be good, too, if from the beginning all of the speakers tried to zero in on what the liberal arts should do for, or should mean to, someone teaching in the ghetto. To some this may seem narrow and too pragmatic, but its very narrowness may sharpen the vision of what we mean by liberal education. Recently I heard a rather good working definition of liberal education. It is the purpose of liberal education to broaden our concepts

of relevance. You will excuse the use of that detested word, "relevance," but in the present context it takes on meaning. Does, or has, or will liberal arts education so broaden the aspiring teacher that, when he enters the ghetto, he is really human enough to understand and appreciate all its relevancies? This question can be asked whether he himself came from the ghetto or from Park Avenue.
3. For the conference to take the direction described in (2) above, the speakers will have to be people who have an ear for the sounds of the ghetto, as well as people who have listened to the social scientists who can construct its models. What I am probably thinking of here is a black, Puerto Rican or Mexican-American poet or novelist. In changing times it does not suffice to rely even on the more farsighted representatives of the traditional culture; some of the more creative people of the emerging culture should be present.
4. As a liberal arts dean, I would like to hear a teacher, a teacher of teachers, a community person tell us what they think of the liberal arts program, its good points, its bad points, and this in detail. Graduate schools put their pressure on us, and we resist, more or less successfully; let the teaching community put its pressures on us, too. Let us see how we react to a new pressure. I am sure that much of the pressure from the graduate schools has been helpful. The teaching community may do a like service for us.

L. *The Community and Students*—Father Henry J. Casso, Mexican-American Legal Defense and Education Fund. (Letter written after the conference.)

"The Year of the Liberal Arts" conference offered a great hope; the liberal arts in this country train 80 percent of the teachers of the public schools. The conference presented the possibility of meaningfully dealing with the development of teachers who are attuned to the social dynamics and challenges of the seventies. The unwillingness of the conference designers to address themselves meaningfully to the crucial issues—bilingual education, culturally differentiated children, American pluralism (versus the melting pot ideology), the quest for youth, minority identity—was disappointing.

LTI (TTT) is committed to educational change. It could have been expected to address itself not only to the "whyness" but the "howness" of the above questions, especially in view of the fact that this conference took place in a portion of the country where these issues are real. The conference's failure to deal with the questions which I have listed was a signal that, in missing the mark, it would be like many other conferences.

Two components to which LTI is committed were absent. Neither community representatives nor youth were visibly involved. If we can assume that it was the decision of each of the forty-eight projects here represented that the community representatives have so little part in the conference and the youth representatives not be invited, then it would seem either that LTI-TTT ideals are not filtering down to the projects, or that these ideals are not being implemented. The implications of either of these possibilities are serious. The one gentleman who had the courage, after two days, to stand and directly raise the question as to why the arts and sciences were asked to be present at a conference on teacher education—since teacher education is not the liberal arts teacher's concern—is a good indicator that the conference missed its mark. If we wish to maximize the effect of the conference, then a follow-through effort certainly must take place; implementing the motions received from the floor during the last plenary session would be a good beginning.

M. *The "Youth" Community*—Group 4.
What do the young (under thirty) want and need?

N. *Two Proposals for Restructuring Undergraduate Education in Relation to the American Community: The General Education Courses and Teacher Training Courses*—Peter N. Gillingham, Executive Associate, Education and World Affairs. (Letter written after the conference.)

It strikes me that a substantial number of the participants accurately reflected a currently widespread state of mind which seems to say, "Stay me with flagons and comfort me with apples, for I am sick of words." I say this in full knowledge that I and many others were instructed, delighted, and moved deeply by such men as Bill Arrowsmith, Paul Olson, Ben DeMott, Charles DeCarlo, and Tim Healy. Furthermore, I myself am thoroughly grateful for the opportunity to be with such men. But it does strike me that what you may want or need now is not any more analysis, or even the most persuasive and soaring synthesis. Instead, I want to try to sketch briefly some fairly specific things you might go to work on in the program which could challenge and engage both those in the schools of education and those in the disciplines and the liberal arts.

In one way, I am suggesting that there may be an analogy here to Aristotle's remark that happiness is not in itself a fit objective for human activity; that it can only be a byproduct of activity directed at other ends. Similarly, both the preliminary reports sent to me and my experience at the conference would suggest that you may best achieve cooperation among the liberal arts, teacher education, schools and the community not as a primary, stated objective in itself, but as a byproduct of certain types of activity which would engage the interest and the allegiance of your various constituencies. On the assumption that I am directing my attention primarily to the schism between teacher education and the disciplines of the liberal arts, I would suggest that two lines of approach might be tried in the undergraduate education of teachers, one primarily in the earlier years and one primarily in the upperclass years. For now I am skipping the underlying hypotheses and most of the details; these can be filled in if any of this fits in with your own thinking.

One area where the TTT Program could go to work is the no man's land of general education and the high-traffic introductory courses in the disciplines of the early undergraduate years. The criticism, debate, and argument of the last forty years is more than familiar, and primarily relevant to the present discussion only in that, to overstate somewhat, no one really cares except in a negative sense about what goes on in this sector; no one, I should say, in the faculty or administration cares, unless they are in special faculties usually separated both from teacher training and the mainline power structure of the disciplines. One could recognize what the primary intellectual needs are of students at that age—reaching as they do heavily into the emotions, the ideational, the action-related—and helping them to get on with their job. Many students at that age are still very much in the middle of trying to develop a sense of who they are and where they come from, both individually and in terms of social groupings. At the same time, they have a strong orientation toward testing themselves in various forms of action, coupled with an increasing sense of pressure about finding feasible and satisfying role relationships with the world of work and of adult endeavor.

Given these conditions, I think it would be possible to find a few institutions and people in them with whom you could work to produce a two-year curriculum, or program or whatever one would call it, which would not only be right for helping future teachers to begin training themselves for their lives and their jobs, but could well be good enough that other students would want to fight their way in. The central focus would be what might be called case studies by the students of how individuals, groups, and even whole societies are coping wth their environment, or have in the past: how they have succeeded or failed, what are the lessons to be learned. A substantial part of this case study material would be brought back by the students themselves into the academic environment from their own involvement in the outside world, in ecological or civil rights or tutoring or other projects and activities. Other case studies would represent experience of others, more remote in space, or time, or both.

In this context, the basic process would center on the students engaging in something about which they are desperately concerned anyway, namely, increasing their comprehension of themselves and their capacity to understand and operate in the world around them. In a sense, the academic process would be structured to help them to generate their own knowledge by putting their own experience alongside both the vicarious experience of others and the relatively more processed information, ideas, methodologies, and systems we think of as academic knowledge. This would not reduce the role of the faculty; if anything it would increase it, as the students came to draw spontaneously and on their initiative upon the skill, knowledge, and insights of the faculty. Within this setting, furthermore, the students would probably get more, rather than less, vital exposure to the conventional academic disciplines, when their first contact came at a time when they were already wrestling with a large, complex, and real problem and then had the experience of seeing how the training and capabilities of an economist, sociologist, historian, classicist, or whatever were able to help them to carry forward more effectively the work they had already embarked on.

The second point I would propose relates to the upperclass years, with or without a graduate component—the years devoted to teacher training. I have done some work on this and am in touch with what I regard as important work by others; for the moment, however, I want to add my voice to what is already being talked about by others, for instance by James Coleman in a paper he gave at a computer conference at Johns Hopkins in late 1969. The basic idea is that the relationship between man and knowledge has changed to a sufficient degree, and the school has been so greatly supplanted as the primary channel for information or even for structured knowledge in the life of the child, that the actual role in the society of schools and of teachers must change substantially within the next quarter century. In effect, the schools must become places which delegate some of the more mechanical skill-inculculation jobs to other (perhaps new) social institutions in order that they can spend a great deal more time performing a function which was not perceived and very possibly not even needed as little as a generation ago—the function of helping the individual to perceive and determine his information and knowledge needs and to seek to fill them from existing sources, to gather the needed information or data anew where necessary, and in particular to orchestrate or synthesize (in substantial measure by filtering out) the bewildering multiplicity of sources and inputs with which he is deluged but whose basic relevance or usefulness to him he often doubts fundamentally. The argument, in other words, is that the teacher even now should be performing a capstone function in which the student will have someone to whom to turn who has been specifically trained to help him to realize that he can learn to cope with his environment, that the school as viewed traditionally is now only one of a number of significant sources of information, data, knowledge, ideas, and attitudes, and that the school and teacher of the future are prepared to help the student to carry out for himself the analyzing, selecting, evaluating, filtering, and synthesizing functions which will enable him to operate effectively and happily in a society which is increasingly shaped and controlled by patterns of effective access (or nonaccess) to relevant and needed knowledge.

O. *Parity*—David J. Swanger, Associate Director, Harvard TTT Project. (Letter written after the conference.)

This was a somewhat Shakespearean affair. On successive days, a number of academic Hamlets—William Arrowsmith, Benjamin DeMott, Charles DeCarlo—mounted the podium to expound upon the existential dilemma of The Liberal Arts: To be or not to be . . . REAL.

The prescription for the liberal arts is that they ought to be real— what else could be said at a conference entitled "The Year of the

Liberal Arts"? In TTT terms, reality is to be bestowed upon those who engage in the business of training teacher trainers, etc. The conference resounded with loud *mea culpas* from the liberal arts people, in recognition of their previous disregard for the business of training teacher trainers, etc. The educationists were the heroes of the conference, having come to Phoenix's sunshine straight from battles with city school boards, proletarian teachers' colleges, and the like.

It appears that TTT is prone to having years. The year we are now in may be belatedly labeled "The Year of the Community." Next year's "The Year of the Liberal Arts" will presumably produce mandates from Washington, site-visit proddings, and proposal directives, all stressing the need for liberal arts involvement in TTT operations. At worst, the effort is faddish; at best, overambitious. In fact, it is probably unrealistic.

Was there any substance to the conference? No. Concrete proposals for engaging liberal arts faculties in the TTT endeavor were sorely lacking from both speeches and small group discussions. In fact, there was only one scheduled opportunity for participation by the delegates, and that flopped. At the end of an aimless hour-and-a-half discussion in my group, a California schoolteacher rose to say that we had failed, and that we were not addressing ourselves to her concerns. The response mustered by our "chairman" was, "You're from the public schools? I didn't know teachers were invited to this conference."

Despite its awesome inconsequentiality, the conference did bring a major TTT problem into some focus for me. The problem is TTT's all-important parity. Created as the rock upon which TTT should rest, parity is more likely to be the shoal upon which it will founder. The concept of parity is rife with internal contradiction—it requires equal partnership, yet insofar as TTT gives money to only one party of the parity relationship (and then only on the basis of an already formed idea), partnership cannot be equal. Another paper would be required to deal with the problem of parity fully; but *apropos* of "The Year of the Liberal Arts," it is clear to me that the TTT mandate makes awkward suitors of schools of education, pushing them towards the creaky door of the liberal arts with only the crassest of bouquets (The Grant) in hand.

Prescriptive suggestions? I think most in order would be a series of colloquies on parity.

III. *Change—How?*

A. *Cooperation vs. Competition*—Group 2.

Most of the conference participants were advocates of cooperative principles, *even if they did not necessarily know how to achieve cooperation*.

B. *Professionalism*—Group 1.

Much of the problem is that of PROFESSIONALISM. Moving the whole *department* is the challenge.

C. *Change in the Young*—Group 1.

The young are aware of the mindlessness of much of our present society and are developing their own coalition.

D. *Experimental Institutions*—Group 2.

Federal funding should be made available to encourage the creation of new models of experimental institutions-within-institutions.

E. *Community and Liberal Arts Change*—Group 1.

Those TTT projects which do not take community needs and wishes into account should not be funded. The potential of the community, its power for demanding change, is great.

F. *Psychological Change*—Group 4.

To what extent do we as professional educators shape the teacher and to what extent do we allow the teacher to shape himself?

G. *The Demands of the Individual Psyche and the Demands of Program*— Group 7.

Programmatic attempts to emancipate and vitalize the preparation of teachers should neither ignore the requirements of a free manhood nor diminish the role of disciplined learning.

H. *Feedback and Change*—Group 4.

Teacher candidates don't get into schools early enough to come back to, say, the English department and let them know what teacher candidates really need for teaching children.

I. *Student Power and Change*—Group 4.

Maybe we will have to rely on the students. One professor stated that the movement in his college toward developing a department of ethnic studies came from students' expression of their needs. The students wanted a curriculum more relevant to their interests and banded together in a show of power to get, for example, black studies.

J. *Student Power and a Proposal for a Shopping Center Education—*
J. N. Hook, University of Illinois TTT. (Letter written after the conference.)

The issue of relevance was raised repeatedly. I enclose some thoughts on that subject that I hope are relevant.

On *Schools as Shopping Centers:* Given the much publicized proliferation of human knowledge—said to double every ten years or less—the once valued ideal of the universal man who is acquainted with every realm of human thought and endeavor is even less attainable than it was in the age of Francis Bacon. In a society infinitely more complex than any previous one in human history, it is not only impossible to approach omniscience but is increasingly difficult to understand one's own relationship to the rest of the world and its three billion diverse human beings.

But some grasp of this relationship, even a superficial one, is essential in the eternal search for one's own identity. Much of the chaos of our time, much of the student unrest, is attributable to the fact that so many questions of identity and of one's relationship to the whole are unanswered. We hear over and over, in various phrasings, How do I fit in? How can I understand what is going on? How can I help to make changes in the things that seem to me to be wrong?

Early academic specialization clearly does not provide the answers; too early narrowness decreases the possibility of understanding an infinitely complicated society. Nor does the too frequent stress on trivia provide the answers (dates in history, the sometimes empty laboratory exercises, the memorization of the characteristics of six kinds of sonnets).

What may help educators and students in the mutual quest is a view of education—in the elementary schools, the secondary schools, and even in much of the work done in our colleges—as analogous with a huge shopping center. Just as a shopping center has grocery stores, hardware stores, drug stores, restaurants, etc., so the educational shopping center has "stores" devoted to the various sciences, to the manual and fine arts, to the humanities. And like the usual shopping center, it has its highly specialized shops, devoted to such things as sociolinguistics or endocrinology.

The first twelve, maybe the first fourteen or fifteen, years of education should be regarded as an extended trip through the shopping center. The tourists find out what is available in the various stores, though at this time they do little more than glance into the speciality shops. Not all the stores will be equally appealing to all students, and they should not be penalized because this is so. (Don't flunk a kid in music because he is tone deaf, or in physical education because he can't high-jump four feet, or in English because he is more hand-minded than poetry-minded.) Education is mainly exploration, but in its early stages it should be far-ranging exploration —like a helicopter flight across terrain rather than a painful on-foot penetration of a rain forest. Show students as much of the shopping-center world as can be shown them. Let them land occasionally at places that especially interest them and poke around to see in more detail what is there; let them revisit some of the places when they wish. But keep them moving—for a long time. Don't rush decisions about the store or stores where the student will want to shop and work for the rest of his life. Let him see the range of choices. What goes on in each store? Why? How are the stores run? Why? What might be better ways to run them? How interested am I in this one, in that one? Which stores need help that I would like to try to offer?

Humanists can be more useful as tour directors than they have been. They are—or are supposed to be—liberal, liberated, humane, broad-minded, farseeing. They are not the only tour directors, of course, but because of their breadth, they can be among the best.

In a shopping center, products change now and then. Some become outmoded. Some have appeal only to a limited few and are stuck away in a drawer to be brought out only on specific request. Some are dispensed with because they didn't belong in the first place.

Our educational shopping center should also change its products as times change. This is the answer to the cry for "relevance." The outmoded, the useless, should be cast out. The still useful but seldom called-for should be available somewhere in a drawer but not pushed at everybody.

The concept of the shopping center will not produce universal men, but it will make possible a better understanding of the world and a better opportunity to find one's own role in it. And no less important, it will have an effect on what is sold. It will make for greater freedom of choice and more intelligent choice. It will help young people to answer more of the questions that they insistently ask and to which they now get too few answers that satisfy them.

K. *Student-Faculty Intellectual Community*—Group 4.
Would interdisciplinary faculty-student seminars help?

L. *A Faculty-School System Community:*
1. If the college professor *could actually go out into the schools,* he *could learn* that way. (Group 4)
2. The best specific I heard was the idea that *every* liberal arts faculty member in a department which prepares some teachers should observe teaching in a high school *at least once* each year. (Donald E. Sikkink, Dean of the School of Arts and Sciences, Saint Cloud State College)

M. How the Liberal Arts College Can Contribute: Teachers and Mechanisms—Richard E. Sullivan, Dean, College of Letters and Science, Michigan State University. (Letter written after the Conference.)

First of all, let me say that I profited greatly from the conference. Although I have long been associated with a liberal arts discipline, I have only recently become aware of the essential neglect of teacher education in the liberal arts. The conference reinforced this awareness and identified more sharply the nature of the neglect. What impressed me most was the remoteness of the liberal arts teacher from the realities of the public school scene. The structure of the conference sessions, juxtaposing the liberal arts spokesmen with public school people and community leaders, was especially effective in revealing the gap between the two worlds. I have returned to my campus determined to try to replicate this confrontation in hopes that such an experience would have a comparable effect on the teaching faculty in my college.

I was especially moved by the presentations of Professors DeMott, Olson, and DeCarlo; these particular speakers impressed on me how vital it is to see to it that particular faculty members with unique insights and understandings be given the key roles in teacher training. I came away from the conference convinced that not all liberal arts professors are suited for the teacher-training role. Perhaps some exploration of this proposition might be worthwhile as the TTT project matures. I would hope that one follow-up of the Phoenix conference would be a continued search for the specific contributions that liberal arts disciplines could and should make to a teacher-training program.

The conference fortified a conviction I previously held that, in any local setting, it is vital to initiate some kind of mechanism that will bring about interaction among representatives of the traditional disciplines on the issue of liberal arts in teacher education. This step is necessary to overcome the narrowness of the traditional disciplines and to get representatives of these disciplines to see that the weaknesses of the individual liberal arts disciplines nourish each other in terms of the problems involved in teacher training. Perhaps some exchange of ideas on this problem would be fruitful in the future.

I would like to see those interested in TTT and the liberal arts try to face the problems of teacher education beyond the terms of disadvantaged segments of society. I do not mean to belittle the desperate importance of this issue, but it seems to me to obfuscate the real issue of what can be done to elicit the essence of the liberal arts as an aspect of teacher training. What I am suggesting is that the liberal arts aspect of teacher education probably transcends this particular social problem.

Finally, what I heard at the Phoenix conference persuaded me that a vital task at hand is that of subjecting those members of university and college liberal arts faculties who are actually involved as teachers of future teachers in specific disciplines to the experience of facing the criticisms of their activities. Teaching historians and artists and economists need to face the realities their products have to meet. More of them should be at conferences, perhaps in place of deans, who can exhort but who cannot do much. Perhaps future planners should think in terms of getting groups from key disciplines in teacher training together for discussion. It is a little too easy to speak of liberal arts in general when much of the problem is really locked in the narrow confines of the particular disciplines.

N. *Change to Make the Liberal Arts Useful to Elementary Teachers—*
   Group 2.

Within the liberal arts faculty, special sections of general courses could be provided offering particular emphasis upon educational aspects of the subject; for instance, a section of chemistry for elementary school teachers. No students need be excluded from such a section, but elementary school teachers could be informed that it would be particularly suited to their needs.

O. *Change to Make the Liberal Arts Useful to Individual Students—*
   Anon.

I have a strong personal feeling about certification requirements, both in the major and in professional education. I continue to puzzle over why we insist on certain exact, specific courses at the same time that we discuss the wide range of individual abilities of our students? Couldn't each student's program be individually designed by his department?

P. *Corporate Competition and Change*—Group 4.

There is an embryonic movement among large corporations to establish their own schools to train the children of employees, because the colleges are not preparing their students the way the corporations feel they should. The administration could shift released war funds to the industrial education effort; if this happens, then the liberal arts won't have to worry about humanizing itself. Large industries are having to take dropouts and train them themselves because the schools did not do the job.

Q. *Change in Student Power*—Group 4.

Should students be given all power and responsibility?

R. *Some Specific Methodisms for Changing the Liberal Arts Input in TTT Projects*—William Hazard, Northwestern University TTT Project (Letter written after the conference.)

Now to the hard part—next steps:

1. At the earliest possible date, get the conference proceedings printed and distributed, and ask each Project Director to turn whatever screws he can to see that the proceedings are read.

2. Give a mandate to the cluster directors[1] as to their responsibility to engineer follow-up discussions, mini-conferences, newsletter material, and similar intracluster pushes; I would assume that normally perceptive cluster directors would catch the hint and deliberately focus on the liberal arts in the next round of cluster meetings this fall.

3. Encourage (in whatever way possible) renewed interest in project-level rapprochement among the parity elements. We have lived, breathed, and to some extent died "community" this year. Perhaps a parallel commitment to the liberal arts is in order. I think judicious pressure at the cluster and/or project level might extract specific evidence of specific commitments, contributions, hang-ups, et cetera, of the liberal arts in the current projects.

I guess I see some monumental problems in producing concrete

[1] The TTT is divided into a series of regional clusters composed of projects from the region. These projects, in turn, give training to each other.

results from this liberal arts focus, but I also see that the benefit to teacher education would be equally monumental, if we can pull off the marriage.

S. *No Grand Strategy*—T. H. Whitehead, Dean of the Graduate School, University of Georgia.

Bringing the liberal arts people and educationists together has taken many years of work here. It has been done by small groups which I had some hand in forming. In my opinion, no grand strategy will work. It is a local matter on each campus which requires a sympathetic administration and the mutual respect of individual faculty members.

T. *AACTE-CONPASS Campus Discussions*—Ed Pomeroy, Executive Director, AACTE. (Letter written after the conference.)

My comments will not be specific, but rather will suggest a focus for action. Each college and university which prepares teachers could become the scene for discussions between liberal artists and educationists. My point is that in Phoenix we heard a lot from others, but had too little opportunity, in the short time available for the conference, to talk with one another. I can envision a national dialogue going on at many campuses based on some of the insights provided by the Phoenix meeting. Perhaps TTT, the AACTE, and the organizations represented in CONPASS could stimulate such discussions.

U. *Model Programs.*

1. *Varying the Time of Entrance:* It could be beneficial to loosen the distinction between education students and liberal arts students. One way of doing this would be to establish multiple model programs within the same institution which would permit some students to enter the field of education as early as the freshman year, others as late as senior year. (Group 2)

2. *Students as Teachers:* Undergraduates in the liberal arts and teacher education should be given increased opportunities to teach one another. (Group 2)

3. *Students Teaching Teachers to Teach:* They [the staff of a specific experimental program] go out and select people from liberal arts and from the community, etc., to work with disadvantaged kids— of 120 participants, they have had only 3 dropouts in three years. The students elect courses in the traditional major and minor programs

with tutorials in such areas as language and other "bridge" courses. The staff translates the program back to the community. A math professor in the program was about to give up when one of the students told him how he thought he could learn. "If I had me," he said, "this is the way I would teach me." (Group 4)

4. *New Models:* I believe that an absolutely essential next step would be to assemble some people to develop an array of models of liberal arts establishments, with each such model being designed to achieve the major objectives spelled out at the conference. Those of us who are in the liberal arts establishment need sets of very specific models indicating how we might proceed. I do believe that liberal arts administrators are very much susceptible to change, but we do need help from the educational community. (Howard J. Pincus, Dean of the College of Letters and Sciences, University of Wisconsin. Letter written after the conference.)

5. *Some Alternative Models:* Prospective teachers can be given greater exposure to the liberal arts only by:

a. Enrolling them in the existing highly professionalized courses which have the preparation of restricted specialists as their goal (and this has not been proven satisfactory), or

b. Providing other availabilities for instruction.

If we conclude that (b) above is the necessary alternative, how could we install such availabilities? Here are some possibilities.

i. A center or an institute for liberal studies, independent of colleges and departments, which could serve the interests of those who do not have exclusively professional goals in humane and social curricula. For example, here at the University of Miami such a center could serve degree candidates in our schools of education, music, engineering, and nursing. I should note, however, that such a center would have to be funded in a way that would avoid direct conflict in budget expense with traditional departments, and provisions would have to exist for the recruiting of faculty and the assignment of rank to those not necessarily accepted by departmental faculties.

ii. A school of education could develop departments of humane studies within its own curriculum.[2] A department of humanities or a department of social studies in a school of education would hardly seem inappropriate.

[2] This was a feature of the early twentieth-century "Bagley Plan." (Ed. note.)

iii. Qualified instructors with excellent credentials could be recruited to teach courses without the formality of structured departments. (All of these possibilities impose inevitable difficulties in recruiting—this latter procedure would likely be least attractive to prospective instructors.)

If HEW and the TTT Program are concerned with these problems as being important, if not vital, perhaps some exploration of these and other unconventional routes to study in the liberal arts for teachers could be sponsored with an appraisal of feasibility and the development of actual plans and guidelines for possible installations. (Robert W. Hively, Honors Studies, University of Miami. Letter written after the conference.)

V. *Joint Appointments*

1. *Arts and Sciences Colleges and Education Colleges:* Mechanisms should be established within universities for bringing together liberal arts and teacher-education faculties. Joint appointments and changes in the reward system are two examples of such mechanisms. (Group 2)

2. *Joint Appointments and Other Ways of Getting Work Out of a Liberal Arts School:* A school of education is a finite entity with limited options, but assuming good intentions and common sense, the following are feasible approaches: (a) joint appointments, (b) liberal arts professors on appointment in the school of education, (c) the assignment of course requirements outside of the school of education, (d) a policy of hiring school of education faculty who have a strong subject-matter background and who have full rank and tenure.

Let us consider these in reverse order. A dean of a large faculty in education could assure subject-matter input by locating people who are in teacher education but who have taught and published in English, philosophy, history, math, biology, music, etc. This is wholly possible and indeed some of the strongest people may be such hybrids. We, the educators, help to cause our problem by our narrow conceptions of what a person's preparation ought to be. To find such persons will require hard work and persistence, but they exist. In the foundations field this is done now, of course, and also in several curriculum and instruction departments around the country. That is the best and most practical way to handle the matter. It avoids interschool strife; it relieves the dean of the burden of receiving a "reject" and it avoids the "borrowing" idea.

Another simple strategy is to require course work in the arts and sciences by the education degree candidates. The courses could be double-listed, in education and in arts and sciences. No problem, and a strong dean of faculties or vice-president for academic affairs will assure that those persons listed to teach education majors will be not only sympathetic but enthusiastic about such service. This does not involve joint appointment, and avoids the recruiting and promotion problems associated with it.

The next alternative is even more appealing; simply keep looking until a first-rate person appears who is secure enough in his field and concerned enough about teachers to accept a full appointment in the school of education. The problem with this is that there may not be enough such people available and the first two alternatives may become the most productive ones.

The joint-appointment approach has merit above all. A person has full faculty status in a department in the school of education and in his subject field. But problems of promotion arise. Where does one work for upward mobility? It appears that the only way to accomplish this is to deal in senior people who are already at the top of the ladder and who can afford to share their talents wherever they are most needed.

Perhaps this is as it should be. A professor of history, for example, in his mid-forties, who has been a first-rate teacher, is tapped and honored by the school of education with a full professorship in his field in order to help reproduce his kind. This forces the education school to deal only in the best and saves it from becoming an out for unsuccessful teachers.

The feeling at the table was that joint appointments were denigrating and threatening to the appointees. This seems to us to be more of a judgment against the schools of education than against the candidates. The solution to this problem may be the solution to the deeper problem, namely, the total image and posture of the school of education. It may be that a half-dozen or so liberal arts people are urgently needed to save the education program from its own faltering intellectual thrust.

No one approach is a panacea, but where there is genuine interest in keeping graduate students in touch with the meat of their teaching fields, one of the above approaches should serve well to meet the need.

Nothing is solved by merely getting Ph.D.s to accept school of education appointments. And it is not enough to devise a scheme.

More is needed. There must be commitment on the part of the administration to have quality teacher education. This will be reflected in the leadership of the administration, the people it attracts to deanships, etc. With that commitment, half the battle is over and any one of a dozen schemes will do. (Group 5)

W. *Other Voices*

1. As in so many educational conferences today, there was much talk here of community and trust and love but to me it all seemed rather aggressively stated. One suspected that it would go rather hard with sinners who couldn't meet the test, that is, those who might choose to state the case for community, trust, and love in somewhat different terms from those of the speakers. (Mortimer Smith, Group 6)

2. In a time when emotion runs high in the country and every public issue is drenched in feeling, we need desperately to apply rational thought to our problems. The poor old liberal arts could help if we gave them a chance. They were not given much of a chance at this conference. (Anon.)

IV. *Changes in Our National Life and University Change*

A. *Cambodia and the Conference*—William Drummond, Associate for Teacher Education, State of Washington. (Letter written after the conference.)

Bill Arrowsmith's opening lecture set the tone and Father Healy's response clinched it so that I no longer dealt with the grubby mechanics of teacher education during the remainder of the conference. President Nixon's decision to go into Cambodia frankly threw me into a psychological depression, and I was angry with the conference and with my colleagues for not changing the conference theme and dealing with that issue. I felt as most of the liberal college students in the nation must have been feeling, "How can we stop all this foolishness, how can we change the course of our national life?" But the next set of speakers came on and I found that they were kindred souls interested in deeper issues; I thought Bernie Watson's response to Charles DeCarlo was magnificent.

The highlight of the conference, of course, was a philosophical conflict which developed during the Saturday morning panel. Arrowsmith hit hard at the elitism of higher education and the basic reformation that's required; I left the conference intellectually refreshed primarily because it gave me a new strategy for work in my state. I am more convinced than ever that the only way we can get over the conflict or the rhetoric of our times is to begin to think about larger issues—issues which give meaning to the flow of life in the sense of "oneness with nature."

B. *Trying to Get People to Talk to Each Other in the Midst of a National Crisis*—Thomas D. Vogt. (Letter written after the conference concerning the last hours of the conference.)

The question was whether lifetime habits could be broken by a conference. And if you had to answer at eight o'clock Saturday morning during an outdoor breakfast for two hundred, you would probably say No. "Hayakawa may not be here in person," said one man who had also just said No himself and now blinked away the glare of the sun on the long, white tablecloth, "which may be all right. We've enough controversy here without him, I guess. But we could certainly use his Abstraction Ladder. Or was it Korzybski's? Anyway, I'd make a display of it, whoever it belongs to. Set it up right over there by the pool, and have everybody sign the particular rung he wants to be on, by the day or hour. That's why we don't know that we're talking about. We're on too many different levels. All unacknowledged."

Under that already hot, blindingly clear Arizona sky, unless you shaded the paper with your head, you couldn't make out much of the morning news, about the trouble in New Haven and the decision on Cambodia. Silverware and glasses flashed like mirrors. Somebody said the sun was even more dazzling over there in Scottsdale, a few miles away, where, "like Andy Warhol says, it costs more."

Overhead, the Ramada Inn's marquee still held WELCOME TTT on the side facing downtown Phoenix. Other greetings were given lower billing. CREATIN' WITH COTTON. KEN-RAD. The sign's second side was blank, unlettered. But it faced a barrio, a mile away, where 17 percent of all Phoenicians (as the paper called its citizens) graduated only 20 percent of their kids from high school, and had only 2 percent of those who go on to college.

In one more hour the last plenary session was to collect the main questions generated by these three days. They were to be fielded by the principal speakers and respondents. But if the skeptic by the pool was right, the cross-purposes so widely felt were not only a product of the particular occupational mix of these two hundred ("Are there any purists here, the people we're really trying to hit?"). To reduce semantic fatalities, before it was too late, perhaps that Abstraction Ladder could have been dragged into the Colonial Room as well, right in front of those television lights which were forcing speakers to shade their eyes and the audience to retreat to the walls. (Beyond that, replicas might have come in handy in the eclectically named smaller rooms—Wistaria, Rodeo, Walnut—where eleven discussion groups of about twenty each, "seeded for personalities to set off fires," had organized these very questions now about to be presented.)

"At the top abstraction level we could put something like 'Liberal Arts: The Humane Tradition.' Okay? The way we think the Greeks and Romans saw them, and so forth.

"Then we could put . . . (take out a few notches, so that everybody can plainly see we're going down) . . . we could put 'Liberal Arts: The Contemporary Custodians.' Custodians of this *long, humane tradition*. Or instead of 'tradition,' we could speak of the humane *habit of mind*, or the *accumulation* of humane wisdom, or whatever we have said it is. In any case, that and today's professional heirs.

"Below that, after another nice and visible gap, we could put 'Liberal Arts: How the Tradition, in the Hands of the Heirs, Can Be, Has Been, Should Be, Applied to the American School System.' I admit, we can get into a dozen fights at every step. And it's my guess that the going will get tougher the further down we drop. But that's all right. This way we should still have a much better chance of knowing what we're getting so mad and tired about."

First, what? Second, who? And third, how? Collecting the sweep of reactions, in all those discussion groups, and in that final question-and-answer session, under those three headings, reveals a vast mosaic of attitudes, resentments, and hopes which needs distance to show much pattern. But as a certain stamp, a repeated impress, occurs and recurs, you finally feel that on this bright and early Saturday morning *No* came too quick.

. . . .

In that Saturday morning breakfast discussion, the definitions kept stretching for what qualified: to Chief Seattle's speech ("How could a man use words like that, without any formal training?"), to Oedipus ("tearing out his eyes, when another organ is at fault"). The conference people reached for some general, distilled impulse. And they also tried to be specific. What of the liberal arts in that English class, where the black girls became worried about losing so many of their athlete boyfriends to the white girls? Was a quick card-flip through the brain for the apt classical source in order? Or the creative story session? With the supplied topic, Eldridge Cleaver's son and George Wallace's daughter. A suicide pact. Like Romeo and Juliet.

"There are subjects that don't lend themselves to helping the feelings of those girls. Teaching solid geometry, I wouldn't know how to fit that in."

There was also division over whether that impulse, as it was historically understood, inevitably carried a pyramidal form, always resting on a broad base of nonparticipants.

. . . .

Who were these people in the liberal arts departments that were being talked about at breakfast? Why for the last fifty years had they relinquished their interest in and responsibility for teacher education? Were they honorable men who had performed functions unappreciated by those who confronted them with blame now? Did they have to be approached differently, then, with far more respect than was being shown? DeMott was to say, "You can't deal with them as though shame should be their response. You have to speak toward their sense of honor. You have to enter their point of view before you can change it." By this light these men had behind them a long history of protest, by personal example, against the cash nexus of American society, in behalf of an extreme commitment to personal integrity. They thus kept values alive tangentially. They had an egalitarian vision. Yes, even from the depths of their faculty clubs. Their removal from society, therefore, proved constructive, just as today it does not. Just as today it proves destructive.

But rudeness toward them, or the injustice of not recognizing their past achievements, could not produce the necessary change. They could not be moved by those who themselves were oblivious. They had to be allowed to reclaim their personal probity. So ran one version, quickly countered by another.

"It's not personal probity put to any use," the thought ran. "Oh, maybe they once kept the American Legion from firing John King Fairbank. Who knows?"

By this view, no institution could be seen changing from within, without confrontation, or at least without the external leverage of independent funding. The whole curricular moss had to be ripped off. The culture had to be deacademicized. In the only Western industrial society that was charging tuition, a vast natural resource was going to waste, which could not be afforded.

Sure, you could have Trappists ("somebody has to do our dreaming"), along with your Jesuits ("traipsing all over northern Europe fighting Lutherans"). But every nickel a university now takes in was also keeping somebody else out. And so the whole gentlemanly preserve had to be opened up. It could not remain so tame. It had to be scared by facts. There was a pervasive personal mindlessness which the liberal arts professor would lapse into so long as there was no larger purpose in his life. "Hold a man responsible so that he'll hold himself responsible." "What we've lost is the redemptive insight."

. . . .

Before breakfast other people had spoken, "The honest topic of this conference is, 'How Can the Liberal Arts Be Applied to the Disadvantaged Communities without Ever Having to Have Them Represented?'"

"We're trying to equalize educational opportunity. To defy sociological predictions."

. . . .

In the midst of Cambodia, of the sun-oppressed breakfasts, the talk, three Hows emerged. *One* method would be to work to modify existing institutions and structures, suspending trial bridges between different bastions of the present educational fortress—the departments. A second would be to set up experiments entirely outside this establishment, whose specific genius was seen to be the defeat, by attack, by agreement, by delay, or by erosion, of any of these attempts which showed signs of life. And a third would be to seek a deep ethical change, a revolution in priorities involving the whole of society's first principles.

Intrasystem changes that could be pointed to were admittedly small, but some did make waves. They often depended on just one man. He was usually a very secure man. He could afford a joint appointment. He could afford to ignore the reward system, most of the time because he had already been rewarded. He could persuade, by his own example, others temporarily to buck the reward system with him. When he died, or left, or tired, his innovations usually followed the same course. A few had become institutionalized. The new College for Educational Development and Change, at new Northern Colorado University (old Colorado State, at Greeley). The Faculty of University Studies, at West Virginia. Similar efforts at Utah, at Chicago. The model at Georgia. The 353 separate groups at Berkeley—scholars from various fields coming together for specific functions, specifically funded, free to select personnel. None were broad-scale assaults. There was also some confusion between which were interdisciplinary and which were merely problem-oriented. But there was usually some agreement to adopt their successes, even if so far departmental funding in excess of 5 percent was a rarity.

All these were attempts to make out of the strictly research-fixated graduate schools, on the one hand (liberal arts professors producing liberal arts professors), and the similar trade-union oriented schools of education, on the other, some recycling agency serving today's teacher-training needs. The repeated caveat stressed how the model had to stay small, and the structure temporary, so that the effect would be definitive and observable. ("We got five years behind in urban education at our university, simply because we went at it too big, by opening all our doors to everybody, for just two days, believe it or not.")

. . . .

If bedrock had now been reached, and Hayakawa's ladder descended, there thus had been a main effort in that descent: a plea for the end of scholarly isolation, perhaps to save that scholarship itself. In this projection of reordered disciplines and disciplinarians, the colleges of liberal arts would act less like a national wall, and more like a national membrane—organic, animate, living, breathing. They would certainly define a form. But it would be thin and pliable, designed to connect, not separate.

The conceptual difference as to how things are changed is contained in two final reactions, from outside this present cultural compound. One comes angrily. And if that authority is right which holds that confrontation is the only route to change, this temper may be its main characteristic: "Don't play me no more of that Trickle Down Rock, man. I've heard it till I'm sick."

Another comes softly, beseeching these men here, and others like them, to be true to their best. "I think, I think that we should not give up knowledge at all. I mean, this is my personal point. . . . Your knowledge, the high professions that you have. I do not want for one minute for you to give up anything. All we want, or I am asking, is that you give us . . . the ones who can't reach you. You come to reach us. Because a lot of us don't know how to come to you."

VII
A BIBLIOGRAPHY:
RAPPING ABOUT THE UNIVERSITY

PETER BROOKS

Rapping about the University

Books about the university are beginning to constitute a new publishing subgenre. The psychology of crisis that reigns in higher education today has spawned analyses of the university's traumas, its relation to student activism, its place in American society, its possibilities for reform and survival. I call them a new subgenre because they are not traditional books about education, but rather urgent analytical confrontations with the institutions of higher learning at a specific historical juncture, and most of them are the work of university men, professors and presidents. Indeed, many of them are limited by an institutional perspective, by a mental set derived from the forms and structures, the implicit assumptions and rationale generated within the university establishment over the years. Many of them can foresee only tinkering with the existing machinery; it is the rare book that breaks through to a radical reassessment and proposal.

In the ranks of those whose analysis is situated well within current practice I would put first of all Clark Kerr's *The Uses of the University*,[1] a crucial statement which deserves considerable attention. In this class, too, would go James A. Perkins's *The University in Transition*,[2] which is essentially descriptive of the style of a "progressive" administrator involved in the process and without much critical perspective on it. Also, Christopher Jencks and David Riesman's

[1] Cambridge: Harvard University Press, 1964.
[2] Princeton: Princeton University Press, 1964.

massive *The Academic Revolution*,³ which is an unequaled source of information, and which does find fault with many current practices, but nonetheless, no doubt because of its sociological perspective, asks few radical questions about the status quo. On the other hand, there are some real dissenters, who from varying perspectives find the status quo radically corrupt: Jacques Barzun, whose *The American University*⁴ is an eloquent if perverse argument for return to a lost purity; Harold Taylor, who in *Students without Teachers: The Crisis in the University*,⁵ has written an extensive critique of current assumptions and a passionate argument for experimental reform; and, most lucid and valuable to my mind, Robert Paul Wolff, author of *The Ideal of the University*,⁶ a book to which I shall frequently return.

Such a line-up is of course unfair, and, more important, it doesn't cover the range of books that should be read by anyone interested in current thinking on the university within the university. For instance, Charles Frankel's *Education and the Barricades*⁷ is a reasoned, modest, and useful analysis of current problems in student power, "relevance," and the restructuring of universities. James B. Conant's autobiography, *My Several Lives*,⁸ provides insights into the transformation of modern Harvard and, in part because of the book's rather bland manner, raises all sorts of unanswered questions about the rationale of this transformation. *Confrontation*,⁹ the Daniel Bell-Irving Kristol volume of essays in response to the Columbia crisis, contains some acute pages by very establishment sociologists, especially in the article by Talcott Parsons. Bell's earlier book, *The Reforming of General Education*,¹⁰ is brilliant and cogent, and I shall come back to it. Some valuable pedagogical techniques can be learned from Joseph J. Schwab's *College Curriculum and Student Protest*.¹¹ One can even glean an occasional idea from Sidney Hook's apoplectic outburst, *Academic Freedom and Academic Anarchy*,¹² which declares total war on the "Movement." The list could be

³ Garden City, N.Y.: Doubleday, 1968.
⁴ New York: Harper & Row, 1968.
⁵ New York: McGraw-Hill, 1969.
⁶ Boston: Beacon Press, 1969.
⁷ New York: Norton, 1968.
⁸ New York: Harper & Row, 1970.
⁹ New York: Basic Books, 1969.
¹⁰ Anchor Books edition, Garden City, N.Y., 1968.
¹¹ Chicago: University of Chicago Press, 1969.
¹² New York: Cowles, 1970.

continued. But with these works we have, I think, enough material to ask some questions about the kinds of thinking on the university presently being carried out in the university.

The most useful of these books are those which are most conscious of their allegiance to an ideal or type of the university, which lay out most clearly the model to which they refer. In this perspective, the wide influence of Clark Kerr's *The Uses of the University* is not hard to understand: Kerr's famous concept of the "multiversity" is a clear delineation of one possible model of the university, a model that has gained wide acceptance and suggests the future orientation of much of American higher education. Kerr's project is ostensibly descriptive, an analysis of the forces at play in the diversified modern university, but it is at least implicitly celebratory as well: the multiversity is the highest expression of American aspirations at the present time, and attention must be directed to furthering and easing its work.

A basic assumption of Kerr's argument is that the American university has in the past—and must in the future—take its shape from the pressures of the whole of American society. "It is interesting," he comments, "that American universities, which pride themselves on their autonomy, should have taken their special character as much or more from the pressures of their environment as from their own inner desires."[13] The University is more reagent than agent, and the play of social forces as expressed in demands for new knowledge and expertise, funding for new projects, pressures for the servicing of social needs, is what determines at any given moment in what direction the university shall expand or exert itself. "The multiversity has many 'publics' with many interests," writes Kerr,[14] and the role of the intelligent administrator is that of mediator among those interests, separating the legitimate from the frivolous, preserving a balance between the immediately relevant and the ultimately beneficial. Students are seen as "consumers" who bring pressures to bear on different areas of the curriculum through their interests and needs. Engaged in knowledge production, adapting to the knowledge explosion, packaging and serving up knowledge as curriculum, the multiversity is at the same time factory, distribution chain, and supermarket. As for the goal of the university, its ideal enterprise and commitment, this need not be questioned: "The

[13] Kerr, *The Uses of the University*, p. 49.
[14] Ibid., p. 27.

ends are already given—the preservation of the eternal truths, the creation of new knowledge, the improvement of service wherever truth and knowledge of high order may serve the needs of man."[15]

There is much to be said in defense of Kerr's multiversity: it corresponds to the democratization of American higher education, it breaks with the snobbery of certain older elitist conceptions of the university's public and function, it sees the university as a force for social and humane progress. The problem is that its progressive nature may very well be undermined by its unquestioningly open, responsive relations to society. The best critique of the multiversity that I know is to be found in Robert Paul Wolff's *The Ideal of the University*. Wolff argues that the university organized to service social needs is bound to respond only to the *felt* needs of society, which may not be its *real* needs, and to respond to needs only insofar as they are translated into effective market demand. The way in which social forces are most often brought to bear on the university make it almost inevitable that it become an instrument of national policy as determined by government and corporate management. The critical interests of society—the need for social organisms that can assume a critical stance toward national policy and the quality of American life—could not come from the multiversity as Kerr conceives it. And the multiversity, one might add, provides no educational ideal on which to found a critique of its *own* practice.

Wolff also gives a cogent analysis of the principle of university governance that necessarily corresponds to the multiversity model. This is the concept of democratic pluralism (Kerr's administrator as mediator), which founds policy decisions on an equilibrium of different interest groups, on moderation among forces. But, Wolff argues, if moderation is a satisfactory way of dealing with interests, it is no good when principles are concerned: here truth is more likely to be found on the extremist fringes than in the middle. The university which insists upon treating different ideals and principles of education as if they were simply interests, hence subject to reconciliation through compromise, ends up engaging in activities that violate its intellectual vision, and offering the intellectually unjustified hodgepodge curricula sometimes called balanced programs, which rightly seem to so many students today a kind of arbitrary game of required irrelevance.

[15] Ibid., p. 38.

I suspect that Clark Kerr's apologia for the supermarket university was a prime cause of Jacques Barzun's writing *The American University*, which begins with a quotation from Cardinal Newman, to the effect that greatness requires unity. The multiversity is abhorrent to Barzun; to it he opposes the conception of a more austere, single-minded, "honorific" institution, withdrawn from the world and the immediate demands for social service. He argues that the university has in the last decade and a half tried to serve too many publics, has tried to play too many roles, with the result that the fabric of the true university has been rent. He clearly articulates his model when he suggests that "if students came from the world they know to a monastic university, full of learning, devotion to teaching, and visible sacrifice to both, they would regain their piety and accept the most arbitrary regimen without a murmur."[16] This argument has considerable bite to it, because one of the prime targets of radical student analysis has been precisely the university's undiscriminating servicing of society's demands, and its consequent inability to locate and nurture its own soul, its incapacity to articulate a justification for the intellectual life, and apprenticeship to its disciplines.

Barzun's critical analysis of the mistaken practices of the service station university is often acute. He is sharply accurate in describing the university's degradation through the muddled professionalism fostered by the graduate schools, the careerism encouraged by structures of promotion and tenure, the pervasive model of "productive scholarship," a metaphor which images all too clearly the academic world's acceptance of models proposed by the Detroit assembly line rather than by the dictates of intellectual worth and need. Barzun has a general label for much of the inflated nonsense that goes on in universities today: "preposterism." For example, it is observed that some fine minds investigate subjects and write books which are original contributions to knowledge; *therefore*, every college teacher shall be defined as someone who has written a book which is an original contribution to knowledge, and the consequent deluge of publications shall be called a knowledge explosion.

But Barzun's book is a strange and maddening one. If his critique is sharp, and if his ideal model is reasonably clear, his analysis of where to go and what to do is foggy. To a large extent, this is because he cannot abide those within the university who should be his allies,

---

[16] Barzun, *The American University*, p. 208.

the critical students. His castigations of the "counter-culture," of student styles and activism (which he insists, quite inaccurately, to be mainly the product of dropouts or marginal students) would be trivial if they did not cut him off from a main source of information and strength in the reform of the university. One has the uneasy feeling that Barzun's critique of the unprincipled, soulless academy is not itself based on any real intellectual principles, but rather on nostalgia for a more elitist, gentlemanly past. What reinforces this feeling is the fact that he rests so much of his case on an institutional analysis, a who-does-what description of the university. This can of itself be entertaining, for we all like to know how our institutions function, be they government agencies or airports, but in itself it doesn't prove anything. It would be significant only within the framework of a deeper analysis of educational ends and means. That is, there is no point in calling for an aloof, dignified, "monastic" university unless you can argue the value of the knowledge it transmits, and the viability of transmitting it in that manner. The social imperatives to which Kerr's university is responding are real, and any argument against its response to them must argue more carefully the nature of the institution within the society. Barzun's model, in his articulation of it, seems finally backward-looking, nostalgically antipopulist, regretful of a paradise lost—which was only uncertainly paradise in any case.

If I have spent so much time on Kerr's and Barzun's models, it is because they represent two reasonably clear sketches of polar cases. They define the ends of the spectrum on which most of the other university books are located, although most of them do not so clearly commit themselves to the pure form of the model. But it is not so much in terms of pure models that I want to pursue discussion of the university books. Rather, I want to see what the models mean when applied to some basic questions raised by "The Year of the Liberal Arts." At the heart of the problems that now confront the universities as institutions of *education* (rather than as professional training schools) are: the place of what have traditionally been called the liberal arts within the university, and of the undergraduate college as a structure within higher education; the relation of undergraduate education to the demands of professionalism and certification; the immediate prospects for reform from the point of view of someone who believes that undergraduate education needs to be reassessed, salvaged, and valorized. These are not new questions;

they have been around for some time. But the crisis psychology of the university today poses them with new force and urgency, and suggests new paths for change.

I have alluded to Barzun's argument that the true business of education has been corrupted by the inflated demands and valuations of professionalism. Wolff maintains even more strongly that college curricula have been adulterated by the demands for preprofessional training, which tend to make college major programs, for example, only downgraded forms of graduate school programs. It is not so much that such programs are too specialized—specialization is at times a necessary part of intellectual discipline—but rather that they see the speciality only in terms of the profession attached to it, so that what goes on in a college English course finally has less to do with the undergraduate and the varieties of experience open to him in literature than with what is valued by the Modern Languages Association, the kind of discourse that appears in its *Publications*, what is said in its professional powwows. Christopher Jencks and David Riesman, too, consider that it is "only a small exaggeration to say that undergraduate education in most universities and university colleges is simply a cut-rate, mass-produced version of graduate education,"[17] and that most curricular "reform" in fact means giving students graduate-type work earlier in their careers.

Professionalism is of course a natural tendency of a diversified functionalist society. By a process that takes place essentially in graduate schools, students and teachers come to regard their investigations and transmissions of knowledge as a guild activity where what counts most is one's reputation in the field, which in turn means staking a claim to a mini-field which one can master and control with the power of a feudal baron. Professionalism is comforting: it enables the professor to behave like any other professional person, to claim status on the basis of certified competence. But it of course means the avoidance of the "naive" and basic questions that mean most to undergraduates: What am I *doing* in reading and talking about Shakespeare or Sartre or Hegel? What kind of an activity am I engaged in? What do I mean by history? And so forth. The preprofessionalism infecting the colleges means that it is assumed that these questions have been answered (sometime, by someone, once and for all) and that students and teachers can get on with the task of acquiring *competence* within a predetermined set.

[17] Jencks and Riesman, *The Academic Revolution*, pp. 247–48.

Faced with the clear demands of American society for professional training, and the very uncertain place of general education within any American university, it is natural that someone like James A. Perkins should argue that, while we must hold fast to the values of a liberal education, we must not assume that it will take the same forms in the university college as in an independent liberal arts college. The university college, he implies, will have to give over most of its resources to those professors who want to do research and to train students in the professional techniques of their specialities. Perkins's argument is not spelled out in detail, but its implication seems to be that general education will become a sort of enrichment program for students specializing at an ever earlier age, and that those committed to a more traditional view of general education will not come to the university college. This solution has analogies with the junior college argument examined by Jencks and Riesman, whereby university colleges would abandon their first two years, generally devoted to a broad distribution among fields, and recruit students from junior colleges. The B.A. would then be deemphasized in favor of preparation for the M.A., and work beyond. Such a reform receives the support of James B. Conant in the last chapter of *My Several Lives*, where he maintains that four years for an education of uncertain orientation and value is too long, and that nonprofessional higher education should be reduced to two years.

This, then, is some of the evidence that the form and content traditional in American college education at least since World War II—four years of liberal study, balanced between exploration of several foundations of human knowledge and apprenticeship into the more specialized tools of one field of knowledge—is much in question. Now, perhaps the most cogent and closely argued defense of the importance of the undergraduate college has been put forth by Daniel Bell in his report on the Columbia curriculum, *The Reforming of General Education*. Bell rejects traditional distinctions between general education as dealing with broad relationships, and specialization as dealing with an organized discipline, in favor of a distinction between ways of presenting material: as "received doctrine or fact" (the specialist's approach) or "with an awareness of its contingency and of the frame that guides its organization." His premise is, then, that "between the secondary school, with its emphasis on primary skills and factual data, and the graduate or professional school, whose necessary concern is with specialization and technique, the function of the college is to deal with the grounds of knowledge: not *what* one knows but *how* one knows. The college can be the unique place where students acquire self-consciousness, historical consciousness, and methodological consciousness."[18] From this stance, Bell analyzes the rise and fall of the general education idea at Columbia, Chicago, and Harvard, then offers a new four-stage curriculum which starts with "History and Tradition," moves to "Introduction to a Discipline," "The Extension of the Discipline to Subjects," and finally a "Third Tier," a synoptic program at the senior level which deals with the methodological and philosophical presuppositions of a field, and shows the application of discipline to problems.

Bell's book is, both philosophically and in terms of concrete curricular proposals, one of the most valuable that we have, and it will continue to deserve serious study. Yet, like Harold Taylor, who devotes several pages of *Students without Teachers* to an attack on Bell, I am disturbed by the conclusions of *The Reforming of General Education*, which outline a vision of the future which casts a disturbing shadow over Bell's proposals, divests them of their "innocence," and nurtures the suspicion that they are the work of a social technologist intent to disarm ideologies and harness students' moral energies to the technologism of the future. Bell foresees a serious intellectual crisis for the university in the "disjunction of culture and social structure," a disjunction expressed in the confrontation of "the technocratic and the apocalyptic." The apocalyptists, says Bell, "abhor the remoteness and coldness of 'social engineering' and prefer to create worlds of 'participation' and 'community.' In the end, however, they lack the technical knowledge, or even the willingness to acquire it, that could test their abstractions against a social reality."[19] This is a chilling judgment, because it suggests that what is best about the student revolt—its intense commitment to recreating community, to finding alternatives to the despair of a technologically engineered "happiness"—will have to be sacrificed. Taylor responds to Bell's "disjunction" with the cry, "Can we not at least entertain the view that subjective experience and desire can furnish the standard for moral truth, or that all moral truth is a fraud created by societies against the true interest of humans?"[20]

[18] Bell, *The Reforming of General Education*, p. 8.
[19] Ibid., pp. 314–15.
[20] Taylor, *Students without Teachers*, p. 159.

For Taylor, reconstruction of college education must proceed from what he calls "radical subjectivism," from the needs and desires of the college's students. He criticizes the analyses of Kerr and Jencks and Riesman for being merely descriptive of the pluralism of purposes and services in the modern university, for failing to set their institutional anatomies against any determination of goals, any choice of the ideals in whose service the organized power of the intellect can be enlisted. What we end up with in Kerr's model (and in most actual practice), Taylor points out, is "an implicit ideology of competition" by which professors and departments indulge in manipulations and strategems, and students are led to regard academic credits as "the exact equivalent of dollars."[21] Essentially, Taylor's solution would be to institute maximum freedom, a medium in which teachers could respond to the interest and interrogations of students, where the curriculum would be "open" and universities would group internal colleges experimenting in different directions.

Taylor's propositions address themselves centrally to the whole question of education as a free process. On this question, the diagnoses of many of the critics of higher education converge: in governing the pluralistic university, in seeking to balance the demands of general education and professionalism, colleges have devised programs which are expressed, and are perceived by the students, far too much in terms of requirements, credits, grades, certificates, hurdles. As Conant puts it, most of our "liberal" arts programs could properly be described as "servile," because they are full of prescribed courses, distribution requirements, credit hours, and so forth.[22] American students, Barzun maintains, "feel they have been in the groove since the sandbox." The questions reiterated to them take the form, "Show me your credentials. Where was this work done? What was your score on the S.A.T., the X.Y.Z., the F.O.B.?"[23] The contamination of college education by professionalism can be seen as part of a larger problem, argues Wolff: the failure to maintain a distinction between the process of education itself, and the use of education for certification. Certification, and the selection of elites which it presupposes, necessitate evaluation, grading, ranking, which, unlike criticism, properly have no place in education itself. The result is the sandbox-to-M.D.,

[21] Ibid., p. 100.
[22] Conant, *My Several Lives*, p. 644.
[23] Barzun, *The American University*, p. 65.

LL.B., or Ph.D. rat race by which American students are constantly pressured into regarding their education as preparation for successful negotiation of the next hurdle. They sacrifice education to competition, they become curricular and extracurricular drudges as they prepare to become acceptable candidates for the next stage. Finally, they arrive in graduate school and are told that their true education lies behind them, that now they can narrow their sights and learn a trade. "What has gone wrong?" asks Wolff. "The answer is simple: Each present was sacrificed to the future, until the presents were all past, and the future an empty present."[24]

Like Bell and like Barzun, Wolff is "deeply committed to a belief in the unique and irreducible character of undergraduate education,"[25] a moment which should be neither a prolongation of high school nor an initiation into professionalism, but rather an extended moment of transition in which the student tests styles of thought and action according to the Socratic dictum that the unexamined life is not worth living. Undergraduate education should be a time for free, and provisory, allegiance to a man and the subject he teaches, a moment when the student can explore any discipline as far as his curiosity and ability will allow him, without necessarily being committed to a career in the manipulation of the discipline's tools and world-view. It is quite clear that this ideal of freedom—almost medieval in its conception of a university of free association—is not extant at most colleges today, although it may be approached at certain consciously experimental independent colleges—the kind that Jencks and Riesman insist upon calling "offbeat" colleges.

When Wolff comes to his "practical proposals for utopian reform," he suggests some radical measures for breaking the whole future orientation of education. High school students would qualify for pools of colleges by meeting the entrance requirements set by the league to which the college belonged, and from this pool they would be selected for a specific college by random. Then would follow three years of rigorous but thoroughly free (and ungraded) undergraduate education, which would lead to no degree. There would be a national competitive examination to select those— whether they had attended undergraduate college or not—who would go on to professional school. These students would then complete a year of special preprofessional training under the aegis

[24] Wolff, *The Ideal of the University*, pp. 93–94.
[25] Ibid., p. 15.

of the professional school, not the college. One may be dubious about the first part of this scheme—the division of high school students into admissions pools according to college leagues might simply push the grade-typing of students to a still lower age—but the plan for freeing college from preprofessional responsibilities seems well conceived. To be sure, it would put much weight on a competitive examination such as the Graduate Records Exam, and would open up the danger of having teachers distort their programs to prepare students, surreptitiously perhaps, for the examination. In many European countries today, teaching is subservient to a national exam.

Jencks and Riesman also argue that there is no reason for education and certification to proceed through the same institutions and the same men, that in many other countries this is not in fact the case. They cite Robert M. Hutchins's effort to separate the two at Chicago, and the system of outside examiners practiced at Swarthmore, which they claim has the effect of making the student "engaged in a collaboration with his teacher to impress the outsider, instead of being an adversary trying to outwit his teacher."[26] This, too, may be subjected to criticism, since preparation for examination by an outsider who will most probably be known only as a professional in some field might encourage concentration on those denominators perceived to be acceptable to, or perceived as necessary by, anyone within the professional field.

Perhaps the main danger of Wolff's scheme, and one that he, as a radical critic of American society, should have noticed, is that a totally free undergraduate education leading to no certifying degree would be in a most unfavorable position in the fierce competition for financial support. The nation's resources, one can reasonably predict, would tend to gravitate toward the "productive" spheres, the professional schools and whatever preprofessional institutes they might be tempted to establish. There is, in other words, a question implicit in Wolff's plans for freedom which he doesn't answer, which is perhaps unanswerable, but needs in any case to be faced, and that is whether American society is willing to finance, support, and protect education which is truly free in the sense that it is gratuitous in any practical estimate, and justifiable only in the quality of the human beings it produces. This was John Dewey's

---

[26] Jencks and Riesman, *The Academic Revolution*, p. 63.

ideal, and it is clearly the ideal of most of the radical critics of American higher education today. Is it realizable?

To make the question more modest: without for the moment striving toward major restructuring of the existing system of higher education, can we reach any conclusions about the possibilities of real reform, the institution of an era of higher rationality and truer freedom in the universities? I am not here concerned with questions of governance or student participation: these are important, but their solution seems to me relatively easy where intelligence and good will exist together, and where goals have been articulated. (Essays in the Winter, 1970, issue of *Daedalus* address themselves to the issue of governance, and several of them—Stanley Hoffmann's is perhaps the most notable—are very good.) More important, both immediately and for the future, I think, is the question of preserving education as a critical function, as training of the mind in a critical stance toward reality, so that those whom Daniel Bell sees as the children of apocalypse can stand in intelligent and effective opposition to those who accept blindly all the consequences of technologism.

Any argument for the preservation of an independent undergraduate education, for the liberal arts college, should avoid taking a protectionist stance, which is perhaps what most effectively vitiates Barzun's argument. No reference to a past paradise devoted to the elitist cultivation of genteel knowledge is adequate to the imperative of quality mass education. As Taylor argues, any educational system must develop more from "the needs of an expanding democratic society" than from "educational plans linked to a clear social philosophy and made by intellectuals." [27] Any justification of the liberal arts must attempt to make them as sharp, as intelligent, as supple as technologism. It must reopen them to praxis, particularly to the act of teaching and training others, and direct them to a redefinition of our cultural situation. It must insist that moral value does still reside in the humanist tradition if we can see it clearly, not in degraded, flabby, academicized forms—if we can recapture the original revolutionary force of its great interrogations.

I think that the university which wants to preserve the liberal arts must become a critical university. The critical university meant to the insurgent French students of May, 1968, an institution that would inculcate a critical stance toward the sociopolitical

[27] Taylor, *Students without Teachers*, p. 27.

realities surrounding it. But it meant also a university that would be constantly engaged in critical examination of its own processes. It would seek ways to make its students and teachers reexamine their cultural and institutional conditioning. It is relevant to us, because we face the problem of how to break through into new ways of doing things, so that what the university regards as eternal structures and forms of knowledge are revealed for what they may be, the result of historical determinants, administrative convenience, ideological assumption, or pure chance. There is in Wolff's book a strong argument against interdisciplinary and problem-oriented curricula, the forms taken by much curricular innovation, on the grounds that they usually fail to give students a sense of methodology and intellectual discipline. This may be so, but we cannot on the other hand accept the disciplines as now defined as the only, or even the true, forms of intellectual discipline—they have indeed been assigned the status of Platonic forms by the professions and the graduate departments, but they may no longer be what we need.

Implicit in all the books I have discussed is the ancient problem of the relation between the knower and the known. Yet it is rarely faced as the radical problem of any teacher and any student. The institution of a critical university would attempt to address itself to the question by encouraging the growth of a counter-university within itself—counter-courses, counter-curricula, perhaps counter-colleges, which would reexamine the bases on which the more standard curriculum was proceeding. Hence the standard work of the university could go forward while at the same time its necessity was being radically questioned. It would allow us to live in our house while we were wrecking and rebuilding it. It would allow a dialectical interplay between structure and nonstructure (between, if you will, Bell and Taylor), would emphasize that education is primarily neither old structures nor new ones, but process. It would put at the center of undergraduate education the principle of the *agon*, or dispute, central to Greek philosophy and literature.

In practical terms, such a conception means that colleges should completely rethink their current ideas on requirements, balance, concentration, distribution. They should perhaps define a core curriculum (or several, for different areas of knowledge), and it should be methodological in orientation. Then they should require this core, if they are certain they can justify it intellectually, and in every other way institute the reign of freedom. The numbers game of eight courses from this department (division, program, or whatever), two courses from each of the other, must be thrown out as the very institutionalization of irrationality. Then the colleges should finance and foster counter-curricula and independent curricula, and the use of faculty time should not be computed in terms of formal course loads. Teachers, too, should be given the opportunity to demonstrate that Milton is just as "relevant" as Mailer, and that it was not Milton, but definitions of education as acquisition of subject matter, that made students think otherwise. Experiments in team teaching and team learning should be encouraged, in order to break from the competitive individualism that is as much part of the academic as the extra-academic structure of America. And students should be involved in trying to transmit to others what they have learned, not simply transmit it back to those who proffered it to them in the first place.

As all of the books under discussion suggest—as Jencks and Riesman, Kerr, Barzun, Taylor and Wolff make explicitly clear—higher education is now in this country a powerful institution, and, like any institution, engaged in the process of its self-preservation. This is not to label it the evil academy (as James Ridgeway would seem to want to do in *The Closed Corporation*[28]), but simply the academy subject to the imperatives of any human institution. It is to say, however, that any true reform is difficult of achievement. It will take constant pressure—from the intellectually committed among the student radicals, from innovative administrators, from faculty dissatisfied by the professionalist determinations of their fields and methods—to create colleges where learning and teaching are mutual processes proceeding in a medium of dedicated freedom.

Parts of this article have been adapted from two book reviews published by the author in *The New York Times Book Review*.

[28] New York: Random House, 1968.

List of Contributors

DONALD N. BIGELOW is the director of the Division of College Programs of the Bureau of Educational Personnel Development, United States Office of Education. He is a historian whose special interest is eighteenth-century intellectual history.

WILLIAM ARROWSMITH was, at the time of the Phoenix conference, a professor of classics at the University of Texas. He is presently a consultant to the Basic Studies Leadership Training Institute and to the Ford Foundation.

TIMOTHY HEALY is vice-chancellor of the City University of New York. He is a Donne scholar.

BENJAMIN DEMOTT is a professor of English at Amherst College. He is also a novelist, critic, and writer on various educational topics.

CHARLES WILSON is vice-chancellor for academic programs at the University of California at Los Angeles.

PAUL OLSON is a professor of English at the University of Nebraska. He was formerly director of the Nebraska University Tri-University Project and of its Project English program.

RICHARD FOSTER is the superintendent of schools in Berkeley, California. He has also been a member of the NDEA National Institute for the Disadvantaged.

CHARLES LEYBA is a professor of education at California State College at Los Angeles. He has also been the director of Project Maestro in the Los Angeles Mexican-American community.

CHARLES DECARLO is the president of Sarah Lawrence College. He was formerly an executive with IBM.

B. OTHANEL SMITH was a professor of educational philosophy at the University of Illinois; he is presently a professor of education at the University of South Florida at Tampa. He was also the major writer of *Teachers for the Real World*, a publication of the American Association of Colleges of Teacher Education (AACTE).

JOSÉ BURRUEL is the assistant dean of students at Arizona State University at Tempe, Arizona.

BERNARD WATSON is the deputy superintendent of schools in the Philadelphia public schools.

PRESTON WILCOX is the president of Afram Associates, an organization concerned with community participation in public institutions.

E. W. POWELL is the dean of instruction at Jarvis Christian College.

HENRY J. CASSO is associated with the Mexican-American Legal Defense Fund.

LESLIE WHIPP is associated with the University of Nebraska English department as a teacher of rhetoric.

ROBERT CROSS is the president of Swarthmore College. He is a historian and has written on the subject of the history of religion in America.

PETER BROOKS teaches French and is master of Pierson House at Yale. He is author of *The Novel of Worldliness* and articles and book reviews on education.